Ordered Liberty

*Legal Reform in the
Twentieth Century*

BORZOI BOOKS IN LAW AND AMERICAN SOCIETY

Ordered Liberty

Legal Reform in the Twentieth Century

Gerald L. Fetner
University of Chicago

ALFRED A. KNOPF   NEW YORK

*This book was originally developed as part of an American Bar Association
program on law and humanities with major funding from the National
Endowment for the Humanities and additional support from the Exxon
Education Foundation and Pew Memorial Trust. The ABA established this
program to help foster improved understanding among undergraduates of
the role of law in society through the creation of a series of volumes in law
and humanities. The ABA selected a special advisory committee of
scholars, lawyers, and jurists (Commission on Undergraduate Education in
Law and the Humanities) to identify appropriate topics and select writers.
This book is a revised version of the volume first published by the ABA.
However, the writer, and not the American Bar Association, individual
members and committees of the Commission, the National Endowment for
the Humanities, Exxon Education Foundation, or Pew Memorial Trust,
bears sole responsibility for the content, analysis, and conclusion contained
herein.*

THIS IS A BORZOI BOOK
PUBLISHED BY ALFRED A. KNOPF, INC.

First Edition
9 8 7 6 5 4 3 2 1
Copyright © 1983 by Alfred A. Knopf, Inc.

LIBRARY OF CONGRESS CATALOGING IN PUBLICATION DATA

Fetner, Gerald L.
　　Ordered liberty.

　　(Borzoi books in law and American society)
　　Bibliography: p.
　　Includes index.
　　1. Law—United States—History and criticism.
2. Law reform—United States—History.　　I. Title.
II. Series.
KF371.F48　　1982　　　　349.73 ′09　　　　82–14820
ISBN 0-394-33194-X　　　347.3009

Manufactured in the United States of America

FOR LESLEE

Preface

This book is an attempt to provide an overview to some of the central points of interaction between the law and other institutions in America. It is an effort to try to suggest a pattern to the host of issues and developments that have shaped American history and law during this century. The essay portion is designed to give the teacher and student a context for relating legal, constitutional, and professional issues to other subjects studied in traditional American history survey and period courses. The book also includes pertinent documents and readings that are representative of twentieth-century legal trends, ideas, attitudes, and developments. They have been chosen with three goals in mind: (1) to show lawyers and legal commentators talking about the law and its functions; (2) to provide excerpts from the Constitution and statutes that exemplify the changing role of law; and (3) to enable the teacher and student to study Court interpretations of the Constitution, statutes, and administrative rules. The bibliographic essay describes the informing literature on the subject.

I would like to acknowledge the advice of a number of persons and the assistance of several institutions: The Port Authority of New York and New Jersey for allowing me to examine material related to the formation of that agency; Yale University Library for permission to consult the Jerome Frank papers; Yale University and Mrs. Alexander Bickel for permission to examine some of Professor Bickel's papers; Mrs. Robert Lee Hale for sharing with me her husband's work at Columbia Law School, which provides a vivid understanding of legal reform in this century; the National Endowment for the Humanities for supporting the ABA Commission on Undergraduate Education in Law and the Humanities; the American Bar Association for sponsoring this program, which resulted in nine books on law and the humanities, of which this is one; and Alfred A.

VIII *Preface*

Knopf, Inc., particularly executive editor David Follmer, for believing in
the educational importance of law as an undergraduate discipline. In this
regard, I would also like to single out the following individuals: Justice
Shirley Abrahamson; Edward Levi; Judge Carl McGowan; Robert
McKay; Geoffrey Marshall; and Stephen Miller.

I owe particular debts to the following teachers and colleagues, who
made helpful critical suggestions about this work: Stuart Bruchey, Columbia University; Barry Karl, the University of Chicago; Stanley Katz,
Princeton University; William Leuchtenburg, Columbia University; and
John L. Thomas, Brown University.

Finally, my warmest appreciation is to my wife, Leslee, who shared
my enthusiasm and endured my frustration from the inception to the com-
pletion of this book.

GERALD FETNER
Chicago, Illinois

Contents

I.

Essay

II.

Documents

III.
Bibliographic Essay

Index

Essay

Introduction to the Essay

This essay is designed to explore the relationship between law and society in America from 1900 to 1980. It is an effort to survey in very broad terms the influence of economic and social developments on the law and legal institutions, and vice versa. The thesis of the essay is that the law and legal institutions became a tool used by those in positions of power during the twentieth century for imposing order on an American society undergoing rapid technological, industrial, and urban growth. Social order consisted of developing new standards of cooperative economic and social behavior that would reduce, if not eliminate, the waste, inefficiency, and injustice associated with the late-nineteenth-century policy of laissez faire. Law and legal institutions were those rules and policies developed by courts, legislative and administrative agencies, and private associations and groups.

It is further contended that the administered solutions worked out by these legal, political, and private agencies during the first half of the century often came into conflict with two fundamental social impulses guaranteed by the Constitution: individual freedom and economic opportunity. This development led policymakers during the second half of the century to seek new guarantees, or entitlements, for those individuals in our society caught in the web of bureaucratic control. Unfortunately, these new freedoms were not achieved without yet another wave of expanded administration. At the end of this period, there was no certainty that these legal controls had, in fact, rationalized economic and social practices and brought

1

freedom and opportunity within reach of all Americans. Rather, one saw the beginnings of a repudiation of the administrative society, to an extent as yet unassessable.

The framework for examining these developments was set at the turn of the century by the Progressive movement, which, very generally, sought to curb the excesses of corporate capitalism and restore a more ethical fabric to American society. The Progressives, and those reform groups and interests that succeeded them, were preoccupied with two sorts of problems. The first, and more prominent, concerned business organization—that is, its size, its trade practices, and its relations with other businesses, labor, government, and the consumer. The second, which was less immediate, dealt with the diverse issue of social welfare. Over the course of the century, this issue came to be a symbol for such things as personal well-being, access to political power, economic opportunity, and individual rights and justice. In seeking to "rationalize" these issues—that is, create a set of standards that would guide policymakers in resolving conflict—political leaders, social reformers, and businessmen came to rely on the legal community.

Unlike the nineteenth-century legal community, which was highly individualistic, dealt little with social causes, avoided public participation, and generally served solely to foster the interests of the emerging industrial and commercial interests, the twentieth-century bar developed, over the years, more distinctive social attributes. The plea that lawyers take a more socially responsive attitude came, at first, from a few thoughtful social critics, political leaders, and jurists, who sensed the need for legal expertise to formulate new economic and social policy. Members of the legal community responded to this call for social invention and intervention by devising a broad array of legal arrangements—statutes, private agreements, arbitration, administrative rules and regulations—to resolve economic and social conflict. At first, those who embarked on this course were the professional elite; by the end of the period, a much broader and diverse group of lawyers were active in some form of socially responsible legal activity.

One first catches a glimpse of this reshaping of attitudes and institutional values in some of the speeches by Woodrow Wilson, before he became President of the United States. In one, titled "The Legal Education of Undergraduates," delivered in 1894 to the American Bar Association, Wilson called for strengthening undergraduate education in the law so that men graduating from college, whether they became lawyers or not, would better understand the law and the legal process. However, in its implications, the address went beyond education. Sensing the temper of the emerging reform spirit of the nineties, Wilson saw the need for a trained body of lawyers who could act not only as technicians but as brokers or managers translating the progressive desire for efficiency into new governing mechanisms that were compatible with democratic traditions. Although sympathetic to the earnestness of reformers and their goals, he feared that their haste, ignorance, and intemperance would cause a reaction against them. (He spoke two years after workers and police had clashed at Homestead and the same year that federal troops confronted striking railway workers in Chicago.) "I feel sure . . . ," he said, "that nothing will steady us like a body of citizens instructed in the essential nature and processes of law and a school of lawyers deeply versed in the methods by which the law has grown, the vital principles by which, under every system, it has been pervaded, its means of serving society and its means of guiding it."[1]

Lawyers were not the only ones affected by this social ideology toward the practice of law. Judges were also urged to adopt a progressive tone—specifically, to weigh conflicts between individual interests with the social consequences in mind. Generally, late-nineteenth-century jurists resisted this plea. Through skillful use of the due process clause to include the substantive as well as procedural protection of property rights, these judges, many of whom were former corporate attorneys, erected a defense against legislative efforts to regulate business for the benefit of those with little economic means or power. With some exceptions, this legal orthodoxy resisted challenge until the late thirties. In contrast, a few judges, most notably Oliver Wendell Holmes, sought to counter judicial invalidation of legislative reform, by urging a return to a narrow interpretation of judicial review, one in which the Court's function is to measure statutory authority against constitutional power, not to interpose its own views about the wisdom of legislation. In those cases where the Constitution did not explicitly or implicitly sanction legislative action, yet did not prohibit it either, the determinant, Holmes

---

[1] Woodrow Wilson, *The Public Papers of Woodrow Wilson: College and State*, vol. 1, ed. Ray Stannard Baker and William E. Dodd (New York, 1925), p. 234.

suggested, should be whether the statute was reasonable—that is, not arbitrary or capricious.

Holmes's opinions, treatises, and speeches, delivered over a career that spanned the post–Civil War period to the New Deal, served to inspire several generations of lawyers to view law not as a fixed system but as one responsive to social need. Although skeptical himself of reform activity, his decisions favoring social experimentation raised the level of expectation of reformers, politicians, and lawyers, leading to successive efforts by these figures to challenge late-nineteenth-century legal formalism. The climax came over the constitutionality of New Deal legislation and led to a crisis between executive and judiciary that surpassed earlier conflicts (e.g., Andrew Jackson's assertion of executive independence of Supreme Court decisions; Lincoln's invocation of the same doctrine to deny the validity of the Court's *Dred Scott* decision) between these two branches of government.

By the time the dust had settled, the judiciary had adopted the position that economic regulation would be accorded the presumption of constitutionality. However, the same status was not extended to government action restricting civil rights and civil liberties, particularly by states and of minorities. This issue, which had its own generative power owing to changing conditions in America in the forties and fifties, led to renewed conflict over the meaning of judicial review. Some judges, such as Chief Justice Earl Warren, believed the courts should take a positive role in rectifying inequities. In effect, he sought the rationalization of Bill of Rights freedoms—that is, the creation of national and uniform standards for the application of these protections and the administration of justice. This objective, which is discussed more fully in the pages that follow, resulted in a more pronounced judicial involvement in policy and social management than the country had ever experienced. Unlike other Courts before it—even during the New Deal—which merely affirmed or denied the existence of constitutional power, the Court under Warren (1953–1969) placed itself at the center of social and political reform (e.g., in superintending the desegregation of schools and the reapportionment of legislatures) in the United States. For some fifteen years, it, not the executive or legislature, determined the shape of American life. Its use of judicial review realized the worst fears of some of our early judges, who considered that power delicate in character and used only under urgent circumstances.

By the end of the period under study, a fierce debate ensued between those who thought the Court had overstepped its authority by intervening in social affairs, and those who thought that in the absence of other methods of conflict resolution and social adjustment, namely the executive and legislature, the courts were the only institution in American society equipped to underwrite basic guarantees of economic and social justice. As one Harvard Law School professor, Lloyd Weinreb, argued, "Far from usurping authority, the courts have on the whole exercised their authority reluctantly. Our political leaders have often been only too glad to leave to the courts responsibility for unpopular measures favoring the weak, powerless, and disfavored of our society."[2] Others pointed to the absence of a political center to account for the increased tendency to resolve conflict through the law.

In its shaping of economic and social issues, the legal community found itself shaped by them. Like business, the organized bar struggled throughout the century to establish internal discipline and order within its own ranks; or, to put it another way, to heighten both its image and its practices as a profession. Bar leaders sought to construct a vision of their work to conform to the Progressive ideal of commonwealth yet, at the same time, avoid any departure from their overriding concern for craft, tradition, and clientele. For example, at the start of the century, they declared themselves opposed to advertising—a stance that may have resulted in a lessening of available legal services for middle- and low-income people. This position reflected a narrow view of the market, and it was particularly ironic in view of the continuing effort during the century by a portion of the nation's lawyers to socialize business practices so that more Americans could share in the productive wealth of the nation. Only toward the end of the period, when the organized bar encountered substantial social and professional opposition to its self-regulatory prerogatives, did it undertake meaningful efforts to reform the economic basis of its work and make access to legal services available to all Americans.

By the end of the seventies, the organized bar had made changes in its attitudes, structure, and methods, all of which promised to revolutionize legal practice in America. But the question remained whether the democratization of legal services would, in fact, promote

[2] Lloyd Weinreb, "Judicial Activism," *New York Times*, February 3, 1982, p. 27.

commonweal or lead instead to new demands for expanded rights (i.e., the notion of "entitlement"). On the eve of having achieved substantial success in modernizing century-old standards and practices, the legal profession found itself confronted by a public perspective toward legal reform that ran counter to its recent achievements. Such noted lawyers and social commentators as Daniel Boorstin urged the legal community to temper the "special urgencies" of the age by adhering to doctrine and technique, and not reflecting in the law so much of the nation's social interests. Like other professional groups in American society, the legal community in the eighties faced the prospect of placing restraints on further efforts at modernization and social reform.

ONE

The Progressive Era: 1900—1918

Lawyers, particularly those in a leadership position, have always played, in one form or another a formulative role in American society. They have often served as a "connecting link," as Tocqueville once observed, between the people and the aristocracy of wealth—which in America has traditionally been the business class. During the formative period of the American republic, many lawyers assumed positions in politics and government while exercising considerable influence in private affairs, particularly those involving commercial development. Daniel Webster was a nineteenth-century lawyer who combined skill in representing the developing commercial interests with a talent for influencing public policy. As a lawyer, he defended corporate property against government interference in the famous *Dartmouth College* case (1819); later, as a senator from Massachusetts, he was an early opponent of slavery.

By midcentury, however, as business demands grew and public policymaking became more intense, lawyers experienced difficulty with this dual public and private role. William Seward found that his activities as governor of New York often interfered with his legal work. Clients and partners were continually forced to readjust their schedules in order to meet his convenience. Seward responded to their annoyance by suggesting that if friends and clients "will not understand that I cannot do their business at the same time that I am overwhelmed with public cares . . ., I see no way but they must learn it by the failure of my best efforts."[1]

[1] William Henry Seward to Richard Blatchford, May 26, 1850, in Robert T. Swaine, *The Cravath Firm and Its Predecessors*, vol. 1 (New York, 1946), p. 121.

After the Civil War, the character of American society changed considerably and so did the lawyer's role. State government involvement in economic development declined; technological advances spurred the industrialization of American business. For the better lawyers, public service no longer seemed as compelling as it did earlier in the century. Instead, lawyers came to play an increasing role in assisting businessmen in such areas as patents, reorganizations, and mergers. Representative of this kind of lawyer was Samuel Carter Tate Dodd, counsel for John D. Rockefeller's Standard Oil Company of Ohio, who was instrumental in creating the famous trust agreements (1879 and 1882) that enabled Rockefeller to unify his various oil interests under one authority. Whether railing against government interference with business or defending business combination as necessary to avoid wasteful competition, Dodd reflected the temper of the late-nineteenth-century corporate–legal community. With regard to the lawyer's relation to government, he observed, "I kept clear of all mingling with politics and legislative business, except when I went to make a public argument before some committee of the legislature, which I did on several occasions."[2] As for business combination, he explained, "The rule in business is emphatically the survival of the fittest. Only thus can the public receive benefit from superior skill and economies in business."[3]

By the turn of the century, the economic and social practices of business had come under scrutiny and criticism from a number of groups and interests. It is hard to generalize about the Progressive movement, since it was geographically and institutionally heterogeneous. Yet if there was one theme that characterized Progressivism, it was the search for and imposition of new standards of ethical behavior for business, government, and the professions. The Progressives sought to bridle the excessive waste, inefficiency, corruption, and human suffering associated with American industrialization. Many Progressive-era spokesmen sounded this theme, none perhaps as forcefully as Theodore Roosevelt. In his book *The New Nationalism*, a collection of addresses delivered throughout the country late in the summer of 1910, nearly three years after he had left the presidency, he pointed to the need to undo special privilege

[2] Samuel Carter Tate Dodd, *Memoirs of S. C. T. Dodd: Written for His Children and Friends, 1837–1907* (New York, 1907), p. 31.
[3] Samuel Carter Tate Dodd, *Combinations: Their Uses and Abuses, With a History of the Standard Oil Trust* (New York, 1888), pp. 12–15.

so that each citizen could give to the commonwealth that to which it is entitled and draw from it that which he deserved. His speeches carried two imperatives: first, control, particularly of corporate activities; and second, efficiency, not only in the use of the nation's manpower and natural resources but in its institutions as well. He called for a "genuine and permanent moral awakening" that would improve the administration of government, business, and the professions. "No matter how honest and decent we are in our private lives," he said, "if we do not have the right kind of law and the right kind of administration of the laws we cannot go forward as a nation."[4]

The Progressives believed that the law and the legal community were central to the moral reconstruction of society. In his influential book *The Promise of American Life* (1909), Herbert Croly, a journalist, claimed that excessive specialization in business affairs had robbed the lawyer of exposure to critical questions of public policy and deprived the public of an important resource. Lawyers were, in Croly's opinion, ideal policymakers. They were trained to be fair, to understand public opinion, and to weigh decisions with dispassion and without political motives. Hence it was particularly disturbing to discover the extent to which lawyers had removed themselves from politics and, even worse, had used state government to win favors for their clients. He saw this as one reason for the loss of influence of state government. A year later, in 1910, in an address before the American Bar Association, Woodrow Wilson criticized the legal community for "being drawn into modern business instead of standing outside of it, in becoming identified with particular interests instead of holding aloof, and impartially advising all interests."[5]

Such Progressive reformers as Wilson and Croly recognized that the lawyer's value as a business adviser, combined with his understanding of the legal process, could and must be put to use in dealing with the critical issues of the day. "Never before in our history," Wilson declared before a bar group in Kentucky in 1911, "did those who guide affairs more seriously need the assistance of those who can claim an expert familiarity with the legal processes by which reforms may be effectually accomplished."[6] Wilson identified two areas he thought would serve as an immediate test of the legal community's

---

[4] Theodore Roosevelt, *The New Nationalism* (New York, 1910), p. 32.
[5] Woodrow Wilson, *The Public Papers of Woodrow Wilson: College and State*, vol. 2, ed. Ray Stannard Baker and William E. Dodd (New York, 1925), p. 245.
[6] Ibid., p. 316.

interest in public affairs. The first was the regulation of modern business. Command of the instruments of business practice was a fundamental objective of Progressives. The second was the reform of legal procedure. Here Progressive-era reformers urged streamlining court procedures so that the administration of justice would operate fairly and effectively. "The actual miscarriages of justice," Wilson noted, "because of nothing more than a mere slip in a phrase or a mere error in an immaterial form, are nothing less than shocking. Their number is incalculable, but much more incalculable than their number is the damage they do to the reputation of the profession and to the majesty and integrity of the law."[7]

The leadership of the legal profession reacted strongly to these attacks. In some cases, they, too, saw their identification as business advisers eroding their public influence and professional status. According to historian Richard Hofstadter, such prominent lawyers as Elihu Root, a turn-of-the-century New York corporation attorney and political leader, viewed public service as a way of enhancing the social position of lawyers.[8] A more telling reason for their interest in public affairs, however, was the desire to temper the pace and shape of reform and prevent the loss of basic professional values. (Later in the century, bar leaders would respond to Great Society social reformers for the very same reason.) "What we lawyers need now," observed William Howard Taft, former U.S. President, now, in 1913, a Yale Law School professor and a representative figure of moderate professional reform, "is to rouse our profession to speak out. We must be heard in defense of the good there is in our present society and in pointing out the social injury which a retrograde step may involve. But we must also put ourselves more in touch with the present thinking of the people who are being led in foolish paths." He went on to urge lawyers to work with the new reformers but in a manner that was consistent "with the maintenance of those principles that are essential to the pursuit of material progress and the consequent attainment of spiritual progress in society and to permanent popular and peaceful government of law."[9]

Those who made this plea and responded to it were the profes-

---

[7] Ibid., p. 315.
[8] See Richard Hofstadter, *The Age of Reform* (New York, 1956), p. 162.
[9] William Howard Taft, *Popular Government: Its Essence, Its Performance and Its Perils* (New Haven, 1913), pp. 236–237.

sional elite. They represented only a small portion of the nation's attorneys. (In fact, the large body of lawyers were individual practitioners whose activities rarely touched policy concerns and whose participation or even membership in organized bar groups was minimal. The membership of the American Bar Association, the national voluntary organization of lawyers, was only 2,000 in 1905, out of over 100,000 practicing attorneys and judges in the nation.) But because they held prominent places in the organized bar and were financially secure as a result of successful practices in metropolitan law firms, these elite lawyers could engage in selective public activity, take positions in favor of government regulation, and advocate reforms of judicial procedure and organization, with the confidence that their opinions would be heeded by political and social leaders.

The fact that leaders of the bar accepted an increased role in public affairs did not mean that they departed from their equally firm belief in corporate capitalism. It must be understood that they were not so much concerned with improving the social responsibility of business as they were with rationalizing economic practices, that is, seeking ways to increase productivity and maximize profits. They accepted some government regulation because they considered it a way of making business more efficient and warding off the possibility of more hostile government action. This attitude, in turn, carried over to the way they viewed the organization of their own professional activities. They were more interested in improving the efficiency of the legal process than in democratizing it. They wanted to improve the administration of justice (by setting standards for ethical conduct, court procedure, and the education of its members)—not so much to broaden the availability of legal services to larger numbers of Americans or to strengthen the position of those with little economic or political power but to streamline legal practice and make it more adaptable to the needs and demands of their business clientele.

======================   ======================

Facing the Problem of Corporate Responsibility

The issue of corporate monopoly and combination provides an excellent illustration of (1) the Progressives' interest in formulating standards and codes of conduct to stem unwanted business practice,

(2) the increased reliance these reformers placed on the law and legal institutions to accomplish this goal, and (3) the need for lawyers to play a larger role in shaping government policy. At the center of this controversy was a dispute over how to enforce the Sherman Antitrust Act of 1890, which Congress enacted to discourage combinations in restraint of interstate trade. The law made any attempt to monopolize interstate trade a misdemeanor. And although it supplemented numerous state laws restraining monopolistic business activity, its importance lay in the recognition that corporate growth was an interstate problem, requiring central control by the federal government.

Although united by their concern that the giant combinations in such areas as steel, oil, sugar, beef, and railroads threatened to destroy traditional American values of free competition and economic opportunity, Progressive reformers and politicians differed over the best way to control these activities. The views of some reformers, such as William Jennings Bryan, a lawyer, politician, and statesman, reflected the agrarian side of Progressivism. They feared both the growth of large corporations—Bryan wanted to dissolve them and return to a nation of small businessmen—as well as efforts to control the giants through federal legislation—he preferred relying on state statutes. More moderate, and realistic, reformers recognized the existence and, in many instances, the value of these combinations. For them, corporations were a natural product of economic forces, which if properly regulated would promote Progressive goals of fairness, cooperation, efficiency, and public welfare. According to Theodore Roosevelt, "The way out lies, not in attempting to prevent such combinations, but in completely controlling them in the interest of the public welfare."[10] Size alone was not the reformers' only concern; they also feared the consequences of interlocking directorates. "The difficulty in this country is not altogether that we have big corporations," Woodrow Wilson pointed out, "but that these big corporations are combined with one another, not by law, but by the fact that their directorates interlace in every direction and that the same combinations of men control the majority of the stock in corporation after corporation."[11] If they ever became sufficiently interlaced, Wilson noted, they would not only stifle competition but

[10] Roosevelt, *The New Nationalism*, p. 15.
[11] Wilson, *Public Papers: College and State*, vol. 2, p. 414.

would diminish the federal government's ability to serve as a counterweight on behalf of the public.

Politicians were not the only ones to have differences of opinion regarding the control of corporations. The judiciary also failed to define a policy that would provide businessmen and their counsel with certainty about the scope and application of the Sherman Act. One of the most important questions courts considered was what business activities were affected by the act, that is, what constituted interstate commerce. In *United States v. E. C. Knight* (1895), the Supreme Court declared that manufacturing, in this case as carried on by the American Sugar Refining Company, was not commerce and not subject to the Sherman Act. In doing so, the Court substantially restricted the scope of application. A second question concerned what constituted restraint, and more specifically, whether size alone created a monopoly in restraint of trade. In 1901, in the *Northern Securities* case, the Court ruled that the formation of a holding company to control two major railroads (the Great Northern and the Northern Pacific) was a restraint of trade, regardless of whether it was reasonable or unreasonable. In 1911, however, the Court decided that the broad language of the act need not be interpreted literally. In other words, "every" restraint of trade did not include all the forms of contracts or combinations that were being evolved from existing economic conditions. Instead, judges could use their discretion regarding what was a reasonable or unreasonable restraint. "To hold to the contrary," wrote Chief Justice Edward White in *Standard Oil Company of New Jersey v. United States*, the decision that declared the Rockefeller trust agreements illegal, "would require the conclusion . . . that every contract, act or combination of any kind or nature, whether it operated as a restraint of trade or not, was within the statute."[12] This conclusion would destroy, he argued, the freedom to contract, which was the best protection against restraint of trade. The *Standard Oil Company* decision left the business and legal community with the understanding that size alone was not a controlling factor in determining restraint of trade, and that each case would be examined in light of existing conditions and practices. The decision did little, however, to resolve the conflict between statutory rule and judicial discretion.

Given the uncertainty posed by executive and judicial policy

---

[12] *Standard Oil Company of New Jersey v. United States*, 221 U.S. 1, 63 (1911).

toward consolidation and business practice, prominent corporation lawyers such as Francis Lynde Stetson, counsel to financier J. P. Morgan, complained of their inability to advise their clients properly. What they feared most was the uncertainty of regulation by litigation. They preferred that Congress create a new federal agency where lawyers could seek advice on impending business agreements and trade practices that might potentially violate the Sherman Antitrust Act. "It is a great deal better," argued Elbert Gary, chairman of the United States Steel Company, "to have regulations by a department which knows all the facts from day to day and which can advise a corporation than it is to have regulation by a law-suit, particularly when the corporation does not know that it is violating the law."[13]

The model proposed by such men as Stetson and Gary was a commission that would have the power to make and revoke declarations regarding the innocuousness of a corporation or business agreement. While this declaration was in force, the Department of Justice would be prevented from prosecuting the business on any matter covered by the decree. The existence of such an agency, they claimed, would go far toward ridding commerce and trade of unscrupulous or inefficient producers. It would assist in the process of business rationalization, which was, after all, what these late-nineteenth-century barons of wealth had been seeking all along.

Some members of the legal community, however, questioned the motives of these corporate lawyers and businessmen. Though they favored the creation of a commission, they urged that it be kept independent of business control. Samuel Untermyer, a particularly aggressive opponent of monopoly (he had served as counsel to the Pujo Committee, which investigated misdealings by financiers), charged that the public was being misled by these corporate lawyers, who merely wished to burden the country with "an inefficient patchwork of compromise legislation,"[14] rather than achieve meaningful reform. Other lawyers, such as Boston attorney Louis Brandeis, questioned the value of commission regulation. Brandeis

[13] U.S., Congress, Senate, Committee on Interstate Commerce, *Pursuant to S. Res. 98: A Resolution . . . to Investigate and Report Desirable Changes in the Laws Regulating and Controlling Corporations . . . in Interstate Commerce, Vol. I,* 62d Cong., 2d sess., 1911–1912, p. 705.

[14] Samuel Untermyer, "A Legislative Program to Restore Business Freedom and Confidence," address before the Illinois Manufacturers Association, Chicago, January 5, 1914, p. 13.

wondered whether such a commission could act as quickly as the courts, particularly since it would be required to conduct extensive and lengthy investigations. And in supervising many industries, rather than a single business, he questioned whether it would be able to handle adequately the special problems of each. Another disadvantage Brandeis envisioned was that such a commission would not be in a position to deal with industry problems until it had built up knowledge and experience in their affairs, and that would involve a considerable amount of time. Others, such as William Howard Taft, pointed out that since the commission would not be able to answer every question, courts would have to step in to supply "the deficiency either by construction of written law or constructive application of the common law."[15] Their concerns reflected the tension that would exist throughout the century between those who favored reform as a consequence of litigation versus those who advocated change using the legislative and administrative processes.

In spite of the differences of opinion regarding the best approach to regulate business, Congress took positive steps to supplement the Sherman Act by passing in 1914 the Clayton Antitrust Act, which outlawed certain business activities, such as interlocking directorates (that is, competing companies with common directors), and exempted labor unions and some labor tactics (e.g., peaceful persuasion) from prosecution. It passed a Federal Trade Commission Act, broadening the crime of restraint of trade from the single issue of monopoly to a series of unspecified unfair trade practices, generally understood at the time to consist of such activities as illegal marketing contracts, resale price maintenance, price discrimination, and false advertising. A Federal Trade Commission armed with prosecutorial power would enforce the act but, in the hope of the bill's sponsors and supporters, in a corrective rather than punitive manner.

They wanted it to lay the basis for a cooperative rather than antagonistic attitude between business and government, provide needed guidance for the new managerial class, and circumvent costly and time-consuming legal and judicial entanglements. "The nation demands such a commission," Wilson pointed out in his message to Congress introducing the legislation on January 20, 1914, "only as an indispensable instrument of information and publicity, as a clearing house for the facts by which both the public mind and the managers

[15] Taft, *Popular Government*, p. 224.

of great business undertakings shall be guided, and as an instrumentality for doing justice to business where the processes of the courts or the natural forces of correction outside the courts are inadequate to adjust the remedy to the wrong in a way that will meet all the equities and circumstances of the case."[16]

The significance of the legislation, as well as of other Wilson administration legislation (e.g., the Federal Reserve Act) lay not only in the effort to control business practice but in the changes it fostered in relations between government, business, and the legal community. First, the legislation gave added weight to the authority of Congress to delegate legislative power to administrative agencies and tribunals for economic regulation. Second, it now meant corporations were required to give details of their activities through submission of documents such as annual reports. The FTC could compel corporations to answer in writing specific interrogatories they issued. Third, corporate lawyers would have to maintain an even keener eye than before on whether business action might run afoul of the law. Finally, there would be a greater need for lawyers and other experts to implement the new administrative machinery. In short, the Wilson legislation signified the impending professionalization of American business, law, and government. This development was shrewdly noted by Felix Frankfurter, who, in 1914, had just joined the faculty of the Harvard Law School. "The one thing we have been learning hard," he pointed out, "is that laws are not self-enforcing. Just as private business is becoming professionalized, not left to native shrewdness and empirical skill, so the great business of government, the intricate problems of public affairs, must be professionalized. We must have a definite supply, organized resources, for men who are to make, and particularly for men who are to administer, the laws."[17]

Cleaning House: Setting Standards for the Legal Community

Passage of this regulatory legislation intensified efforts already under way by the organized bar to upgrade professional standards and

---

[16] Woodrow Wilson, *The Public Papers of Woodrow Wilson: The New Democracy*, vol. 2, ed. Ray Stannard Baker and William E. Dodd (New York, 1926), pp. 85–86.
[17] Felix Frankfurter, "The Law School and the Public Service," *Harvard Alumni Bulletin*, 18 (November 11, 1914), 115.

improve the administration of justice. In dealing with this issue, bar leaders argued strenuously for the prerogative of setting guidelines through the bar's own self-regulatory mechanisms, that is courts and voluntary bar associations rather than legislative action. According to one prominent lawyer and scholar, Columbia Law School dean Harlan Fiske Stone, law was a self-contained body of principles that, when studied and applied systematically and consistently, would promote the kind of social justice reformers demanded. In a series of influential lectures at Columbia in 1915 (later published as a book called *Law and Its Administration*), Stone argued that changes in the law must be made by those trained to deal with it—namely, lawyers and judges—rather than by social reformers and politicians. Although not opposed to using legislation to resolve some issues, Stone preferred the common-law approach—that is, judge-made law—for dealing with social conflict (e.g., torts, civil disputes, crime). Like other Progressives, he linked improvements in judicial administration and social justice to ethics, procedure, and education. In this respect, he represented what might be considered the more moderate response to the Progressive critique of the legal profession.

Improving the ethical behavior of lawyers and ridding the profession of unscrupulous practitioners became a goal of local, state, and national associations of lawyers. Leading this effort was the American Bar Association (ABA), which set up a committee in 1905 to devise a code of ethics for the profession. The Canons of Ethics, as they were called on their introduction in 1908, were designed to ensure the proper conduct of practitioners. Among other things, the canons stressed the allegiance owed by the lawyer to his client. "Entire devotion to the interest of the client, warm zeal in the maintenance and defense of his rights and the exertion of his utmost learning and ability,"[18] were the standards lawyers should use in representation. With the canons, the profession sought to control the economic and moral basis of legal practice by prohibiting lawyers from soliciting business by circulars or advertisements. "The most worthy and effective advertisement possible," the canons stated, ". . . is the establishment of a well merited reputation for professional capacity and fidelity to trust."[19]

Though it might lessen the opportunity for unscrupulous attorneys to get a professional foothold, this rule also hindered efforts by

---

[18] *Reports of the American Bar Association*, 33 (1908), 576.
[19] Ibid., p. 502.

less well connected lawyers to establish themselves. Similarly, though it reduced the chances of the public being taken advantage of, it also suspended meaningful efforts to make legal services available to larger numbers of Americans. In one sense, the canons were a professional trade-off: they provided a means for ensuring the quality of services, yet they hindered the expansion of those services to middle- and low-income groups. This development delayed one very important step in the process of professional modernization. Nevertheless, the canons provided the profession with some important policy guidelines. Their success can be measured by the fact that by 1916, thirty state bars had adopted them.

To implement the canons, however, required machinery which could deal with issues that arose daily. During the first and second decades, many state and local bar groups established committees of grievances to accept complaints about violations of conduct. In New York City, the County Lawyers' Association created a Committee on Unlawful Practice of the Law (1912) to act as a clinic in answering questions concerning legal ethics. To a degree, the committee functioned almost like an economic regulatory commission, insofar as it sought to fill in on a day-to-day basis the broad guidelines of ABA policy. Committees of lawyers were also established to guard the profession against the "unauthorized practice of law," including the work of notaries, bill collectors, and real estate brokers. In this way, the profession sought to reduce unwanted competition.

Streamlining judicial procedures was also viewed as a desirable means of improving the administration of justice, achieving moderate social reform, and maintaining the common-law system. Among the most serious problems confronting courts were excessive litigation and delay in disposing of cases, resulting in some instances in delays of two or more years. William Howard Taft laid part of the blame for this situation to state legislatures, which had sought to deprive the courts of their power at common law. "Codes of procedure of immense volume and exasperating detail keep litigants 'pawing in the vestibule of justice' while the chance of doing real justice fades away," he complained.[20] Harlan Stone proposed that procedural rules be liberalized and made less technical so that trial proceedings could run more quickly and smoothly. He urged that judges be given greater authority to set limits on the time of argument allowed to

[20] Taft, *Popular Government*, p. 226.

counsel. Moreover, he suggested that state appellate courts, some of which were powerless to correct a lower court error except by sending the case back for retrial, be given authority to modify or reverse lower-court judgments.

In addition to upgrading performance and clarifying judicial procedure, bar leaders also urged the creation of standards for legal education as yet another way to rid the profession of unqualified lawyers and contribute to the public good. To set law school entrance and curriculum standards, the ABA in 1893 had created a Section on Legal Education and Admissions to the Bar. This development was followed in 1900 by the formation of the American Association of Law Schools, which also promulgated its own set of rigorous guidelines. Both groups sought to upgrade law school entrance requirements and courses of study. Nevertheless, because entrance to the bar was controlled by states, standards varied considerably. For example, Indiana's constitution provided that every voter was entitled to admission to the bar as a matter of right. In contrast, New York State consistently raised its standards during the first two decades of the century. The standards set by schools also varied. Some were content to follow the minimal standards of the state bar. Others, such as Columbia Law School, established standards higher than New York State rules for admission.

Bar leaders saw such structural changes as a way of meeting the profession's public responsibility. Their proposals helped define the shape of twentieth-century legal reform: judicial procedures, court organization, ethics, and legal education standards became continuing areas of concern, and a measure of the profession's desire to accommodate its affairs to public and private pressures. Nevertheless, this approach encountered criticism from liberally oriented lawyers. One reviewer of Stone's *Law and Its Administration* suggested that the author's emphasis on procedure would do little to improve the condition of the average man. Rather, it would reinforce what the law did best, protect the interests of those with property and wealth. "He would improve the machinery of law and make it more efficient, but he seems to think that nothing else is really needed. To be more efficient in doing the old things is . . . cold comfort to those who have seen the inadequacy of doing some of these at all."[21]

---

[21] Quoted in Alpheus T. Mason, *Harlan Fiske Stone: Pillar of the Law* (New York, 1956), p. 118.

As a matter of policy, bar associations generally advised lawyers against professional involvement in or advocacy of economic and social policy issues (e.g., state ownership of industry, the single tax, prohibition, and the redistribution of property), which as one prominent New York bar leader observed, "agitate the thinkers or the economists or the social philosophers."[22] The professional leadership's concern for social welfare or protection of the poor usually centered on legal aid, a movement that began tentatively in the late nineteenth century but gained strength prior to World War I because of increased professional, public, and philanthropic support. But as in the case of ethics, education, and the courts, legal aid attorneys were concerned with procedure rather than with substantive efforts to improve the economic position of the poor. "It is not of chief importance whether the legal organizations win or lose their appeals," declared Reginald Heber Smith, a leading figure in the movement. What matters is that "our common law system should have a fair chance to work itself out . . . by having those issues fairly argued . . . from both points of view."[23] Although they won victories that benefited poor people and provided an alternative to the "shyster" or "ambulance chaser" (the stereotype of the lawyer who preyed on people of little means), legal aid societies were not geared to or inclined to engage in activities that would result in fundamental changes in social conditions.

Counsel to the Situation: The Lawyer as Social Engineer

In contrast, there were a small number of lawyers who believed that the bar had failed for nearly a generation to participate in constructive work to solve the social and economic problems of the age. They believed that lawyers should commit themselves to a higher moral obligation than their clients' interest and be as inventive in the interests of the public as they were in the interests of business. They contributed their services, often without compensation, to assist a broad group or class rather than an individual client. Very often, the individuals they sought to protect were unorganized and ill-equipped

[22] Charles Boston, "The Lawyer's Opportunity," in *Addresses and Writings,* Book II: 1912–1916, New York County Lawyers' Association Collection, p. 97.
[23] Reginald Heber Smith, *Justice and the Poor,* 3rd ed. (New York, 1924), p. 207.

to protect themselves against unscrupulous or unfair businessmen, government bureaucracies, or hostile corporations. These lawyers worked on developing mechanisms—whether in the form of legislation, administrative agencies, or voluntary agreements—that would mediate conflict and strengthen the economic position of lower-income Americans. Their activities constituted a form of legal aid far different from the work of legal aid societies, which were not designed to benefit any individual or group in a substantive manner.

The impulse for this form of sociological jurisprudence came from a number of sources, including such jurists as Oliver Wendell Holmes, such academics as Roscoe Pound, and such practitioners as Louis Brandeis. Holmes's influence in shaping a modern conception of jurisprudence is without parallel. Unlike his late-nineteenth-century contemporaries, he did not view law as a set of mechanical principles. His own personal experiences—as a soldier in the Civil War, as a practitioner and teacher of law, and later (1883–1902) as a Massachusetts state court judge—shaped his view of law as a process rather than a body of principles. His war experience also sharpened his ideas about thought and action. "It is one thing to utter a happy phrase from a protected cloister; another to think under fire—to think for action upon which great interests depend."[24] From this statement, it is not difficult to understand his famous dictum that "the life of the law has not been logic: it has been experience," which he developed in his influential book, *The Common Law* (1881). Holmes forged this philosophy during the same period of time that Christopher Langdell, dean of the Harvard Law School, was introducing the case method approach to the study of law. Under this system, students study a series of excerpts from appellate court decisions arranged chronologically by subject to determine the operating premise. The case approach reinforced the late-nineteenth-century perception that law was an applied, yet completed, body of principles.

Recognizing that lawyers and judges need to understand that law involves making choices between competing social interests, Holmes questioned this conception of legal education. Addressing the 1897 Brown University graduating class, he observed, "If lawyers' training led them habitually to consider more definitely and explicitly the social advantage on which the rule they lay down must be justified,

---

[24] Quoted in Felix Frankfurter, *Mr. Justice Holmes and the Supreme Court* (Cambridge, Mass., 1938), p. 14.

they sometimes would hesitate where they are now confident, and see that really they were taking sides upon debatable and often burning questions."[25] Though his ideas challenged the legal orthodoxy and formalism of his age, they were not meant to encourage a nonrational or instinctive approach to legal study. Thus, sociological jurisprudence was not a radical departure from existing legal philosophy. It still relied on a system, but on one that was not fixed; that is, one which was ready to incorporate changes derived from social and economic experience.

Sociological jurisprudence took on greater shape around the turn of the century, thanks to the work of Roscoe Pound, a lawyer and teacher in the law department of the University of Nebraska and, by 1911, a professor at Harvard Law School. Pound urged legislators, lawyers, and judges to take more account "of the social facts upon which law must proceed and to which it is to be applied."[26] He asserted that legal systems were prone to become rigid and that, when this occurred, it was beneficial to infuse them with experience from outside, particularly through the insights of economics and the social sciences. He looked to law teachers to help reshape juristic thinking so that judges and other lawmakers would see that law was a creative social institution rather than a mechanical system. His ideas stimulated a new generation of liberal-minded lawyers who came to maturity during the first and second decades of the century believing that by relating law and the social sciences, institutions could be reshaped to meet the economic and social needs of Americans.

Again, it must be understood that liberal lawyers worked within the same context of corporate capitalism as did such old-guard lawyers as S. C. T. Dodd and such moderate reformers as Stone. They were not interested in revising property rights in a radical manner or introducing public ownership of wealth. Like other corporate lawyers, they too supported measures to improve business efficiency, reduce waste, and integrate productive units. They differed from their corporate bar colleagues insofar as they believed the health of the nation depended as much on the economic well-being of the worker and his family as it did on increasing productivity and profit. If they sought ways of strengthening this group, it was more to

[25] Oliver Wendell Holmes, *Collected Legal Papers* (New York, 1920), p. 184.
[26] Roscoe Pound, "The Scope and Purpose of Sociological Jurisprudence, III," *Harvard Law Review*, 25 (April 1912), 513.

provide a counterpoise to business than to weaken it. In their interest to be fair, they saw value in protecting businessmen and investors as well as workers and consumers.

Louis Brandeis is an outstanding example of such a lawyer. He made his career as an attorney in Boston during the early part of the century a fulfillment of this philosophy. The roots of Brandeis's interest in legal reform appear to go back to his days as a law student at Harvard Law School (1875–1877), where he was exposed to the thinking of Holmes. Later, as secretary of the Harvard Law School Alumni Association, Brandeis was influential in having Harvard establish a chair for Holmes. As he once told a friend, "Knowledge of decisions and powers of logic are mere handmaidens—they are servants not masters. The controlling force is the deep knowledge of human necessities."[27] These necessities were glaringly apparent during the late nineteenth century in the struggle being waged by workers for social justice. In fact, it was the excessive violence toward workers occasioned by the use of Pinkerton agents at the Homestead plant outside of Pittsburgh during an 1892 strike that made Brandeis think deeply about the social responsibilities of the lawyer. "It took the shock of that battle," he told an interviewer in 1914, "where organized capital hired a private army to shoot at organized labor for resisting an arbitrary cut in wages, to turn my mind definitely toward a searching study of the relations of labor to industry."[28]

Unlike those liberal reformers who viewed government regulation as the best counterweight to business acquisitiveness, Brandeis sought, when he could, to work out nongovernmental solutions to social conflict, that is, methods that minimized government control of business and business dependence on government. For example, during the period from 1904 to 1907, he helped develop a Sliding-Scale Rate Bill for determining the selling price charged by Boston Consolidated Gas. Brandeis proposed establishing a 7 percent per year standard dividend rate; for every five-cent reduction in price, the rate would increase by 1 percent. Under the system, Brandeis hoped management would be encouraged to be more efficient, leading to reduced costs, lower prices for consumers, and larger returns to stockholders. Thus all would benefit. He also thought the

---

[27] Louis Brandeis to William Harrison Dunbar, February 2, 1893, in *Letters of Louis D. Brandeis, vol. 1: 1870–1907: Urban Reformer*, ed. David Levy and Melvin Urofsky (Albany, N.Y., 1971), pp. 106–109.

[28] L. S. Richards, "Up from Aristocracy," *The Independent*, July 27, 1914, p. 130.

plan was a viable alternative to municipal ownership. As he observed in a letter to a supporter of municipal reform, "The great gain is not confined to cheaper gas. We expect to get, what is more important, purer politics, because the bill will have the effect of eliminating the Gas Company from the field of politics."[29]

Regardless of which side he might represent, Brandeis tried to accommodate all interests. As labor counsel during the 1910 New York garment industry strike, he urged the union to give up its demand for a closed shop. Searching for common ground upon which to mediate the dispute between manufacturers and workers, he directed the participants toward acceptance of what he called the preferential or union shop. Under this arrangement, employers would commit themselves to hiring union workers in situations where they had a choice between equally qualified union and nonunion candidates. To oversee this arrangement as well as govern the operation of the industry generally, Brandeis advocated the creation of internal, self-governing mechanisms. Such mechanisms included a board of grievances to settle disputes that could not be handled by lower-level committees of employers and employees; a board to oversee sanitary conditions; and a board of arbitration, which, like a court of last resort, would hear appeals from the grievance committee. Each of these mechanisms sought to prevent either party from resorting to a strike or lockout. Brandeis counted on good faith and accommodation to make the plan work. He underestimated, however, the individualism of the garment industry. In 1916, the protocol was abandoned. Its failure once again raised the question of how effective cooperative and voluntary methods could be in solving serious economic problems.

The protocol experience also raised another issue that hovered over each new effort to by-pass the courts for settling social and economic conflicts: who would manage administrative agencies? Lawyers thought that they were in the best position to perform this task, since they were skilled in fact-finding, weighing evidence, and arriving at independent judgments. This mediational role was, after all, what Progressives such as Croly had argued was missing among practitioners. Businessmen, on the other hand, thought that although lawyers might possess these skills, they did not understand the nature

---

[29] Quoted in Alpheus T. Mason, *Brandeis: A Free Man's Life* (New York, 1946), p. 140.

of business and were inclined to "legalize" issues, that is, cast them in a judicial rather than economic context. This was a matter of paramount importance throughout the century as lawyers became involved in designing administrative mechanisms and expected, therefore, to have the responsibility for implementing them.

Brandeis's belief in applying rational and scientific methods to business and industry carried over to the field of legislation, where he was a strong advocate of improving methods of drafting social welfare laws and defending them against constitutional or legal challenge. In this regard, he served as a model for a number of young, progressive-minded lawyers who were eager to participate in public affairs. Although they may not always have designed the laws, these lawyers did play a critical role in adjusting the ideas of reformers to accord with constitutional and statutory limitations. They understood that effective legislation required skill in harmonizing new laws with existing ones, as well as knowledge of the legal situation into which the legislation would fit. This meant that lawyers needed to be trained in this new method of legal work or exposed to it through some practical experience.

A growing number of lawyers found the opportunity to acquire these skills while serving as advisers to politicians, social reformers, and legislative investigatory commissions. Some participated in state legislative drafting or reference bureaus, or in privately funded agencies such as the one that Columbia University established in 1911. The Columbia group provided advanced law students with the chance to study legislative methods and conduct research work in administration and legislation. Students worked in libraries and in the field among economists, administrators, and other knowledgeable people. The group involved itself in such diverse areas as workmen's compensation, shipping, uniform state laws, uniform probate of wills, criminal procedure, law enforcement, and administrative procedure. The success of this five-year experiment helped establish the group on a permanent basis, reinforced the importance of research as a component of modern legislation, and provided a valuable outlet for public service.

These socially conscious lawyers also helped advance the manner in which the laws were presented to courts for review. In addition to establishing the constitutional and legal authority for the laws, they presented to the courts an array of nonlegal data showing their social and economic purpose and the circumstances surrounding the legislature's action. In *Muller v. Oregon* (1908), where Brandeis introduced the method (hence the term "Brandeis brief"), hundreds of reports, domestic and foreign, from committees, statistical bureaus, commissioners of hygiene, and factory inspectors were produced to support legislation prohibiting night work for women. In spite of their dislike for this type of legal argument, even some conservative lawyers were, by the teens, resorting to this technique—but more as a way of countering the strategy of such reformers as Brandeis and Frankfurter.

For the most part, moderate and conservative leaders of the bar remained generally opposed to social welfare laws and those who advocated them. This sentiment was vividly demonstrated by the uproar in 1915 over President Woodrow Wilson's nomination of Brandeis to the United States Supreme Court. Although eventually confirmed, the hearings on his nomination exposed the deep resentment felt by members of the bar toward Brandeis's political, social, and even religious beliefs (he was the first Jewish justice). Even a moderate such as Taft confided to a friend that he thought Brandeis was emotional, socialistic, unscrupulous, and a threat to the integrity of the court. But an even more telling objection concerned Brandeis's role as a counsel to the situation. Many opponents of the nomination claimed that Brandeis had used his corporate connections to gain valuable information, which he then used against them. Such charges suggested how difficult the role of mediator or people's attorney could be.

Sociological Jurisprudence and the Courts

The issue of sociological jurisprudence created a dilemma for judges, who, like their colleagues at the bar, were criticized by Progressives for not weighing legal conflicts with the interests of society in mind; that is, they too were accused of favoring businessmen over workers and consumers; of standing in the way of changes in common-law rules and needed social welfare legislation. Some Progressives, among them former President Theodore Roosevelt, urged that judicial decisions by state courts be recalled when they failed to promote the readjustment of economic and social conditions. Others, such as Roscoe Pound, offered a more moderate solution. Pound explained that the judiciary tended to protect business interests because judges trained in the common law were accustomed to reflecting concern for individual rather than social rights. He believed that courts must secure individual interests only to the extent that they were social interests. In other words, although courts could never escape dealing with the rights of the individual, they should take better care to ensure that by upholding these rights they also upheld the general security and welfare of American institutions.

During the Progressive period, courts were faced with a variety of new issues resulting from the transformations caused by industrialization, technology, and urbanization, as well as by changes in business practice. In some cases, courts, particularly at the state level, handled these issues by effectively modernizing old rules to suit new conditions. In other instances, judicial resistance to modifying established principles led reformers and politicians to resort to legislation. In the field of product liability, some state courts began to revise the doctrine of privity by acknowledging that manufacturers of products that might be inherently dangerous if defective were liable not only to the vendee, that is, the one with whom they had contracted to sell the article, which in most cases was a dealer, but also to the one for whom the product was ultimately destined, that is, the consumer. This change in legal doctrine came about in part because judges recognized that an increasingly larger number of manufactured goods were being handled by middlemen or distributors before reaching the consumer. In a 1916 case involving an injury to the owner of an automobile with a defective wheel, Benjamin Cardozo, a progressive-minded New York State Court of Appeals judge declared, "If the nature of a thing is such that it is reasonably certain to place life and limb in peril when negligently made, it is then a thing of danger. Its nature gives warning of the consequences to be expected. If to the element of danger there is added knowledge that the thing will be used by persons other than the purchaser, and used without new tests, then, irrespective of contract, the manufacturer of this thing of danger is under a duty to make it carefully."[30] Although not every state court subscribed to this new theory at once, it did signal a change in judicial thinking regarding liability, and it demonstrated the effectiveness of common law adjudication.

Courts, however, did not always adjust the common law to meet

---

[30] *MacPherson v. Buick Motor Co.*, 111 N.E. 1053 (1916).

changing economic and social conditions. A case in point was occupational injury, where judicial resistance resulted in the passage by state legislatures of workmen's compensation laws. Throughout the nineteenth century, American courts generally held that an employer's liability for injury to his workers was limited by his responsibility to exercise reasonable care. To produce further protection against suit, courts fashioned such doctrines as (1) the fellow servant rule (a master was not liable for injury to an employee caused by the negligence of another employee); and (2) the assumption of risk (even when an employer was negligent, if the employee knew of the danger when he or she took the job there was no cause for action). Like the doctrine of privity in product liability, these rules were formulated in a simpler age, when the relation of master and servant were more proximate. With industrialization, not only were master and servant farther removed but the causes of possible accidents arising from negligence became more complex and variable. Nevertheless, courts resisted imposing an absolute liability on employers. As a result, a number of state legislatures enacted a variety of compensation laws, obligating the employer, independent of fault, to compensate the injured worker. In addition to resolving the legal and economic aspects of the problem, compensation laws were designed to reduce the social conflict that attended accident litigation, particularly the employee's fear of employer retaliation and loss of his job if he or she brought suit. By neutralizing this acute economic, personal, and social issue, state legislatures took an important step toward harmonizing employer–employee relations and promoting industrial safety and security.

But passage of regulatory laws and creation of administrative agencies did not remove judges from having to deal with broad issues of social welfare, since controversy inevitably developed over the constitutionality and implementation of these statutes and administrative rulings. In a way, the conflict between advocates of legislation and supporters of judicial action was spurious. As one thoughtful observer, Felix Frankfurter, pointed out in 1915, "[I]n the last analysis, the whole field of law is for judicial development, because of the reviewing power of the courts." He suggested that it was necessary that statute law and law developed through judicial opinion harmonize. Judges, he noted, should not lose sight of, nor be "uninfluenced by the reasons back of this legislation."[31] Nevertheless, judges asked to review the constitutionality of regulatory legislation were caught up in the dilemma of having to separate their attitudes as citizens (and, in many instances, former corporate lawyers) from their professional responsibility of deciding whether the laws were constitutional. Thus, while states circumvented common law courts in dealing with workmen's compensation, they could not circumvent judicial review. (In one notable instance, the New York State Court of Appeals in *Ives v. South Buffalo Railway Company* [1911] found a New York state compensation law unconstitutional.) This area of judicial decision making grew throughout the century, as legislation and administration came to supplant common-law methods for dealing with economic and social issues. Judicial decision making concerning the constitutionality of regulatory legislation became a source of public controversy affecting both law and politics.

A classic example of this conflict over judicial review of social welfare laws was *Lochner v. New York* (1905), where a majority of the judges of the United States Supreme Court, the final arbiter of the constitutionality of state regulatory laws, invalidated a law limiting the daily hours of work of bakers to ten. In the opinion of a majority of the judges, there was not a sufficient relationship between the hours of work and the health of the bakers to justify state intervention. "Clean and wholesome bread," declared Justice Peckham, "does not depend upon whether the baker works but ten hours per day or only sixty hours a week."[32] The Court decided that for the statute to be valid, it must relate directly to a legitimate end. They rejected the claim that the trade of a baker was sufficiently unhealthy to warrant interfering with the freedom of contract between employer and employee.

In dissent, Justice Oliver Wendell Holmes, who had joined the Court in 1902, differed with his colleagues over both the question of the law's constitutionality and the role of the Court in reviewing such legislation. As a rule, he believed judges should be detached and neutral in their attitude toward these laws, regardless of whether as citizens they would oppose or favor them. "I strongly believe," he

[31] Felix Frankfurter, "The Law and the Law Schools," *American Bar Association Journal*, 1 (1915), 536.
[32] *Lochner v. New York*, 198 U.S. 45, 57 (1905).

said, "that my agreement or disagreement has nothing to do with the right of a majority to embody their opinions in law." Moreover, he criticized his judicial colleagues for injecting their ideas about social and economic theory into the decision process. "[A] Constitution is not intended" he went on, "to embody a particular economic theory, whether of paternalism and the organic relation of the citizen to the State or of *laissez-faire*."[33] From his standpoint, legislation was constitutional if a "rational and fair man" thought it was reasonable. Since most of his colleagues were less willing to confine their judicial power to such a simple test, cases involving questions of regulation became clouded by lengthy examinations of the wisdom of particular legislative actions.

In spite of its decision in *Lochner*, the record of the Supreme Court during the last decade of the nineteenth century and first decade of the twentieth century with regard to state regulation was not entirely reactionary. In fact, the Court upheld a variety of regulatory laws involving (1) the protection of women (e.g., eight-hour laws and prohibitions on night work and on work during certain periods before and after childbirth), (2) the purity of foods, (3) rates and management of railroads, (4) public improvements, (5) health and safety conditions, (6) zoning, and (7) professional licensing. One survey found that out of 560 state statutes adjudicated under the due process and equal protection clauses between 1887 and 1911, the Court upheld over 530.[34] These statistics suggest that the Court responded affirmatively to the growing need for administrative solutions to social and economic problems. But the same study found that the Court also invalidated 3 laws relating to social justice and 34 relating to the private rights of property, suggesting that in these vital areas of public policy the judiciary was not of one mind.

Although the Court might uphold legislation expanding the scope of government control over business, it refrained from acknowledging the existence of an outright authority on the part of states, under the police power, to protect the consumer and the worker. For example, the Court refused to uphold state price regulation unless it could be shown that the nature of the business substantially affected the public interest. In *German Alliance Company v. Lewis* (1914), it

---

[33] Ibid., p. 75.
[34] Charles Warren, "The Progressiveness of the United States Supreme Court," *Columbia Law Review*, 13 (April 1913), 309.

upheld the constitutionality of a Kansas law regulating the fire insurance business because losses caused by fire, the Court reasoned, could be spread over a wide area of the community. As a result, contracts for hazard insurance had greater public consequence than normal contracts between private citizens.

In contrast, the same Court was unwilling to extend this reasoning to a situation where a statute made it a misdemeanor for employers to require employees, as part of their contract of employment, to refrain from joining a union. In *Coppage v. Kansas* (1915), the Court showed that on some issues it held views much closer to the ideology of laissez faire and social Darwinism than to that of sociological jurisprudence. In the opinion of the majority, employers and employees came to the bargaining table as equals, and the government had no authority to interfere with this relationship, even if past circumstances had rendered one party more powerful than the other. Public policy, Justice Mahlon Pitney argued, did not justify the leveling of inequalities, as long as private property was the basis of social relations. The decision not only hindered any meaningful labor organization for the next decade and a half but revealed how deep a schism existed within the legal profession over the issue of individual property rights and governmental regulation.

Even when the Court acknowledged the constitutionality of administrative control over private economic affairs, it scrutinized the actions of the agencies involved. In the field of rate regulation of railroads and public utilities, the Court adopted the position that rates could not be set in such a way as to yield a return on investment that would be confiscatory. In other words, if the commission used a formula that did not result in a fair return on the fair value of the property, the rate order constituted a deprivation of property without due process.* The Court was deaf to critics who argued that courts should defer to the judgment of experts. They were equally unconvinced by the claim that the effect of all regulation is to reduce the income of the property owner or investor. These critics argued that it was erroneous policy to allow an agency to set rates yet, at the same time, not permit it to limit earnings. Conservatives could not easily reconcile their understanding of due process, which meant that

---

* As used by the courts, due process of law referred not only to the procedure used in passing or enforcing a law but to the very substance of the law. If the nature of a law or rule was unreasonable, capricious, or arbitrary, then the law was without due process.

property owners were entitled to the full and beneficial use of their property, with legislative efforts to weaken this right.

Nevertheless, even the modest and gradual acceptance by the Court of state regulation troubled some business lawyers. They were unprepared to advise their clients to share decisions about prices, a traditional management prerogative, with untried administrative agencies or courts of general jurisdiction. According to Louis Marshall, a prominent New York constitutional lawyer, the introduction of price-fixing laws meant that the legislature may "say to the farmer or to the grocer that, irrespective of the contract price at which he may sell to a customer milk, potatoes, wheat, or any other of his products, the purchaser may contest the reasonableness of the price and be limited in his payment to the sum that a court or jury may eventually determine to be the just and reasonable price." "There is not a business conceivable," he concluded, "however private it may be, that could not with equal right be made dependent upon the action of the legislature."[35] For Marshall and other business lawyers, social improvement would develop, as it always had, by adhering to such values as stability, certainty, and business freedom.

In contrast some members of the legal community strongly favored acknowledging once and for all that states, under the police power, were authorized to regulate economic affairs in any rational way they saw fit, unless restrained by explicit constitutional provisions to the contrary. "The legislative or police power is a dynamic agency," declared Judge Cuthbert Pound of the New York State Court of Appeals, one of a small number of progressive-minded lower court judges. If we continue to restrict the range of state legislative power, he asserted, we will, in effect, have forced the state to surrender "one of the attributes of sovereignty for which governments are founded and made itself powerless to secure to its citizens the blessings of freedom and to promote the general welfare."[36] Pound considered this argument sufficient to uphold a 1920 New York law preventing landlords from raising rents unreasonably during a severe housing shortage induced by wartime conditions.

This is not to suggest that Pound and other liberally oriented

[35] Louis Marshall, *Brief for Amici Curiae, Marcus Brown Holding Company v. Marcus Feldman et al.*, 256 U.S. 170 (1921), in *Records and Briefs*, United States Supreme Court, October term, 1920, pp. 49 ff., 80, 85–91.
[36] *People ex. rel. Durham Realty Corporation v. LaFetra*, 230 N.Y. 429, 442–443 (1921).

judges were ready to abandon their authority to review legislation. Like conservatives, many of them doubted the value of sociological jurisprudence. But unlike conservatives, they feared the consequences (e.g., social disorder, labor unrest) if the profession continued to lag behind other social and economic institutions in modernizing its practices and attitudes. The time had come, Cuthbert Pound exhorted in judicial opinions, law review articles, and bar association addresses, for lawyers to challenge authority in order "to loose 'the dead hand of the common law rule.'" "Call it sociological justice or any other hard name from the vocabulary of technical philosophy . . . ," Pound asserted, "the courts have always in a greater or less degree given ear to those who contend for a modification of the old rule to conform to modern conditions."[37]

The first two decades of the twentieth century were a turning point for legal institutions. The legal profession sought to meet the Progressive challenge to its organization and status by seeking ways of accommodating both its activities and those of its business clients to pressing economic and social needs. The bar responded by establishing stronger ties to government—in some cases, as a means of rationalizing business practices; in others, to assist government in efforts to improve working and living conditions for a majority of Americans. They also sought to reconstruct their own organization on a more ethical and efficient basis. In each instance, there was a growing reliance on administration and standards. These efforts, however, did not reduce the substantial tension within the judiciary, as judges struggled to resolve questions concerning demands for improved social conditions versus respect for property rights, and demands for national control of business versus demands by business for freedom and self-regulatory prerogatives. These issues grew more intense during the twenties and thirties, as changing economic and social conditions forced politicians, businessmen, lawyers, and reformers to search for additional methods of fulfilling the shaping vision of Progressive-era reform.

---

[37] Cuthbert Pound, "The Relation of the Practicing Lawyer to the Efficient Administration of Justice," *Cornell Law Quarterly*, 9 (April 1924), 242.

TWO

The Years Between the Wars: 1919—1941

Although the moralistic fervor of Progressivism declined after World War I, its more rational side—that is, the development of standards and methods for managing a more efficient and cooperative society—was not lost. If anything, these ideals carried over into the twenties and thirties with renewed intensity, as business, government, and the legal profession sought ways of modernizing and rationalizing their activities and functions. With the growing separation of ownership from management, business sought methods of operating according to scientific theories of organization and behavior, rather than relying on late-nineteenth-century theories of unrestrained competition and laissez faire. Enlightened businessmen looked for proven ways of organizing resources, reducing waste, and maximizing profit. Economic planning and forecasting of market behavior became twin corporate goals. To accomplish these goals, corporate leaders sought the advice of a new array of managers, technicians, scientists, economists—and lawyers.

Corporate lawyers helped promote the spirit of this new competition by working out the details to implement such cooperative techniques as trade associations and commercial arbitration. Both were designed to assist business planning and growth, and reduce industrial conflicts when they arose. Lawyers aided corporate leaders in seeking government help against unwanted trade practices, yet opposed federal or state regulations that interfered with traditional business prerogatives, such as setting production levels, prices, and wages, or limiting a corporation's ability to acquire additional capital and markets. Lawyers were retained to shield corporations from antitrust prosecutions, as well as from the growing public demand for such social welfare legislation as minimum wages.

Above all, businessmen bitterly resisted unionization, and turned to their legal counsel to head off further labor organization. For a time during the twenties, business and some parts of organized labor were able to cooperate in promoting harmonious relations. But this situation applied mostly to craft unions. In the growing industrial trades, the conflict between labor and business did not abate, and it is here that the point of contact between labor, business, and the law was most acute. In other words, the cooperative spirit of the twenties masked the deep social tension that still existed between those who believed in the sanctity and inviolability of property and the liberty of contract, and those who maintained that these rights could be regulated on behalf of larger social interests. Once again, the judiciary was caught in the middle of the controversy, and its reaction to this issue during the twenties and thirties largely determined the outcome and shape of economic and industrial relations.

Planning, cooperation, and social responsiveness affected other areas of the law and legal institutions. Some lawyers played a role in strengthening government enterprise, particularly in commercial areas into which business was unwilling to venture. As demands for public services increased and it became apparent that business could not provide them, local and state governments sought new mechanisms for financing and organizing large-scale enterprises. Here, too, many socially conscious lawyers came to play a constructive role in devising new instrumentalities, often fashioned out of existing, though dormant, constitutional and legislative powers. Rather than litigation, which they considered costly and time-consuming, these lawyers championed collective and coordinated solutions, arrived at scientifically, for dealing with issues of economic and social organization. They favored preventive rather than punitive action, and continuity rather than the disruptions of a courtroom trial and appeal. As a result, there was a burgeoning of administrative mechanisms and law.

During this period, the organized bar continued to look internally for ways of reconstructing its own social, professional, and educational standards. There were brief and abortive attempts to revise legal education and legal doctrine so that they took greater account of social and economic circumstances. Lawyers urged that legal rules, particularly when they affected private relations, be updated and made more uniform from state to state. In this respect, law teachers emerged as effective resources for legal reform. Some lawyers proposed organizing bar association activities on a corporate basis— that is, in such a way that membership in professional groups would be compulsory rather than voluntary. These lawyers believed that such a system would, among other things, enable the legal profession to respond better to social change. The scheme had only modest success, for, as a whole, the organized bar preferred voluntary rather than compulsory organization as a means of regulating and controlling legal standards and behavior. Nevertheless, the highly individualistic character of the legal profession enabled a small portion of that community to play a critical role in organizing and modernizing economic resources and institutions.

Business Planning and the Law

World War I helped forge a strong sense of cooperation between business and government and a belief in the value of economic planning. To meet the war effort, the Wilson administration assembled a vast number of agencies to handle the nation's credit, financial, labor, trade, and industrial relations policies. Committees of businessmen, lawyers, and academics worked together with government officials to develop codes and other forms of industrial agreements for the regulation of the economy. Taking time off in 1918 from his faculty position at Harvard, Felix Frankfurter led the War Labor Board in creating mechanisms for self-government in industry. After the war, business engaged in new efforts to rationalize its activities by the integration of productive units within industry. Consolidations and mergers occurred in a number of areas, including the automobile, iron and steel, motion picture, food product, and telecommunications industries, as businessmen looked for ways of obtaining additional capital to renovate and build new plants and expand their markets nationally. Investment bankers, searching for ways to employ excess capital, found these large corporations an attractive investment.

As might be expected, business supported efforts to relax enforcement of the antitrust laws. The Justice Department and the Federal Trade Commission geared their policies toward enforcing the unfair trade practice provisions of the antitrust laws rather than their antimonopoly provisions. Both agencies used sparingly their powers to prosecute holding companies. When they did prosecute, as in the government's suit against the United States Steel Company, they met resistance from the Supreme Court. In one notable case, the Court held that the United States Steel Corporation, a holding company (that is, one controlling the stock of several companies) formed in 1901 to integrate production among twelve iron and steel manufacturers, had not violated the antitrust laws. Although the corporation had in the past sought unsuccessfully to restrain trade, the Court noted that at the time of the suit, it was engaged in no illegal activity. Moreover, the Court rejected the government's contention that size alone was determinative of monopoly. "The Corporation is undoubtedly of impressive size," wrote Justice McKenna, "and it takes an effort of resolution not to be affected by it or to exaggerate its influence. But we must adhere to the law and the law does not make mere size an offense."[1]

The apparent relaxation of the antitrust laws gave businessmen and their lawyers the opportunity to experiment with new forms of cooperative activity, one of which was the trade association. Trade associations were voluntary organizations of business competitors who joined together to share information about accounting practices, business standards, commercial and industrial research, public relations statistics, and trade promotion. With the help of lawyers, businessmen developed a structure, almost a form of legislation, to provide standards and ethics for the guidance of individual industries. A typical agreement might provide for a statement of the reasons why the association was being formed. Like a statute, the trade association agreement presented a series of facts concerning the problems within an industry and the need for coordinating activities. It provided the ground rules for membership and laid out prohibitions on certain unfair practices such as price discrimination. By incorporating essential features of public policy in these agreements, businessmen hoped to strengthen their claim to self-regulation.

---

[1] *United States v. United States Steel Corporation*, 251 U.S. 417, 451 (1920).

To enforce the terms of the agreement, the association might adopt a resolution calling for arbitration of disputes. In Chicago, for example, the Central Committee to Promote Commercial Arbitration encouraged trade associations to follow the State of Illinois Arbitration Act, and the rules and regulations of the committee. These provisions called for the mutual submission of claims by the parties to an arbitrator followed by a hearing in which "evidence . . . may be taken and the proceedings . . . conducted in a mercantile way without regard to legal technicalities." But arbitrators were permitted to submit questions of law to an appropriate court, and the answers were to be binding. The final award would be made in accordance with the arbitrator's "own sense of the equities of the case, taking into consideration such trade customs and usages as may be applicable."[2] Advocates of commercial arbitration believed it maintained the relationship of harmony among businessmen, which litigation, by virtue of its coercive and combative character, could not. They viewed it as a constructive means for using the law to strengthen rather than exacerbate commercial relations. Thus it fitted the spirit of cooperation, rather than confrontation, that many lawyers hoped to promote.

Businessmen hoped that trade associations and commercial arbitration would provide methods for achieving the kind of planning and coordination they found difficult under normal competitive activity. They looked to the government and the courts for acceptance of these methods and further endorsement of the policy of cooperation. But the Justice Department and the judiciary were not fully prepared to relax their enforcement of the antitrust laws to favor trade association activities. In one of the most prominent decisions, early in the decade, *American Column and Lumber Co. v. United States*, the Supreme Court rejected the argument of a newly formed association of hardwood manufacturers that their organization was created solely to exchange and disseminate information about market conditions so that members could make "intelligent" decisions about production and prices. The association believed that their activities reduced cut-throat competition and provided a more cooperative atmosphere

[2] "Arbitration Rules and Regulations of the Central Committee to Promote Commercial Arbitration of Chicago, Illinois," *Journal of the American Judicature Society*, 2 (August 1918), 58. See also "Commercial Arbitration in England," *Journal of the American Judicature Society*, 2 (August 1918), 53.

for the conduct of business. Members were required to make full disclosure of intimate details about production, which the association compiled, analyzed, and disseminated, in reports and at conferences, in order to predict market conditions and prices.

The Court considered the character of the information (future market conditions, production estimates, and future prices) and the use made of it (assimilating the data and making specific recommendations) characteristic of a "competition suppressing organization." Other factors also led to this conclusion. The closeness of business competitors with one another, the tendency of producers to follow the lead of the more powerful competitors, and the opprobrium of being judged unfaithful to the others in the group were, the Court argued, elements of coercion that were used to compel compliance with the association's proposals. "Genuine competitors," the Court concluded, "do not make daily, weekly, and monthly reports of the minutest details of their business to their rivals. . . . [T]hey do not contract . . . to submit their books to the discretionary audit and their stocks to the discretionary inspection of their rivals for the purpose of successfully competing with them."[3]

In dissent, Justices Holmes and Brandeis, who had joined the Court in 1916, argued that the association merely employed a rational technique for regulating production: urging restraint when demand was low and encouraging expansion when demand was high. Holmes observed, quite perceptively, that this was nothing more than an "allwise socialistic government" might do to promote the public welfare. In his opinion, the association did not try to take advantage of the market by profiting unfairly but sought ways of conforming to it. Both judges commended the association for trying to substitute knowledge and education for ignorance and suspicion. Their attitude reflected the view held by the many businessmen, lawyers, and political leaders who believed the Sherman Act should be used only to prevent agreements that were patently coercive and "unlawfully" narrowed the market. More generally, it represented a general movement during the twenties and early thirties either to relax or to suspend the antitrust laws.

A few years later, the Court modified its position toward trade association activities. "Free competition," declared Justice Harlan

---

[3] *American Column and Lumber Company v. United States*, 257 U.S. 377, 410 (1921).

Fiske Stone, who had been appointed to the Court in 1925 after serving as attorney general in the Coolidge administration, in *Maple Flooring Manufacturers Association v. United States* (1925), "means a free and open market among both buyers and sellers for the sale and distribution of commodities." Competition, he argued, is no less free when businessmen try to make themselves more knowledgeable about the essential factors of commercial transactions.[4] He distinguished the facts in *Maple Flooring* from those in *American Column* by the character of the information exchanged and the use made of it. In *Maple*, the defendants exchanged information regarding the cost of production, transportation, surplus inventory, and the price of the goods in the market—all of which the Court considered perfectly legal. What is more, no evidence was produced to show that the members of the association sought to use this information to interfere with commerce or to restrain trade. In other words, the Court found no evidence of concerted action on the part of the member manufacturers to control production or prices. Nevertheless, Stone cautioned businessmen that improper use of the trade association method would subject them to antitrust prosecution. Once again, businessmen were given no absolute guarantee that their activities would not run afoul of the law. Each case would be judged separately, which, for businessmen, reduced the sense of security and freedom from antitrust prosecution they had been seeking since the turn of the century.

The Court's trade association opinions also reflected its doubts about allowing private groups authority to create legal obligations on individuals or groups who might not be fairly represented by the agreement. The Court was reluctant to give business a free hand to set standards of industry practice that would be imposed on other producers, workers, and the public. What guarantees existed that these standards would be developed with the same rigor and detachment as legislation? The tendency of powerful elements to dominate the weaker groups existed as much in the trade association as it did if the businesses were merged. Self-regulation left open the possibility that new ideas and new interests would not be permitted to develop. The Court wished to avoid this possibility and at the same time keep alive honest efforts to rationalize business practices. No matter how

[4] *Maple Flooring Manufacturers Association v. United States*, 268 U.S. 563, 583 (1925).

attractive cooperation and rationalization were, efficiency would not be won at the expense of free and fair access to the market for all producers and consumers.

Labor, Law, and Other Social Interests

The business community's prospects for success in planning and efficiency depended in large part on its ability to curb labor conflict, of which there had been a substantial amount immediately following the conclusion of the war. The prevailing business attitude toward labor was one of resistance, preferring to treat workers as an item of cost, to be liquidated when market conditions warranted, rather than as a partner in the productive process. In the view of most business-men, unions represented an obstacle to business freedom; when they accepted labor, it was usually in the form of company-controlled unions. Some entrepreneurs—Henry Ford, for example—also saw laborers as consumers and sought to increase their purchasing power through higher wages. Ford understood that consumption was as important as production. There was little wisdom in increasing production through scientific management if there was no market to absorb this productive capacity. Nevertheless, his attitudes also reflected a form of paternalism and sprang from a desire to prevent labor unrest and unionization. Many labor groups, generally those with skilled craft workers, accepted this form of welfare capitalism. Like business, they were benefiting from the rise in prices and wages during the twenties, and from the expansion in foreign trade. And like business, many of these crafts (e.g., boilermakers, bricklayers, carpenters, and printers) exercised their own form of opportunism by limiting entrance into their professions through long apprenticeships and high initiation fees.

Such, however, was not the case with the growing number of industrial unions, which were composed of unskilled workers; they were more militant in pursuing labor organization. But their activities were circumscribed by unsympathetic courts, which, among other things, viewed many of these unions as communist-inspired. In *American Steel Foundries v. Tri-City Central Trades Council* (1921), for example, the Supreme Court strengthened business's hand against strikes where picketing was accompanied by violence and intimidation. It ruled that picketing was not included as a protection afforded by section 20 of the Clayton Antitrust Act. Writing the majority opinion, William Howard Taft, who had just become chief justice, observed, "Congress wished to forbid the use by the federal courts of their equity arm to prevent peaceable persuasion by employees . . . in promotion of their side of the dispute. . . . This introduces no new principle into the equity jurisprudence of those courts. It is merely declaratory of what was the best practice always. Congress thought it wise to stabilize this rule of action and render it uniform." According to Taft, the very phrase "peaceful picketing" was a contradiction in terms. Picketing connoted a militant and sinister purpose. Taft did suggest, however, that the act allowed for peaceful persuasion, as long as such persuasion did not involve methods that would lead to intimidation and obstruction.[5]

The problem for some labor leaders, however, was the uncertainty of what the Court meant by intimidation. Given the explosiveness of a strike situation, such an interpretation of the picketing process served as a powerful constraint and inhibition. In *American Steel*, for example, the Trades Council contended that the alleged violence was the result of strikebreakers. In contrast, other union heads remained undisturbed by the decision. They saw it as an indication that the Court would not tolerate violence and intimidation but would accept union efforts to give proper notice of a labor dispute. Benjamin Schlesinger, president of the International Ladies' Garment Workers' Union, thought the decision upheld labor's right to picket as long as it was done peacefully. "Organized labor has never approved of violence or intimidation by pickets in labor troubles, and is glad to see a ban placed on it by the courts."[6]

In addition to restrictions on picketing, courts also weakened unionization by granting businessmen injunctions halting strikes when it could be shown that the activities threatened to disrupt the flow of commerce and result in irreparable harm. In *Duplex Printing Press Company v. Deering* (1921), the Supreme Court ruled that labor's exemption from the antitrust laws under the Clayton Act applied only to strike activities involving an employer and employee

---

[5] *American Steel Foundries v. Tri-City Central Trades Council*, 257 U.S. 184, 203 (1921).

[6] *New York Times*, December 6, 1921, p. 21.

directly related by contract, thereby outlawing secondary boycotts and sympathetic strikes. The injunction was also a powerful deterrent to unionization, since it had the effect of weakening organizational momentum. An effort by one state, Arizona, to restrict the use of this form of equity relief was turned back by the Court in *Truax v. Corrigan* (1921), constituting yet another setback to the labor movement in the twenties.

Only a handful of judges throughout the country protested these restrictions on labor. Among Supreme Court justices, Holmes and Brandeis were the leading opponents of the Court's antilabor policy. For example, Brandeis disagreed with the Court's position in *Duplex*. First, he thought the Court was intruding into a matter that was more properly legislative. Second, he defended labor's need to organize in spite of the fact that it might inconvenience the community. "The conditions developed in industry," he argued, "may be such that those engaged in it cannot continue their struggle without danger to the community. But it is not for judges to determine whether such conditions exist, nor is it their function to set the limits of permissible contest and to declare the duties which the new situation demands." Brandeis urged the parties to look to the legislative branch for relief. The legislature's role was to "substitute processes of justice for the more primitive method of trial by combat."[7] As for state efforts to limit use of injunctions, he maintained, in a dissenting opinion in *Truax v. Corrigan* that no state is obliged "to protect all property rights by injunction merely because it protects some."[8]

Although Brandeis was one of the most outspoken proponents of judicial restraint, he was less reluctant to interpose the judicial function when the question involved legislative restrictions on personal freedoms. Postwar frenzy over foreign influence had led to a rash of legislation restricting Bill of Rights freedoms. For example, in 1923, Brandeis joined the conservative majority in using the due process clause to overturn the laws of several midwestern states prohibiting the teaching of foreign languages to any students below the eighth grade in public or private schools. The Court characterized the laws as arbitrary, capricious, and unrelated to the welfare of the community or young children. In dissent, Holmes chided his brethren, as he had done in *Lochner* in 1905, for substituting their views of

[7] *Duplex Printing Press Company v. Deering*, 254 U.S. 443, 488 (1921).
[8] *Truax v. Corrigan*, 257 U.S. 312, 374 (1921).

social welfare for the community's. "I think I appreciate the objection to the law," he wrote, "but it appears to me to present a question upon which men reasonably might differ and therefore I am unable to say that the Constitution of the United States prevents the experiment being tried."[9]

Writing anonymously in the *New Republic*, Harvard law professor Felix Frankfurter warned that judicial nullification of antiliberal laws was not necessarily an "encouragement to liberalism." Rather, it encouraged laissez-faire jurists to think their invalidation of economic legislation was justified. "In rejoicing over the Nebraska . . . [case]," he wrote, "we must not forget that a heavy price has to be paid for these occasional services to liberalism." Like Holmes, he thought the Court confused constitutionality with propriety. "Such an attitude," he observed, "is a great enemy of liberalism." A liberal society, he argued, was not won in courts but in the public mind, which he equated with the legislature. He admitted that the foreign language laws were silly; but he thought that once the postwar hysteria subsided, they would be repealed by a liberal resurgence. In contrast, the Court's invalidation of liberal economic laws was more far-reaching, durable, and authoritative, and less easily remedied.[10] Legislative restrictions of personal freedoms, although not a predominant concern of the Court in the twenties and thirties, gained greater attention during and after the forties. As they did so, the issue of judicial review of such laws emerged as a consideration of substantial importance.

Government Planning and Legal Engineering

During the twenties, political leaders also came to realize that certain economic activities did not lend themselves to organization, development, and coordination through private enterprise alone. The demands of Americans for a higher standard of living outpaced the ability of business to develop such areas as interstate commercial activity (e.g., railroads, bridges, tunnels), hydroelectric power, hous-

[9] See *Meyer v. Nebraska*, 262 U.S. 390 (1923); and *Bartels v. State of Iowa*, 262 U.S. 404, 412 (1923).
[10] "Can the Supreme Court Guarantee Toleration?" *New Republic*, 43 (June 17, 1925), 85–87 (unsigned editorial).

ing, and recreation. Businessmen found the return on investment in these enterprises small and often not worth the risk. Government development also had drawbacks. State, county, and municipal governments found that financing such projects through taxation was unpopular; and constitutionally imposed debt limitations weakened their ability to raise private capital.

For example, conditions in the port of New York illustrated the failure of private enterprise to rationalize freight traffic in and out of the New York metropolitan area—that is, to develop methods for shipping and delivering goods more quickly and less expensively. Internecine conflict among shippers, particularly railroads, impeded efforts to reduce inefficiency. The geographic location of the port, between two states and among several municipalities, placed special burdens on shippers and reduced the chances of effective planning. To remedy this situation, New York and New Jersey legislators appointed a commission in 1917 to investigate the problem and recommend a solution. Their work resulted in a proposal to create an "authority," a legal and financial entity that combined corporate and political characteristics. The Port of New York Authority, the entity they created, was charged with producing a rational and comprehensive plan for port development in the New York area.

The "authority" exemplified legal instrumentalism, that is, the adaptation of law to meet existing economic and social conditions. As a "body corporate and politic," the authority was both a corporation and a government instrumentality. Its directors and investors had limited liability. And it had to raise its own capital, which meant that like a corporation, it had to convince the financial community and other investors that its enterprises would result in revenues over and above the costs of operation and maintenance, and adequate to amortize the debt. Thus the authority had a corporate mentality insofar as it needed to make a profit. This meant choosing projects that were revenue-producing and self-liquidating. Although its activities would benefit the public, the authority was not designed to be a social service agency. Those who took advantage of an authority service, such as a bridge or freight terminal, would have to be in a position to pay for that service. As a private corporation, the Port Authority was not subject to civil service requirements, which strengthened its hand in filling staff positions.

What gave the authority its public character were valuable governmental privileges. The legislation creating the Port of New

York Authority empowered it with the right of eminent domain, which meant that like any governmental unit, the Port Authority need only pay a fair market price to acquire property for its projects. In this way, the authority substantially reduced the cost of construction and gained a competitive advantage over private groups engaged in related activities. The authority's revenue bonds were made tax-exempt, which also enabled it to reduce construction and operating costs substantially. For businessmen and investors seeking a safe investment and fair return, tax-exempt bonds were attractive, even if the interest earned was lower than the prevailing corporate rate. The Port Authority also claimed immunity from payment of federal income taxes. These privileges and immunities enabled the Port Authority to lower construction, operating, and maintenance costs, as well as to reduce the cost, in the form of tolls or rents, to those who used its services.

Another feature that made the authority representative of the trend toward cooperation was the fact that it came into existence as a result of the compact clause of the Constitution. Although expressed as a negative restriction on the states—no state is allowed to enter into agreements with other states without the approval of Congress—the clause became a tool used by policymakers to resolve, without resorting to federal control, intergovernmental conflicts affecting the economy of contiguous governmental jurisdictions. For example, the Colorado River basin states entered into a compact in 1921 providing for the equitable apportionment of the waters of the Colorado River and for administrative mechanisms to supervise and implement the policy. Such agreements among states also helped reduce conflicts concerning the protection of fish, the development of parks, and the improvement of navigation. It also served as a means of dealing with economic problems stemming from technological development. In the provision of hydroelectric power, policymakers found interstate agreements helpful for establishing administrative procedures for the regional transmission of electric power.

Policymakers believed these agreements and the accompanying administrative machinery were superior to regulation through litigation. According to Harvard Law School professors Felix Frankfurter and James Landis, both of whom took active roles in advising political leaders about the advantages of interstate cooperation, "The judicial instrument is too static and too sporadic for adjusting a social-economic issue continuously alive in an area embracing more than a half dozen States."[11] Unlike legislators and judges, administrators had the time to give careful study and consideration to issues that emerged daily. These legal engineers understood that government, like business, needed continuity; litigation interfered with continuity.

But just as some lawyers feared that the trade association provided no protection of the rights of minority interests, some students of the administrative process feared that these agencies, set up to foster a higher standard of living and improved economic conditions, might in the course of their work abuse minor interests. Even though he was a strong proponent of the administrative process, Frankfurter warned that in areas affecting minor interests, care should be taken to construct proper administrative techniques. "The vast interests confided to bodies like the Interstate Commerce Commission, the Federal Trade Commission and State public service commissions, just because they are so vast, are not likely to suffer much nor long from incompetence or injustice in our legal system. The incidence of law . . . is most significant at the lowest point of contact."[12] The very qualities of independence and efficiency that made the authority and the compact clause attractive mechanisms to achieve economic and social order also made them potential sources of unwanted social control. Independence from traditional sources of political power and representative democracy meant that such government instrumentalities as the authority could more easily abuse the power and privileges entrusted to them.

An excellent example of such a situation is the career of Robert Moses, a New York urban planner. From the thirties to the early sixties, as head of the Triborough Bridge Authority, Moses led planners and architects in developing most of New York City's present-day bridges, tunnels, roads, and recreational facilities. Moses used skills acquired as a legislative draftsman during the Progressive period to convert the Triborough Authority from a device used to finance the construction of a single bridge into a means for the continued financing of multiple public projects. Although he accomplished a great deal, he often did so at the expense of the rights and interests of many citizens whose property lay in the path of a proposed project. These people found themselves powerless against

---

[11] Felix Frankfurter and James M. Landis, "The Compact Clause of the Constitution—A Study in Interstate Adjustments," *Yale Law Journal*, 34 (May 1925), 701.
[12] Felix Frankfurter, "The Task of Administrative Law," *University of Pennsylvania Law Review*, 75 (1927), 618-619.

the Triborough Authority and unable, as were many politicians, to use the political process to weaken Moses's power. It would be an error to attribute the entire blame for this situation to the authority technique. There are numerous examples of politicians and other administrators who have aggrandized governmental power. And the authority, used properly, helped many states and municipalities to finance projects that exceeded normal taxing and spending powers. Nevertheless, the very features that made the authority a valuable instrument also made it susceptible to manipulation. It was a product of an age that stressed efficiency, rationalism, and the idea of a commonwealth. These are difficult values to achieve without sacrificing democratic interests. In this respect, Moses symbolized these values carried to an extreme.

Bar Integration and Planning

By the late twenties and early thirties, the legal profession began to show a similar concern for modernizing and rationalizing its activities through cooperative methods. Bar leaders experienced the same pressures as businessmen and government administrators to integrate, consolidate, and coordinate their work. Corporate law firms increased in number, by consolidating smaller firms, often with a particular specialization, into one organization. Just as business became concerned with planning, scientific management, and division of labor, law firms started to organize their work according to such specialties as taxation, trusts and estates, trade regulations, labor law, and real estate. Modern record keeping and time methods of billing were introduced. Specialization took place not only in substantive areas but according to clientele. Lawyers shifted their attention from the courtroom to the conference table. Skill in negotiation became more valued than courtroom oratory. Corporations and government agencies created distinct law departments, and lawyers came to be present in nearly every economic or policy decision made by these organizations. The profession became a technical subsidiary of business and government.

Among other things, the profession sought to integrate the standards governing its activities, by expanding the membership of local and state bar groups and strengthening their affiliation with the

American Bar Association. The ABA undertook a national bar program to unify the activities of bar associations. Even such fiercely individualistic members as John W. Davis—a noted conservative constitutional lawyer, ABA president, and unsuccessful presidential candidate—saw value in enlarging the self-regulatory activities of the bar association in order to improve professional standards. He wrote,

> In these days when such vast efforts are being made to impose a regimental discipline on society, one hesitates to suggest any addition to the number who must submit to that necessitous fate. . . . No one yet has been so temerarious as to suggest to the profession the adoption of a *code* of unfair competition or a regulation of the hours and conditions of labor. The Code of Ethics is probably the outer boundary of regulatory possibility. Nevertheless, would it not be a distinct gain if every lawyer were compelled by public opinion . . . to enroll as a member of his local bar association; and if to that local association should be confided the power and duty of disciplining its members, as a court of first instance, including in its reach the penalty of disbarment, subject always to appropriate court review? Under such a regime would there not come in time an approach to common standards and a heightened *esprit de corps* everywhere?[13]

Some bar leaders thought that lawyers should be required, as part of admission to the bar, to join their state bar association. To effect this goal, they proposed the creation of state-chartered bar groups or "integrated" bars. Many of those who favored this approach argued that state bars would promote a collective sense of social responsibility, which would improve the formation and enforcement of bar association codes. (Voluntary groups could only recommend standards; the legislature and the state courts were responsible for legislating and enforcing them, respectively.) Proponents of integrated bars faced the same problem as trade association leaders seeking to create industry-wide standards enforceable against all units of an industry.

Advocates of corporate bars argued that the compulsory format would attract more young lawyers into association activities and serve as a safeguard against commercialism and specialization. Many of these lawyers—for example, public-spirited New York attorney

[13] John W. Davis, "The Need for a Closer Coordination of the Bar," *American Bar Association Journal*, 20 (January 1934), 8.

Julius Henry Cohen—wondered how the young corporate lawyer who joined one of the new law factories that were emerging during the twenties would develop a concern for the public interest. How would he view legal problems in their social context if his activities were centered on protecting the special interests of his clients? How could he interpose broader social values if he depended on retainers from corporations for his livelihood? How could he take a role in governmental affairs when he was the repository of commercial confidences? Presumably, by participating in a compulsory rather than voluntary group, lawyers would have an opportunity to be exposed to a view of the world and legal issues beyond that of their immediate client, and consequently would adopt a social perspective, perhaps even participate in public activities.

Opponents of integrated bars were unconvinced by these arguments. Some—for example, Robert Jackson, an upstate–New York attorney—argued that rural lawyers had little interest in bar association activities. Attending meetings in remote cities and competing with big-city attorneys and their associates, were two reasons, Jackson claimed, why the average country lawyer shunned association activities. Jackson preferred the representative system of voluntary associations to the democratic, mass-meeting format of integrated bars. Other bar leaders, among them Louis Marshall, suggested that integrated bars would not strengthen the participatory role of the average lawyer. In his opinion, the same leaders would emerge in state-run bars as in voluntary groups; and as a matter of principle, voluntarism was much preferred to compulsion. Some lawyers feared, too, that integrated bars would allow unqualified and disreputable lawyers to mingle with elite lawyers and even gain leadership positions. These arguments were strong enough to convince the New York state legislature in 1927 to defeat a bill creating an integrated bar.

Nevertheless, some states, notably North Dakota, Idaho, Alabama, and California, did enact state legislation creating corporate bar associations. There is little evidence to show that these groups were any more effective than voluntary groups in policing their profession and upgrading the social consciousness of attorneys. Some state bars—California, for example—sought to take a hand in disciplining members. This was objected to by those lawyers who considered it an usurpation of judicial authority. The California Supreme Court ruled that the state bar could act only as an intermediary to take evidence and report its findings to the courts. Disbarment was a judicial prerogative. In a way, this situation is analogous to the problem encountered by trade associations seeking to exercise punitive action against members who violate codes of ethics. Here is another example of legislatures and the courts being unwilling to allow private groups (even if they are professional groups) complete authority to regulate their activities.

Lawmaking, Research, and Education

All of these efforts to impose order and continuity in the affairs of business, government, and the legal profession showed how reliant policymakers were becoming on administration and enforcement. The multiplication of statutes, rules, regulations, standards, and codes meant that administrators needed to understand the purpose of the law and how to implement it. As coordinated administration in business, government, and the professions became the method of adjusting economic and social relations, policymakers found themselves more in need of research information and analyisis, particularly of a legal character. Lawyers seeking to understand the mechanics of operating an administrative network of economic supervision required objective and verifiable data, rather than speculation or partisan claims. Properly done research studies would enable lawyers to place the work of administrative agencies in the context of developments in the law, generally. As Frankfurter observed, "Here, as in other branches of public law, only here probably more so, we must travel outside the covers of lawbooks to understand law."[14] Research became the vital link between lawmaking and administration; it also became closely related to professional training.

The growth of administration and the need for research studies helped strengthen the status of law teachers within the profession. Though viewed initially as legal technicians, law teachers were by the twenties beginning to be valued as researchers who could relate law to economic and social development. The opportunity to initiate, direct, and shape critical legal policies studies gave the professoriate an important advantage over lawyers and judges. The reference to

[14] Frankfurter, "Administrative Law," p. 620.

law teachers, as with practitioners, is to an elite group; to those who, by virtue of their training, experience, and position, influenced the shape and character of their craft. The most influential teachers, as one might expect, were those who held faculty appointments at prestigious university-based national law schools such as Harvard, Yale, Columbia, and the University of Chicago. These teachers had available substantial research facilities, financial support, and publication outlets. They taught the brightest students, many of whom went on to prominent careers in business and government. They maintained contacts with metropolitan law firms (to whom they often served as consultants) and to local, state, and national bar groups. Many of them attracted the attention of politicians and social reformers, who looked to them for advice on critical policy issues.

Unlike practitioners and judges, teachers were in a position to provide assistance because they had more time for thoughtful reflection and more independence, since they were not in the position of representing a client or weighing conflicts between competing interests. This is not to suggest that law teachers did not take sides on troubling questions of economic and social policy. Quite the contrary. Many took strong positions on policy issues and played the role of informed critics of the profession. They analyzed the opinions of judges with a view toward understanding the trend of the law on issues and pointing out errors in logic or policy. Judges welcomed these scholarly criticisms—which usually appeared in law review articles, symposia, and letters to judges—particularly because their insulation from professional activities made it difficult always to gain reactions to their work. Law teachers' comments on judicial decisions, conservative jurist William Howard Taft observed, have "pricked the consciences of judges and aroused them to a sensitiveness to challenge and an earnest desire to reach conclusions that can be defended against criticism of professional teachers who are masters of the legal science."[15]

The support of prominent philanthropies also stimulated the growth of research and enhanced the position of the law teacher. The Carnegie Corporation and the Rockefeller Foundation helped subsidize the work of the American Law Institute, a group created in 1923 to adjust law to modern conditions by undertaking a scientific

---

[15] William H. Taft, "Legal Education and the University Law School," *Minnesota Law Review*, 10 (May 1926), 556.

restatement of such areas as property, torts, contracts, agency, conflict of laws, trusts, and business associations. According to Columbia Law School dean Harlan Fiske Stone, one of the leaders of the effort, the restatement of the law "must [review] in detail and with precision accepted rules and doctrines, eliminating or modifying the rule or doctrine not supported by reason or adapted to present-day social institutions and needs."[16] In 1920, the Commonwealth Fund established a Legal Research Committee to initiate education activities in the law. Among its first efforts was sponsorship of a series of studies in the adminstrative process, under the direction of a group headed by Frankfurter. The group viewed studies in this area as "a prerequisite for an appraisal of what administrative law really does, so that we may have an adequate guide for what ought to be done."[17] The eight volumes produced between 1924 and 1943 covered the activities of such major agencies as the FTC and the ICC, as well as more discrete and local administrative functions, such as building regulation in New York City. But the character of these studies was far more than educational; they were designed and written to effect policy changes in lawmaking and administration.

As teachers found themselves engaged in research and teaching involving policy, they were inevitably faced with the need to relate their work to economic and social affairs. The urge to see law as a part of experience, rather than as simply logic, had been one of the contributions of early-twentieth-century sociological jurisprudence. But sociological jurisprudence was more an affirmation of the relations of law to society than a change in methods of legal research or education. According to Harvard Law School professor Samuel Williston, early law teachers such as Christopher Langdell had "recognized . . . that the purpose of law is to supply human needs, and that, in general, rules of law must conform to those needs, whether the law consciously adopts existing *mores* or, as undoubtedly sometimes happens, *mores* shape themselves in conformity with legal rules."[18] Williston suggested that law has always been associated with

---

[16] Quoted in Alpheus T. Mason, *Harlan Fiske Stone: Pillar of the Law* (New York, 1956), p. 122.
[17] See Gerard Henderson, *The Federal Trade Commission* (New Haven, 1924), p. vii.
[18] Samuel Williston, "The Judge and the Professor," *Reports of the American Bar Association*, 58 (1933), 607.

public policy, but never to the extent that it overshawdowed doctrine and the rule of law.

Some scholars, however, began experimenting during the twenties and thirties with the idea that legal research and education should delve more deeply into the factual situation and policy surrounding a judicial decision, rather than concern itself solely with stated principles. Known as "legal realists," this group, which included faculty at Yale and Columbia law schools, tried to relate law to economics and the social sciences in a systematic way. They believed that legal development sprang from the actions of men rather than from doctrine; principles were a means—the warrant for arriving at conclusions for entirely political or personal reasons—rather than an end. Though it struck some traditionalists as irreverent, some legal realists even suggested that the basis of judicial decision making might rest on such visceral reactions as what a judge had for breakfast. Most important, realists placed great emphasis on building a series of factual situations that could be identified and used as a method of predicting judicial behavior. This functional approach, legal realists claimed, would undo the mechanistic character of the case method. The desire to have a system, observed Chicago lawyer Jerome Frank, who popularized legal realism in such works as *Law and Modern Mind*, "should not lead the discerning into assuming that it exists or must exist." University law schools, he argued, should make students aware of the "uncoordinated and non-interrelated phenomena with which they will have to deal."[19]

For a variety of reasons, including the fact that standards of legal education and professional licensing were set by the organized bar, realists did not succeed in making meaningful changes in law school curriculum. Responsible critics, such as William O. Douglas, himself a law professor at Yale and Columbia in the late twenties and early thirties, faulted the realists for attempting to substitute an attitude about the law for technique. Douglas suggested that acquaintance with economics and the social sciences, although indispensable, could be acquired by outside reading; analysis of doctrine and its application, that is, the system of law, could not. Therefore, the latter should remain the principal goal of legal education. Robert Hutchins, who was dean of the Yale Law School in the twenties and later president

---

[19] Jerome Frank to Felix Frankfurter, January 6, 1932, Jerome Frank Papers, Yale University Library.

of the University of Chicago, pointed out that the realists' fascination with the social sciences must be tempered by the fact that social scientists have not yet shown lawyers how to use the data they have collected. Finally, Felix Frankfurter suggested that the realists were wrong to insist that by ordering cases to create a system, one established a rigid formula; any reputable law teacher, Frankfurter argued, knew that this system could be replaced as soon as a better one was devised. Order was a convenience, Frankfurter maintained. In retrospect, legal realism appears to have been a symptom of the anxiety many lawyers felt over the need to adapt law to changing social and economic developments. The reasons for its emergence may be attributed, at least in part, to the economic crisis confronting the nation at the end of the twenties.

Law and Politics in the Thirties: The NIRA Experience

As the country struggled to find organized means of dealing with the effects of the Great Depression, which had begun in 1929, questions regarding judicial decision making and legal reasoning became part of the larger problem of economic and social reform. The economic chaos created by the depression exacerbated the issue of judicial review of state and federal legislation. It highlighted the continuing struggle between those who favored national control and standards, and those who thought the states were better equipped to handle regulatory concerns. Advocates of cooperation and planning, with or without government support, clashed with those who favored a regulatory approach. Even advocates of regulation were divided between those who believed economic relations were best accommodated by the commission or administrative method and those who favored litigation primarily through enforcement of the antitrust laws. Many of these combatants were leading lawyers and law teachers. Each vied for the attention and support of the new President, Franklin Roosevelt, who took office in March 1933. Although one cannot point to any group or party that was clearly victorious in the end, one can conclude that these lawyers, teachers, and judges played a strategic role in the formation of new governmental policies and programs and that, in the process, they clearly demonstrated what might be called Wilsonian statesmanship.

Faced with the growing imbalance in production, prices, and employment brought on by the depression, the Roosevelt adminstration at first chose to rely on the cooperative methods that lawyers and businessmen had experimented with during the twenties. "One of the beneficial results of the acute economic crisis through which we are passing," observed New York attorney Julius Henry Cohen, a long-time advocate of cooperation, "is the fact that we have been obliged to face powerful economic realities. We see clearly that there must be planned production in industry."[20] Cohen pointed to a recent dissenting opinion by Louis Brandeis in *New State Ice Company v. Liebmann* (1932), a case involving state regulation of the ice business, as a symbol of the kind of attitude that was needed to bring the economy into balance. Although the Court overturned an Oklahoma statute designed to control prices in the ice business by requiring state licensing, Brandeis thought the legislative effort was clearly constitutional and even worthwhile. His opinion stressed experimentation and rationality in business–government relations, and despite objections from old-guard conservatives in the legal community, these were the values that guided the early New Deal reformers.

The cornerstone of early New Deal legislation was the National Industrial Recovery Act of 1933 (NIRA), which sought to incorporate "cooperation" as a part of government policy, using the trade association concept. Government legal architects found the trade association an inadequate means of implementing a public policy of industrial self-government, since its authority extended only to participants to the agreement. The trade associations' rules were not enforceable against the industry as a whole. The NIRA tried to remedy this shortcoming by extending to industrial representatives the authority to legislate standards and practices of fair competition binding on all members of an industry doing business interstate. It also sought to establish means for handling labor conflicts. One result of the law was the virtual suspension of prosecutions under the antitrust laws.

The act once again renewed controversy over whether business could be left to regulate its own activities. Was it constitutional to permit members of an industry to design codes of fair competition which would be binding on all members of that industry engaged in interstate commerce? Could these standards be made to have the

---

[20] Julius Henry Cohen, "Ice," *Boston University Law Review*, 13 (January 1933), 18.

same effect as law? According to David Podell, coauthor of the NIRA, the majority of members in a business could impose rules of fair competition on the minority as long as the rules did not lead to monopolistic conditions.[21] And Benjamin Javits, a New York lawyer and advocate of industrial self-government, argued that as long as the industry developed its codes with the public interest in mind, and with justice to competitors, workers, and consumers, "it can bind the minority who do not consent."[22] However, at least one influential group within the American Bar Association, the Standing Committee on Commerce, questioned whether the NIRA codes protected the rights of the minority and pointed out that, "The protection of the individual from the exercise of unrestricted power is essential if our form of government is to survive."[23] The statement foreshadowed the bar's growing concern over the absence of standards of due process and judicial procedure in administrative activity.

Even more troubling was how to reconcile the conflict that developed between lawyers for the National Recovery Administration (NRA)—the agency set up to administer the act—and businessmen over procedures for enforcing the codes. Businessmen sought to implement the codes in ways that violated due process. According to Donald Richberg, one of the authors of the NIRA and successor to General Hugh S. Johnson as chief NRA administrator, "The early legal division policies of a cautious advance in dangerous, unexplored areas of administrative law enforcement were submerged in a general desire within and outside the NRA to get rid of legalistic methods and 'the law's delay' and to use effectively and promptly this new instrument."[24] This situation troubled Richberg, who thought the success of the NIRA depended on balancing self-regulation with effective and judicially sound enforcement procedures. But in practice, businessmen sought to rid the NIRA of legalistic procedures; they used the authority given them by the government to dominate the industries they were to protect. Businessmen also abused their power by interfering with union organizational efforts. "[B]usiness management," Richberg observed, "given new powers and granted

[21] David Podell, "Essential Factors in Determining Constitutionality of Recovery Act," *American Bar Association Journal*, 20 (March 1934), 283.
[22] Benjamin Javits, *The Commonwealth of Industry: The Separation of Industry and the State* (New York, 1936), p. 52.
[23] *Reports of the American Bar Association*, 57 (1934), 441.
[24] Donald Richberg, *The Rainbow* (Garden City, N.Y., 1936), p. 169.

an opportunity for a more effective control than ever before of private enterprise by private planning, was not only generally intolerant of interferences by organized labor and by the government, but sought continually to exercise public authority to discipline its own ranks."[25]

The conflict that developed in the administration of the NIRA is not hard to understand when one realizes the differences between business and law. In business, decisions are made quickly and in response to conditions existing at the moment. Decision making is based on the best available information and predictions of market behavior. The actions of influential competitors and consumers may also be taken into account. One of the reasons businessmen sought to reduce competition was so they could have more control over market conditions. In law, decisions are made after a rigorous process of information gathering, in which the force of the law is brought to bear to compel interested parties to divulge as much information as they have. The process is slow and often complicated by numerous procedural technicalities, all of which are designed to ensure parties their day in court. Fairness, rather than profit, is the motivating factor that moves the legal process along.

The Supreme Court dealt with these issues in *Schechter Poultry Corporation v. United States* (1935), where it nullified the NIRA. Under consideration was the "Live Poultry Code" for the New York metropolitan area, which was designed to correct what were considered unfair and disruptive competitive methods in the largest market for live poultry in the United States. The defendants, who were in the business of buying poultry, slaughtering it, and selling it within the New York area, were charged with violating code provisions dealing with inspection (the Schechters were selling diseased chickens), minimum wages, and maximum hours. According to the government, the violations had weakened industry efforts to raise prices and strengthen consumer purchasing power.

Aside from reviewing the important questions of whether the Schechters were engaged in interstate commerce and whether Congress could delegate to the President what amounted to legislative power, to which it responded in both instances negatively, the Court examined the issue of the constitutionality of the codes. Although it recognized the value of voluntary, cooperative activities by combina-

[25] Ibid., p. 177.

tions of businessmen, it could not accept giving businessmen the power of legislators. The Court's opinion was written by Chief Justice Charles Evans Hughes, a former associate Justice of the Supreme Court, who had given up his seat on the Court to run unsuccessfully for President in 1916 and was appointed chief justice by President Hoover in 1930. The fact that business was familiar with conditions within industry, argued Hughes, did not justify permitting it, in the form of trade or industrial associations, to make laws, even if they might be "wise and beneficent."[26] It was not the same as the Congress delegating to instrumentalities of its choosing the power to make "subordinate rules within prescribed limits" and apply legislative policy to a set of facts.

In the case of the NIRA, there was a complete absence of legislative policy to guide the formulation of rules, and an absence of proper administrative procedures for examining and testing the validity of rules of fair competition. The Court found that establishing fair rather than unfair codes of competition also went beyond any recognized authority to legislate. Finally, the Court suggested that there was a fundamental difference between Congress seeking the opinions of business before it legislates, and allowing business to legislate for itself. This calls to mind Holmes's analogy between the trade association and an "allwise socialistic government." The Court was unwilling to accept such an analogy. Once again, it placed a limit on the freedom accorded business to regulate its own affairs. Regardless of the emergency, the Court would not countenance economic experiments that violated due process and the Sherman Act.

Commission Regulation Enhanced

Growing disenchantment with business self-regulation—a disenchantment heightened by Supreme Court invalidation of New Deal legislation—strengthened the position of those policymakers and lawyers who favored commission regulation. The Progressives had conceived of the commission as an intermediary between business and the courts. More than that, they envisioned the commission as

[26] *Schechter Poultry Corp. v. United States*, 295 U.S. 495, 537(1935).

playing a preventive role in resolving economic conflicts. Thus, the Federal Trade Commission (FTC) was seen as a vehicle for eliminating unfair trade practices in a cooperative and voluntary manner. In practice, the FTC found its mission impeded by its dual role as an investigatory and planning agency, and a prosecutorial and judicial organization. Investigating issues, establishing a set of facts, and making a judgment regarding those facts compromised the agency's impartiality. Efforts to ensure standards of due process failed. Commission personnel arrived at decisions regarding an alleged trade abuse without giving business the opportunity to respond effectively to its charges. Unable to frame its remedial orders in terms that described the economic and market conditions, the commission resorted to legalizing issues. This practice limited its ability to execute its role as a cooperative, informational agency.

In spite of these shortcomings, the Roosevelt administration began by 1935 to resort to commission regulation in a series of new legislative enactments, one of the most important of which was the National Labor Relations Act or, as it was more commonly known, the Wagner Act. In the act, Congress sought to embody the same principles contained in earlier Progressive legislation, such as the Federal Trade Commission Act and the Clayton Act, of using the federal commerce power to rationalize trade practices. In this case, it aimed at eliminating one of the most disruptive aspects of interstate commerce: labor–management conflict. The Wagner Act sought to establish uniform standards in relations between employers and employees. Employers were prevented from engaging in activities that constituted unfair labor practices, such as interfering with the workers' right to form and join labor organizations and bargain collectively through representatives of their own choosing. Like the FTC, but unlike the NIRA, the Wagner Act created an agency armed with punitive powers yet guided by a mission of promoting industrial harmony. The National Labor Relations Board was given authority for certifying when a majority of workers in a unit had agreed on a representative of their choosing. The act did not deal with the protection of minority interests, such as workers who wanted either a different bargaining representative or no union at all.

The act was passed at a time when organized labor was pressing its effort to extend its reach to ever larger numbers of workers in ever more diverse industries and crafts. In the period between its passage,

1935, and the Supreme Court decision upholding its constitutionality, 1937, the nation saw waves of sit-down strikes and other labor violence. At the same time, the issue of judicial review was being studied as Congress held hearings in early 1937 on Roosevelt's plan for reforming the judiciary. Angered by the reversal the Court inflicted on New Deal legislation, and buoyed by his stunning election victory in November 1936, Roosevelt sought a method of ridding the Court of the influence of those judges—James McReynolds, George Sutherland, Willis Van Devanter, and Pierce Butler, all over seventy years old—whose attitude toward regulation had been shaped by nineteenth-century economic and legal theory. The plan he proposed called for the President to appoint additional judges in all federal courts where there were incumbent judges of retirement age who did not choose to resign. With regard to the Supreme Court, Roosevelt proposed that once a justice reached age seventy, he would be given six months to retire. If he did not, the President would be permitted to appoint an additional justice, up to a maximum of six new appointees. At the time the bill was proposed, there were six justices who would have qualified for retirement. If passed, the bill would have enabled Roosevelt to appoint enough new judges to weaken the Court's conservative majority. The court-packing plan revealed how closely related were law and politics.

While hearings on the court-packing plan were proceeding, in April 1937, the Supreme Court handed down decisions on the Wagner Act cases. Writing the majority opinion in *National Labor Relations Board v. Jones & Laughlin Steel Corporation* (1937), Hughes upheld the act on the grounds that the effect of unfair labor practices on employees could substantially affect the free flow of commerce. In examining conditions in the steel industry, the Court found that industrial strife at Jones and Laughlin, a major steel company, had more than an indirect or remote impact on commerce. "When industries organize themselves on a national scale," Hughes declared, "making their relation to interstate commerce the dominant factor in their activities, how can it be maintained that their industrial labor relations constitute a forbidden field into which Congress may not enter when it is necessary to protect interstate commerce from the paralyzing consequences of industrial war?" Congress and the Court, Hughes maintained, would have to examine questions of federal power over commerce in the light of experience and practical-

ity rather than in an "intellectual vacuum."[27] The decision gave
Congress virtually plenary power to regulate the economy, and
served to promote unionization. Though Hughes's switch is often
viewed as motivated by fear of the court-packing plan, a more
accurate assessment was rendered years later by Owen Roberts, a
decisive member of the *Jones & Laughlin* majority. "Looking back,"
he said, "it is difficult to see how the Court could have resisted the
popular urge for uniform standards throughout the country—for
what in effect was a unified economy."[28]

In addition to upholding federal power, the Court also acknowledged the validity of state economic regulatory authority. In 1934, in
Nebbia v. New York, the Court had upheld a 1933 New York law
setting up a board to establish minimum prices for the retail sale of
milk. "[N]either property rights nor contract rights," declared Roberts, "are absolute; for government cannot exist if the citizen may at
will use his property to the detriment of his fellows, or exercise his
freedom of contract to work them harm. Equally fundamental with
the private right is that of the public to regulate it in the common
interest."[29] By 1937, the Court had added minimum wages for women
to the list of areas protected by state regulation. The liberty safe-
guarded by the Constitution, Hughes declared, "is liberty in a social
organization which requires the protection of law against the evils
which menace the health, safety, morals and welfare of the people."[30]
Although in subsequent cases dealing with state legislation the Court
did not abandon entirely the notion of substantive due process, it said
in effect that in economic matters, the presumption of constitutionality rested with the state.

These decisions climaxed the long struggle by legal and economic
Progressives to force the Court to accept economic management and
administrative control. Advocates of administration were hopeful—
as Woodrow Wilson had been in 1914 when he introduced his plan for
a federal trade commission—that the new agencies created by the
New Deal (some fourteen in number in the years from 1933 to 1940)
would foster a partnership between business and government. They
played down the weaknesses of commission regulation, in particular

---

[27] *National Labor Relations Board v. Jones & Laughlin Steel Corporation*, 301 U.S. 1,
41–42 (1937).
[28] Owen Roberts, *The Courts and the Constitution* (Cambridge, Mass., 1951), p. 61.
[29] *Nebbia v. New York*, 291 U.S. 502, 523 (1934).
[30] *West Coast Hotel Co. v. Parrish*, 300 U.S. 379, 391 (1937).

the relaxation of standards of due process in agency hearings and the combination of investigatory and prosecuting functions with adjudicatory responsibilities in one body. These shortcomings were a small price to pay for the economic benefits that would be derived from allowing experts the freedom to formulate policy. Such supporters of the administrative process as James Landis and William O. Douglas believed that agency personnel would operate as managers rather than police. They foresaw forensic talent yielding to executive skills, and lawyers, whether they represented business or government, acquiring knowledge of statistics, finance, accounting, marketing, production, and labor. In the opinion of Douglas, who headed the Securities and Exchange Commission, a New Deal agency, between 1936 and 1937, regulatory bodies would help fill the need for governance in industry that regulation through courts could not accomplish. He summed up the meaning of these developments: "The material factor is that government has moved permanently into the control over new social and business areas. This new problem of control does not require, nor can it countenance, the techniques of common-law litigation and adjudication."[31]

By the early forties, the legal profession, which had been reluctant to accept commission regulation, was making it a part of its daily work. Law schools introduced courses in administrative law; and the American Bar Association replaced a committee on administrative law with a section, signifying its recognition of the permanency of this area of legal activity. The ABA lobbied vigorously to improve the procedures of the administrative process, and it succeeded in securing passage of the Administrative Procedures Act of 1946, which separates an agency's investigatory and prosecuting functions from its adjudicatory functions. Lawyers now became increasingly involved in monitoring federal agency developments. The term "Washington lawyer" came into prominence along with "Philadelphia lawyer" and "Wall Street lawyer." It referred not only to lawyers in Washington but also, more broadly, to lawyers whose clients were affected by the activities of federal administrative agencies. Thus a Washington lawyer could be found in almost any metropolitan area of the nation. His or her work would involve litigation as well as lobbying to influence legislation. The Court of Appeals for the District of Columbia grew in importance because it was given original

[31] William O. Douglas, *Democracy and Finance* (New Haven, 1940), p. 287.

jurisdiction to hear appeals from the orders of federal agencies, regardless of the geographic location of the litigant.

Many of those lawyers and judges who accepted commission regulation did so because they were uncertain whether there was any better alternative. "I don't think we can have any absolute guaranty of fair treatment, whether we leave it to the court or to other bodies," Columbia University law professor Robert Lee Hale observed. "Somebody must in the nature of things have power to act arbitrarily—the company, the legislature, the commission or the court. I find it hard to predict in whose hands that power is least likely to be abused."[32] For the moment, he was willing to let the agencies have the benefit of freedom from judicial supervision. Judges expressed a similar attitude toward administrative expertise. According to federal appeals court judge Augustus Hand, "I feel sure that nothing will be gained by an assumption by the courts of supervisory jurisdiction that is not fairly granted by the terms of the constituent acts. For the present, parties must be left to 'fry in their own fat' until the legislative branch sees fit to change the procedure or the administrative tribunals become more circumspect."[33]

Competition and Antitrust Revival

Departure from the NIRA's business self-regulatory approach spurred efforts to revive enforcement of the antitrust laws. Lawyers who favored such action attributed the economic depression of the thirties, and in particular the downturn in the economy in 1937, to the lack of market competition. Although they did not urge a return to unrestrained competition, they favored stronger enforcement of the Sherman Act as a way of preventing organized power groups from unreasonably restraining trade. These lawyers feared the cartelization of American industry, that is, combinations of businessmen and labor unions, often with government assistance or support, setting prices or limiting production in order to take advantage of market conditions. They argued that cartelization interfered with the development of new products and new merchandising techniques, lowered

[32] Robert Lee Hale to Richmond Weed, June 3, 1942, Hale Papers.
[33] Augustus Hand, "Lawyers in a Revolutionary Age," *Pennsylvania Bar Association Quarterly*, 18 (1946), 46.

productivity, raised prices, and generally disadvantaged the consumer. Better to let the market operate on its own, they explained, even if there are losers, rather than try to manage it so that everyone comes out even.

Among the most prominent figures of this group was Thurman Arnold, a lawyer and Yale Law School professor, who, from 1938 to 1942, headed the Antitrust Division of the Justice Department. Arnold claimed that as a process for regulating industrial and labor groups, litigation was superior to trade associations and even commissions. "Under the cloak of distributing statistical information," he noted, "trade associations have kept business within a ring and established a quota for every member."[34] Similarly, commissions were effective only in specialized areas, such as prohibiting unfair trade practices; they were ill equipped to render judgments on broad economic policies. "Commissions do not have protective symbolisms which enable them to escape attack in applying a broad formula to business in general."[35] Moreover, Arnold pointed out, big business knows the ins and outs of the administrative bureaucracy and can easily win favor.

Arnold considered the Sherman Act a better legal and economic formula, since it covered every field and expressed a general policy and attitude enforceable by the courts. Because of their ability to shroud their work with ceremonial and symbolic gestures, courts were in a better position than government commissions to compel respect and compliance with their decisions. Armed with voluminous testimony regarding monopolistic conditions in industry—testimony that had been developed by the Temporary National Economic Committee, a group set up by Roosevelt in 1937—and with increased congressional funding, Arnold and his staff engaged in an extensive campaign to enforce the Sherman Act. In each case, their goal was to upset agreements that unduly restricted the distribution of goods and services.

In 1938, the Antitrust Division brought suit against a Chicago cartel composed of the Milk Wagon Drivers Union, several milk producers and distributors, and the Chicago Board of Health, charging them with a conspiracy to fix the purchase and resale price of milk, and prevent the delivery of milk to retail grocery stores. The

---

[34] Thurman Arnold, *Democracy and Free Enterprise* (Norman, Okla., 1942), p. 68.
[35] Thurman Arnold, *The Bottlenecks of Business* (New York, 1940), p. 100.

issue arose from the union's opposition to the vendor system of milk delivery with which some producers, distributors and deliverers had begun experimenting during the early thirties. Under this system, independent vendors bought milk from distributors and sold it to retail grocery stores. The costs of distribution were considerably less than the traditional door-to-door system, and retail prices were nearly half as much. Concerned by the loss of their business, the Milk Wagon Drivers Union engaged in boycotts and strikes, some involving considerable violence and intimidation, to weaken the vendor system. The Supreme Court upheld a lower court indictment, thereby permitting operation of the vendor system and dramatically reducing milk prices in Chicago. In the process the Court justified, at least temporarily, the validity of Arnold's contention about the effectiveness of Justice Department enforcement of the antitrust laws.

With America's entry into World War II, concern for monopoly lessened. Policymakers once again realized, as they had during World War I, that cooperation between business and government was necessary. Although some feared that this relationship would lead to a fascist economy once the war ended, such was not to be the case. After the war, the conflict continued between business's desire to control its own affairs and government's efforts to keep open the channels of competition. Looking back at the first fifty years of the century, one saw evidence of how much the law and legal institutions had become tools for broadening economic opportunities for increasing numbers of Americans. Property rights had been revised short of revolution, but not without substantial labor violence and near constitutional crisis. Parts of the Constitution, particularly the commerce clause, had gained new vitality. In contrast, it appeared that the due process clause had withered as an impediment to government economic regulation. But the solution of troubling economic issues did not relax social tensions. Beginning in the forties, policymakers confronted a new group of issues, largely of a personal rather than economic character. In dealing with them, they relied on the law and legal institutions to impose such Progressive values as a belief in rationalism, nationalism, and the efficacy of standards and administration.

THREE

The Age of Egalitarianism: 1942—1980

By the forties, it was becoming apparent that the law and legal institutions had been used effectively to establish a new social order in which laissez-faire economics and social Darwinism were no longer tenable policies. The price paid for curbing the waste, inefficiency, and inequity associated with these philosophies was a complex web of administrative agencies and administered solutions. Broader numbers of Americans were now able to share in the good life, protected by a new concern on the part of the federal government for social welfare. Indeed, the facts seemed to bear witness to these conclusions. Rising income and expanded production and employment during the forties, largely made possible by the war and by rapid unionization, enabled Americans to accept big business, big government, and big labor. But while the gradual resolution of economic chaos made people less concerned with such issues as economic democracy and the redistribution of wealth, other forces were making them sensitive to a group of issues that were largely non-material.

The assault by both fascist and communist countries on traditional concepts regarding the legal protection of individual rights contributed to making thoughtful Americans more sensitive to moral rather than material issues. In a speech shortly before his appointment to the Supreme Court in 1939, William O. Douglas observed, "A strong, efficient, well-balanced national economy will ever be one of our indispensable assets. But without the meaning and guidance of a vigorous set of spiritual values, I doubt that the other will alone enable us to meet successfully our 'rendezvous with Destiny.' "[1] For many, the new war raging in Europe was convincing evidence that the materialism of the twenties and thirties had distracted Americans from the more fundamental things in life. James Reston, reporting for the *New York Times* from London in the early forties, warned Americans that the prelude to victory was to recognize that the war was being fought not so much to preserve the economic order as to secure fundamental liberties. "[I]f we had been more concerned with the four freedoms, which seemed so intellectual, and less concerned about money, which seemed so practical, we should not be doing the job all over again today."[2] By war's end, other publicists were also urging Americans to rededicate themselves to the preservation of basic liberties. "I know of no generation in American life," Max Lerner wrote, "which is in a better position to understand what brought the Bill of Rights into existence than ours—if it makes the effort."[3]

In addition to being stirred by the war, renewed interest in personal freedoms was stimulated by the growth of the administrative state, which worried many observers, including some former New Deal lawyers. In particular, they wondered whether the proliferation of agencies was making it more difficult for the individual to express his or her interests. Could the average American make a judgment about policy when the facts needed to do so were controlled, and possibly manipulated, by government bureaucracies? As Douglas noted, "[T]he past twenty years have seen the issues grow in complexity and multiplicity, until they threaten to outstrip the capacity of the voter to evaluate them."[4] Was the system of countervailing power of business, government, and labor providing an opportunity for effective participation? "Is enough play left in the joints of our highly organized society," asked Benjamin V. Cohen, one of a number of former lawyers responsible for New Deal legislation, at a conference on freedom and the law at the University of Chicago in the early fifties, "to enable the individual to move and to venture?"[5]

---

[1] William O. Douglas, *Democracy and Finance* (New Haven, 1940), p. 293.

[2] James Reston, *Prelude to Victory* (New York, 1942), p. 38. Roosevelt's "Four Freedoms" included freedom of speech, freedom of religion, freedom from want, and freedom from fear.

[3] Max Lerner, *Public Journal: Marginal Notes on Wartime America* (New York, 1945), p. 63.

[4] Douglas, *Democracy and Finance*, p. 265.

[5] Benjamin V. Cohen, "Comments," in *Conference on Freedom and the Law*, University of Chicago Law School, Conference Series, No. 13 (May 7, 1953), p. 78.

The impulse to secure constitutional guarantees of individual freedom triggered once again the question of public responsibility and placed the law and legal institutions in the position of having to redefine their professional role in the face of new social pressures. Conflict over whether these were legislative or judicial questions again created divisions among lawyers and jurists. Some in the legal community believed the judiciary should remain neutral in weighing questions that involved legislative or administrative restrictions on personal freedoms. Others sought to establish new standards that would guarantee individual freedom yet maintain internal order and social discipline. Still others, dissatisfied with legislative inaction and distrustful of judicial efforts to balance order and liberty, opted instead for affirmative judicial efforts to secure constitutionally guaranteed rights and expand the area of permissible conduct. Legislative action did come, albeit late, in the form of congressional legislation to ensure civil rights and equal opportunity. New administrative mechanisms were created to implement these policies, and lawyers for both government and the private sector faced decisions regarding the best way to enforce rights under these laws—that is, through accommodation or through litigation. Finally, protecting social interests also became an issue that forced the organized bar into a major reassessment of its role in American life. At the end of this period, the struggle between professional and public responsibility, the commonweal and individualism, seemed no closer to solution than at the start. Accommodation seemed the best approach, particularly in a period of growing scarcity. Yet individualism continued to affect decision making, because Americans still prized opportunity and feared restraint.

A Court Divided

Perhaps no institution in America during the postwar period mirrored better the conflicts and tensions concerning individual rights than the United States Supreme Court. Since the late thirties, the Court had accepted the twentieth-century liberal ideology that property and contract rights could be impaired, altered, or regulated for the benefit of the public. Economic regulatory legislation, argued Justice Stone in *United States v. Carolene Products Co.*, would be considered constitutional as long as it was related to a rational governmental purpose. But in a footnote he ventured to add that the scope for operation of this presumption of constitutionality might be narrower when it concerned Bill of Rights protections. Stone went further, suggesting that in those areas where legislation restricts access to the political process or where it discriminates against religious, national, or racial minorities, particularly in such a way as to reduce their chances for redress through legislative or political means, there might be a need for a "more searching judicial inquiry."[6]

Throughout the forties and early fifties, the Supreme Court struggled with whether or not there was a concept of preferred freedoms. In other words, did protection of intellectual rights (freedom of speech, press, and religion), procedural rights (the right of defendants to be protected against unwarranted police action or improper judicial procedure), and civil rights (the right not to be discriminated against by government because of race, creed, or national origin) require and justify greater judicial scrutiny than protection of property rights? If judges invoked the due process clause to invalidate legislation restricting such rights, would they not be committing the same error of which they accused laissez-faire jurists? This question became particularly troubling for the Supreme Court, because by the early forties it was composed of such former New Dealers as (1) Hugo Black, a senator from Alabama before replacing conservative Van Devanter in 1937; (2) Felix Frankfurter, Roosevelt's long-time unofficial adviser, who succeeded Cardozo in 1938; and (3) former attorney general Robert Jackson, appointed in 1941 to fill Stone's seat when the latter was elevated to chief justice, replacing Hughes. Although they shared similar views on judicial review of economic regulation, these Roosevelt appointees differed over the question of judicial review of personal freedoms and the related matter of whether the Fourteenth Amendment's due process clause incorporated Bill of Rights protections.

Since the twenties, the Court had selectively accepted the doctrine of incorporation. In *Gitlow v. New York* (1925), the Court declared that the due process clause incorporated certain Bill of Rights protections. "[W]e may and do assume that freedom of speech and of the press . . . are among the fundamental personal rights and 'liberties' protected by the due process clause of the Fourteenth Amendment from impairment by the States."[7] Nevertheless, it added

---

[6] *United States v. Carolene Products Co.*, 304 U.S., 144, 152 (1938).
[7] *Gitlow v. New York*, 268 U.S. 652, 666 (1925).

that the right was not absolute, and where it could be determined that the public welfare required legislative protection against those who would incite to violence or anarchy, states had the power to restrict speech accordingly. In 1932, in *Powell v. Alabama*, it ruled that the right to counsel guaranteed by the Sixth Amendment could be made applicable to state criminal proceedings when special circumstances required. *Powell*, an appeal from the infamous Scottsboro trials, involved the denial of counsel to defendants in a capital case who were judged to be indigent, feebleminded, and ignorant.

A more coherent statement of the Court's position on the subject of incorporation came in 1937 in *Palko v. Connecticut*, a case in which the Court rejected the claim that the Fourteenth Amendment's due process clause incorporated the Fifth Amendment's protection against double jeopardy. Writing the opinion of the Court, Justice Benjamin Cardozo, appointed by Hoover in 1930, declared that the due process clause did not absorb all Bill of Rights protections but only what was needed to maintain a system of "ordered liberty." This concept, Cardozo argued, should be the "rationalizing principle" judges use in weighing claims for incorporation.[8] Cardozo seemed little worried that justice would be denied. "Few would be so narrow or provincial," he said, "as to maintain that a fair and enlightened system of justice would be impossible without [applying to the states all the freedoms and protections of the Bill of Rights]."[9] Nor did he fear that such a principle would lead to a renewal of the judicial activism of the twenties and thirties. Thus, in 1942, the Court refused to extend the *Powell* rule in a case where the defendant was normal and not charged with a capital offense. Further evidence of the Court's reluctance to adopt national standards of criminal justice was the decision in *Adamson v. California*, where it declined to absorb in the due process clause the Fifth Amendment's protection against self-incrimination. Thus, unlike federal courts, state courts could direct a jury's attention to a defendant's failure to testify and explain the truth or falsity of incriminating evidence.

Roosevelt appointees generally divided into three groups. One group, led by Felix Frankfurter, believed that justice could be maintained without adoption of the Bill of Rights in the Fourteenth Amendment. In fact, Frankfurter went so far as to suggest that only an eccentric mind believed that the Fourteenth Amendment incorpo-

---

[8] *Palko v. Connecticut*, 302 U.S. 319, 325 (1937).
[9] Ibid.

rated the entire Bill of Rights. In *Adamson*, he argued that to suggest that the due process clause of the Fourteenth Amendment was merely a shorthand expression for applying to the states protections afforded citizens against the federal government was ludicrous. First, it was historically inaccurate, since it was rejected by judges who were witnesses to the process by which the amendment was formulated. Second, to maintain such a theory would invite the danger of destroying our federal system. "A construction which gives to due process no independent function but turns it into a summary of the specific provisions of the Bill of Rights would, as has been noted, tear up by the roots much of the fabric of law in the several States, and would deprive the States of opportunity for reforms in legal process designed for extending the area of freedom."[10]

Frankfurter also pleaded, as Holmes had done, for judicial restraint. He argued that legislative experimentation was legitimate regardless of whether personal or economic rights might be disadvantageously affected, as long as they were not constitutionally impaired. As a judge, Frankfurter retained his faith in a progressive commonwealth, where individual interests sometimes had to take second place to national interests. In *Minersville School District v. Gobitis* (1940), Frankfurter wrote the majority opinion upholding the right of Pennsylvania to impose a flag salute on all schoolchildren, regardless of whether their religious affiliation might preclude such observance. "The mere possession of religious convictions which contradict the relevant concerns of a political society does not relieve the citizen from the discharge of political responsibilities."[11] He added, very boldly, "We are dealing with an interest inferior to none in the hierarchy of legal values. National unity is the basis of national security."[12] Frankfurter believed that redress for injustice or discrimination should be directed in nearly every instance to the legislature, not the courts. "To fight out the wise use of legislative authority in the forum of public opinion and before legislative assemblies rather than to transfer such a contest to the judicial arena, serves to vindicate the self-confidence of a free people."[13]

In contrast, Black and Douglas took the lead throughout the forties and early fifties in urging that due process be used broadly as a

[10] *Adamson v. California*, 332 U.S. 46, 67 (1947).
[11] *Minersville School District v. Gobitis*, 310 U.S. 586, 594–595 (1940).
[12] Ibid., p. 595.
[13] Ibid., p. 600.

substantive protection against interferences with individual liberties by states. They saw no contradiction between this position and their equally strong contention that due process should not be used as a defense against economic regulatory legislation. Black maintained that the Bill of Rights was a set of absolutes written into the Constitution in language that was unmistakably clear; whereas, the Constitution provided no similar protection against economic regulation. Black feared the *Palko* doctrine because he thought it would put too much discretion in the hands of judges. On the other hand, he did not believe in judicial restraint when the rights in question, such as speech, press, and religion, were protected literally by the Constitution. In a dissenting opinion in *Adamson*, Black argued that invalidating state regulation, as the old laissez-faire Court had done, on the basis of a limitless notion of reasonableness or "natural law," was not the same as invalidating statutes according "to particular standards enumerated in the Bill of Rights and other parts of the Constitution."[14] Leaving it up to the courts to determine what constituted "ordered liberty," Black argued, gave them a license, as they had had in the past, "to roam at large in the broad expanses of policy and morals and to trespass, all too freely, on the legislative domain of the States as well as the Federal Government."[15]

In between these two ideological and judicial philosophies were the views of Associate Justice Robert Jackson. In some instances, he sided with Black and Douglas about the importance of judicial activism; at other times, he was closer to Frankfurter in sensing the need to trust legislative judgment and experimentation. For example, he saw little value in drawing distinctions between economic rights and personal freedoms. Property rights were as much a personal right as the right to free speech. "[E]ven if we think property sometimes has undue protection against regulation," he argued, "the question remains, how far so-called rights of property can be swept away without encroaching upon the rights of the person as well."[16] Jackson avoided endorsing fully either judicial restraint or the doctrine of preferred freedoms. Instead, he favored balancing selectively when individual rights came into conflict with legislative or administrative action.

[14] *Adamson v. California*, 332 U.S. 91 (1947).
[15] Ibid., p. 90.
[16] Robert Jackson, "The Task of Maintaining Our Liberties: The Role of the Judiciary," *American Bar Association Journal*, 39 (November 1953), 963.

He worried, for instance, about the growth of local ordinances, which might, for a variety of reasons—including the fact that they affected fewer people than state or federal legislation—be more difficult for the average individual to challenge. Bill of Rights protections, he argued, were not meant to exempt local officials from the standards of concern for individual rights that applied to federal officials. "[T]he small and local authority may feel less sense of responsibility to the Constitution, and agencies of publicity may be less vigilant in calling it to account. . . . There are village tyrants as well as village Hampdens, but none who acts under color of law is beyond reach of the Constitution."[17] He expressed these views in 1943, shortly after joining the Court, in *West Virginia State Board of Education v. Barnette*, a case involving an effort by the Jehovah's Witnesses to have declared unconstitutional state and administrative regulations requiring school students to salute the flag and recite the pledge of allegiance, in violation of their right to freedom of speech and religion.

Writing the majority opinion, which, incidentally, overturned the Court's earlier decision in *Gobitis*, Jackson considered the salute a symbolic form of expression protected by the First Amendment. "To sustain the compulsory flag salute we are required to say that a Bill of Rights which guards the individual's right to speak his own mind, left it open to public authorities to compel him to utter what is not in his mind."[18] Similarly, he was less certain than Frankfurter of the value derived from overemphasizing national standards, particularly if it meant restricting minority rights and cultural diversity. "We can have intellectual individualism and the rich cultural diversities that we owe to exceptional minds only at the price of occasional eccentricity and abnormal attitudes."[19]

Yet there were times, he believed, when local administrative officials had to be trusted, even if individual interests were restricted. His experience as chief American prosecutor at the Nuremberg trials of Nazi war criminals in 1946 strengthened his belief in social order. In *Kunz v. New York* (1951), Jackson dissented from the majority opinion, which ruled unconstitutional a New York City ordinance requiring a permit to speak in public places. He argued that prior

[17] *West Virginia State Board of Education v. Barnette*, 319 U.S. 624, 637–638 (1943).
[18] Ibid., p. 634.
[19] Ibid., pp. 641–642.

municipal control was not inconsistent with the First Amendment. A local community might have an interest in protecting its citizens from disturbances caused by public speeches, and he pointed to a number of communities that had enacted similar laws. The law simply enabled the police to make certain that the speaker had an opportunity to speak and that the crowds were orderly. The case in question involved a speaker who had been refused a permit only after municipal authorities determined that his previous behavior had led to numerous complaints. Kunz was a virulent religious fanatic who uttered inflammatory remarks against Catholics and Jews. Jackson thought that the administration of the law had been fair, and that there were limits to free speech. The city, Jackson contended, was merely seeking to protect its citizens "against fanatics who take possession of its streets to hurl into its crowds defamatory epithets that hurt like rocks."[20]

Jackson recognized that the cold war and McCarthyism posed a serious threat to civil liberties, but he thought that these conditions were no reason to broaden Bill of Rights freedoms and give them greater protection than in the past. He feared that the Court was attempting to define standards for protection of First Amendment freedoms when, in fact, no standards existed. The urge to establish national standards of permissible civil and personal freedoms was an outgrowth of the Progressive ideology of social rationalization, internal discipline, and commonweal. But unlike in the economic arena, where the Court eventually subscribed to the position that the legislature and administrative agencies were the best judges of appropriate standards, in the area of civil rights and personal freedoms it found legislative and administrative action wanting and began increasingly to assume an active and often remedial role in protecting these rights. By the early fifties, Jackson's nonideological approach was coming into greater conflict with the Court's tendency toward judicial activism.

The Warren Court Influence

President Eisenhower's appointment of Earl Warren as chief justice in 1953 helped solidify a Court that had lacked strong leadership

[20] *Kunz v. New York*, 340 U.S. 290, 313 (1951).

under its two previous chief justices, Harlan Fiske Stone and Fred Vinson, and strengthened the position of those who favored an active judiciary. Although his record on social issues as governor of California was a mix of liberal and conservative values, Warren's attitude toward his role was an activist one. By the time he came to the Court, he had apparently fused his belief in action with a stronger conviction about the need for government protection of the public good. Unlike Frankfurter, he was not troubled by the concept of judicial activism. Nor did he think it necessary, as Black did, to look for literal constitutional restrictions on government in order to invalidate legislation. Rather than take the path of least resistance, Warren was ready to challenge legislative interference with vital human freedoms. According to Arthur Goldberg, who was to become in 1962 part of the Court's liberal majority, Warren "conceived that whatever the justification in other ages or times for seeking out ways of avoiding decisions on the merits of a case, the tenor of the modern world demands that judges, like men in all walks of public and private life, avoid escapism and frankly confront even the most controversial and troublesome justiciable problems."[21]

Warren pushed his brethren to define a new concept of fairness and equality before the law, one that would be applicable to all citizens regardless of their race or religion, whether they lived in a city or in a rural community, and whether they were subject to federal, state, or local authority. "The fundamental principle of representative government in this country," he declared, in what he considered one of the Court's most important decisions, the reapportionment case of *Reynolds v. Sims* (1964), "is one of equal representation for equal numbers of people, without regard to race, sex, economic status, or place of residence within a State."[22]

Under Warren, the Court did more than restate constitutional protections. Its decisions—particularly those in which it ruled school segregation unconstitutional (*Brown v. Board of Education*, 1954), required apportionment of legislative bodies according to the principle of "one person, one vote" (*Baker v. Carr*, 1962; *Reynolds v. Sims*, 1964), and applied federal standards of law enforcement to state courts and officials (*Mapp v. Ohio*, 1961; *Gideon v. Wainwright*, 1962; and *Escobedo v. Illinois*, 1964)—reflected its interest in fash-

---

[21] "Remarks by Honorable Arthur J. Goldberg, Tribute to Chief Justice Earl Warren," Lincoln Memorial, Washington, D.C., June 29, 1969, p. 3.
[22] *Reynolds v. Sims*, 377 U.S. 533, 560–561 (1964).

ioning a set of national standards for the protection of all Americans. In relying, as no previous Court had ever done, on the equal protection clause of the Constitution to curtail government discrimination, the Warren majority seemed intent on creating an egalitarian society in fact as well as theory. In order to do this, the Court went beyond invalidating restrictive legislation; it asserted an affirmative responsibility for implementing the legal and social principles it enunciated.

Its affirmative concept of judicial power emerged a year after the landmark decision of *Brown v. Board of Education*, where it held that separate but equal facilities in public education institutions did not meet constitutional standards. In the second Brown decision (1955), it charged the lower federal courts with the authority and obligation to oversee and supervise the implementation of school desegregation throughout the country. By virtue of their proximity to local conditions and their ability to fashion equitable remedies, Warren argued, federal courts were in the best position to deal with the issue of desegregating schools and adjusting and reconciling public and private needs. He urged lower federal courts to study the manner in which school administration was utilized to accomplish the new desegregation standards. This would involve studying "the physical condition of the school plant, the school transportation system, personnel, revision of school districts and attendance areas into compact units to achieve a system of determining admission to the pubic schools on a non-racial basis, and revision of local laws and regulations which may be necessary in solving the foregoing problems."[23] The decision established the authority of federal courts to provide both prohibitory as well as remedial relief.

Similarly, in *Reynolds*, the Court expressed its confidence in and desire for the federal judiciary to implement its reapportionment rulings. "Lower courts," Warren stated, "can and assuredly will work out more concrete and specific standards for evaluating state legislative apportionment schemes in the context of actual litigation." The Court encouraged litigation to resolve conflicts over apportionment. "Developing a body of doctrine on a case-by-case basis," Warren concluded, "appears to us to provide the most satisfactory means of arriving at detailed constitutional requirements in the area of state legislative apportionment."[24] As in the desegregation cases, judges

---

[23] *Brown v. Board of Education, II*, 349, U.S. 294, 300–301 (1955).
[24] *Reynolds v. Sims*, 357 U.S. 533, 578 (1964).

were urged to take into account a number of factors relating to local conditions, as long as the fundamental constitutional principle of apportionment by population was followed.

By entrusting judges with so much discretionary authority, the Supreme Court, in effect, converted lower federal courts into administrative tribunals. This approach troubled conservative jurist John Marshall Harlan, an Eisenhower appointee, who, in a dissenting opinion in *Reynolds*, argued that the Court was involving itself in determining questions for which it was decidedly unsuited. "[T]he vitality of our political system . . . is weakened by reliance on the judiciary for political reform; in time a complacent body politic may result."[25] But the Court acted as it did because, in its estimate, state and federal legislatures were already complacent.

Warren's reapportionment decisions were particularly noteworthy because as governor of California he had supported the state's apportionment system even though it gave some groups disproportionate power. Warren admitted that he had done so because as a political figure he was under an obligation to do what worked. "Politics has been said to be the art of the possible, and in it we accomplish what we can accomplish by compromise and by getting agreement with people." As a judge, however, he thought he had an obligation to uphold the Constitution and the principles it set forth. In this realm, there was no room for compromise. Unlike politics, which was not an exact science, judicial review required a more exacting search for applicable principles. If a law violates constitutional principles, he observed, "we no longer can compromise, we no longer can change to bring people into agreement, we have to decide the matter according to the principles as we see it."[26] One sees in Warren's assessment of his judicial role the reason why many responsible critics of the Court were troubled by its decisions. For many legal figures, judicial acceptance of legislative action, even if it appeared inequitable, was defensible as long as there was a rational basis for it.

In addition to its race and reapportionment decisions, the Court also sought to rationalize criminal justice by applying national standards to state and local jurisdictions. With regard to the question

[25] Ibid., p. 624.
[26] Anthony Lewis, "A Talk with Warren on Crime, the Court, the Country," *New York Times Magazine*, October 19, 1969, p. 127.

of admissible evidence, the Court held in *Mapp v. Ohio* (1961) that the Fourteenth Amendment's due process clause prohibited unreasonable searches and seizures by local and state officials, and that evidence obtained through such means was not admissible in a state court. The Court found that the Fourth Amendment's right to privacy was applicable to the states through the Fourteenth Amendment, and that safety from unreasonable searches was an essential part of privacy. Though the amendment itself did not speak of exclusion of evidence, the Court concluded that this was a privilege extending from the right. "To hold otherwise," declared Justice Tom Clark, a member of the Court since 1949, "is to grant the right but in reality to withhold its privilege and enjoyment."[27] The Court also stressed the need for standards of cooperative behavior in federal–state law enforcement. The existence of strict rules of evidence for federal officials in federal courts and less rigorous rules for state officials in state courts encouraged disobedience of the Constitution, Clark argued, and made no sense. "Federal–state cooperation in the solution of crime under constitutional standards will be promoted, if only by recognition of their now mutual obligation to respect the same fundamental criteria in their approaches."[28]

In 1963, the Court extended to state courts the Sixth Amendment's guarantee of right to counsel in criminal cases. In *Gideon v. Wainwright*, the Court eliminated the special circumstances test established in *Powell*. One year later, it took the even bolder step of extending the Sixth Amendment's protection to the interrogation process. In *Escobedo v. Illinois*, Justice Arthur Goldberg ruled that the right to counsel was as important to a suspect accused of a crime as it was at a later stage in the criminal justice process, when the suspect was formally indicted. In *Escobedo*, the accused had implicated himself in a murder plot by admitting knowledge of it, which under Illinois law was grounds for a murder indictment. Goldberg claimed that had the suspect been allowed to consult with his lawyer prior to the interrogation, he would have been advised of his right against self-incrimination.

The case was particularly controversial because it meant police officials would have to advise clients of their right to counsel immediately after an investigation moved from the general to the

[27] *Mapp v. Ohio*, 367 U.S. 643, 656 (1961).
[28] Ibid., p. 658.

accusatory stage with the intention of eliciting a confession. Goldberg chided those who claimed that extending the right to counsel to the interrogation process would reduce the chances of law enforcement officials obtaining convictions. "If the exercise of constitutional rights will thwart the effectiveness of a system of law enforcement, then there is something very wrong with that system."[29] He encouraged authorities to consider means of obtaining convictions through skillful investigations aimed at uncovering external evidence rather than through extorted confessions.

In dissent, Justice Byron White urged restraint in applying the *Gideon* rule. "The right to counsel now not only entitles the accused to counsel's advice and aid in preparing for trial but stands as an impenetrable barrier to any interrogation once the accused has become a suspect. From that very moment apparently his right to counsel attaches, a rule wholly unworkable and impossible to administer unless police cars are equipped with public defenders and undercover agents and police informants have defense counsel at their side."[30] He predicted the decision would have a crippling effect on law enforcement. Whether it did or did not has been difficult to assess. What is certain is that the Warren Court's criminal procedure decisions were more controversial than its civil rights and reapportionment decisions, which found general acceptance. Unlike civil rights and reapportionment, where the beneficiaries were disadvantaged blacks and underrepresented urban dwellers, the beneficiaries of the Court's criminal procedure decisions were more likely to be members of the nation's criminal elements. By the end of the sixties, the Court's predisposition toward protecting the rights of those suspected or accused of crime weakened whatever consensus it had been able to achieve with its other opinions.

Extension of Federal Control to the Social Arena

Warren Court decisions and the civil rights movement had political as well as judicial influence. They lent greater strength to the need for executive and legislative action to combat discrimination and broaden economic opportunities. Under the leadership of Lyndon

[29] *Escobedo v. Illinois*, 378 U.S. 478, 490 (1964).
[30] Ibid., p. 496.

Johnson, a President imbued with the mission of broadening the New Deal, the federal government embarked on an ambitious "war on poverty" to meet the critical needs of the country in education, transportation, health, natural resources, government organization, urban development, and agriculture. In Johnson's words, the legislation would offer the nation's poor "a genuine opportunity to change their lives—programs to train them for jobs, the means of giving their children a better chance to finish school, a method for putting medical clinics and legal services within their reach."[31] But these developments also meant a massive extension of the administrative process, not unlike what had taken place during the New Deal. Like the New Deal, the Great Society legislation opened up substantial opportunities and responsibilities for the legal profession. It also served to challenge the organized bar with new obligations and duties that would help shape their internal structure throughout the seventies.

The cornerstone of the Great Society was the Civil Rights Act of 1964, which went further than any other legislation of its kind in fostering equality among all Americans. The law forbade racial discrimination in jobs, strengthened constitutional prohibitions against voting discrimination, and prohibited racial segregation of public facilities. It included fair employment provisions and prohibitions against housing discrimination. At the heart of the law was a provision that assured blacks the same rights of access to any place of public accommodation as whites. It also provided for a commission that would investigate alleged violations of the law, "study and collect information concerning legal developments constituting a denial of equal protection of the laws, . . . appraise the laws and policies of the Federal Government with respect to denials of equal protection of the laws," and act as a national clearinghouse. In addition to the Commission on Civil Rights, Congress created an Equal Employment Opportunity Commission (EEOC) to enforce those provisions dealing with discriminatory hiring.

Although Congress hoped that these social changes could be brought about peacefully, through cooperation and persuasion, it also recognized that in the event substantial resistance developed, more appropriate enforcement machinery, such as litigation, would be needed. The EEOC, for example, was charged with eliminating

---

[31] Lyndon B. Johnson, *The Vantage Point* (New York, 1971), pp. 328–330.

any unlawful practices "by informal methods of conference, conciliation, and persuasion." If voluntary compliance failed, the commission could institute appropriate legal proceedings. Similarly, the
attorney general was authorized to initiate civil proceedings when he
deemed a person or group of persons unable to do so on their own.
This meant that if an individual lacked the finances to institute legal
proceedings or retain "effective" legal counsel, or stood in jeopardy
of losing his or her job or encountering physical harm, the government would act on that person's behalf. This statutory provision
marked an effort to surmount one of the inherent weaknesses of the
litigation process: the inability of the average citizen to initiate
effective remedial assistance.

Another significant feature of the Civil Rights Act was that it was
passed as an exercise of Congress's commerce power, rather than as
an exercise of the enforcement provision of the Fourteenth Amendment. In selecting this power, Congress evidenced its interest in
considering racial discrimination in the same class of abuses as
restraints of trade and as price discrimination. The fact that racial
discrimination in public facilities was a moral and social wrong,
Justice Clark wrote in *Heart of Atlanta Motel, Inc. v. United States*
(1964), upholding the constitutionality of the law "does not detract
from the overwhelming evidence of the disruptive effect that it has
had on commercial intercourse." And in light of this burden,
Congress had sufficient warrant to use its authority in this area. In
contrast, Justice Douglas preferred to detach civil rights from a
grant of economic power. He saw civil rights as part of the "higher"
law of the Constitution. "[T]he right of people to be free of state
action that discriminates against them because of race," he observed
in a concurring opinion, "like the 'right of persons to move freely
from State to State . . . occupies a more protected position in our
constitutional system than does the movement of cattle, fruit, steel
and coal across state lines.' "[32] He argued that the power to prohibit
racial discrimination in public facilities should rest on the enforcement provision of the Fourteenth Amendment.

By linking the prohibition against racial discrimination with the
commerce power, it appeared that Congress underscored the relationship between the protection of the civil rights of minorities and
their economic rights. Moreover, the nature of the act itself seemed

---

[32] *Heart of Atlanta Motel, Inc. v. United States*, 379 U.S. 241, 279 (1964).

to build on such Progressive-era and New Deal measures as the Federal Trade Commission Act and the National Labor Relations Act. Like those measures, the Civil Rights Act was class legislation designed to rationalize behavior that touched economic, social, and personal concerns. Like those acts, it contained elements of both the cooperative and the litigative approaches to government regulation. Like those acts, it sought to remove morality and emotionalism from highly charged economic and social relations by substituting procedure and objectivity. And like those acts, it sought to promote as well as punish. In this case, it sought to promote harmony of the races at the point where disharmony would disrupt the commercial, and hence general, welfare of the American republic.

The civil rights movement generated other legislation—such as the Voting Rights Act of 1965, strengthening access to the ballot for all minority groups, and the Civil Rights Act of 1968, guaranteeing fair housing to all minority groups. But guarantees of access to public facilities, schools, voting, and housing remained empty declarations without substantive efforts to correct disparities in economic position. A panel of distinguished Americans, assembled by the Rockefeller Brothers Fund, had reported in 1961 that the extension of civil liberties was not enough to "ensure an individual's allegiance to democratic principles." "Without the proper social structure," the panel argued, "civil liberties can seem empty abstractions. . . . A full-fledged desire to give meaning to civil liberties calls for continuing concern, not only with legal safeguards but with the economic and social conditions that can make those liberties instruments that ordinary citizens actually prize and use." Only "through access to the necessary resources of talent, wealth, and influence in the community," the panel reported, can legal guarantees of civil liberty have value.[33] By the mid-sixties, these conclusions were generally accepted by the nation's leaders. The civil rights movement, which had begun as an effort to ensure to minorities and other disadvantaged people protection against discriminatory legislation and better access to the political process, became part of a larger program to broaden economic opportunities. And a large share of the responsibility for implementing these policies fell naturally to the legal community.

[33] *Prospect for America: The Rockefeller Panel Reports* (Garden City, N.Y., 1961), p. 425.

New Legal Activism:
Private Action in Defense of Public Rights

Legal reformers seized the opportunity afforded by Warren Court decisions and civil rights legislation to launch a broad campaign to expand individual and civil rights. In doing so, they helped exacerbate the issue of whether legal reform should be pursued through the courts or through the legislature. "Each successful appeal to the courts in lieu of the political process," Harvard Law School professor Archibald Cox observed, "added to the momentum from previous steps. More and more of the problems of government were being presented to and handled by the federal courts as questions of constitutional law."[34] The situation was reminiscent of Progressive-era legal reformers who, encouraged by the dissenting opinions of such jurists as Brandeis, Cardozo, and Holmes, sought to readjust the distribution of economic power. But the scenario of legal reform had changed.

Unlike the Progressive-era generation of legal reformers, whose concern had been drafting and defending economic regulatory and social welfare legislation, the new group of legal activists focused their attention on areas, such as race relations, where legislation and administration had, in their view, been used to constrain individual freedom and initiative. Whereas the older generation of liberal activists had supported judicial restraint in order to win their battle for the constitutionality of legislative authority, the new generation supported judicial activism as a way of limiting legislative authority. They equated judicial activism with justice. "For them," wrote federal judge Skelly Wright, "there was no theoretical gulf between the law and morality; and, for them, the Court was the one institution in the society that seemed to be speaking most consistently the language of idealism which we all recited in grade school. . . . They have seen that affairs can be ordered in conformance to constitutional ideals and that injustice . . . can be routed."[35]

Once again, research and education became powerful weapons for promoting social reform. Law reviews and journals increased in

---

[34] Archibald Cox, *The Role of the Supreme Court in American Government* (New York, 1976), p. 36.

[35] J. Skelly Wright, "Professor Bickel, the Scholarly Tradition, and the Supreme Court," *Harvard Law Review*, 84 (February 1971), 804–805.

number to meet the need for publication outlets and the demand for information. Judges not only relied on them for edification but, with greater frequency and more openly than before, began supporting their conclusions with these research findings. It was not uncommon to find young, activist law students using their editorial control of law school journals and reviews to exert considerable influence on the judiciary in favor of improved social and economic rights for minorities. Some law schools added courses on civil liberties, to make students more sensitive to these issues. The legal staffs of such major civil rights groups as the National Association for the Advancement of Colored People, the American Jewish Congress, and the American Civil Liberties Union were increased, as was the Civil Rights Division of the Justice Department. Activist judges welcomed the supporting information provided by these groups and supplemented their "friend of the court" briefs by inviting experts—not just in the law, but in the social sciences, health, and medicine—to present testimony and reports on critical policy issues.

Fueled by a substantial influx of public and private funding— the latter largely from foundations—research centers, usually located at prominent university law schools, were created to further education and policy goals in these social areas. The New York University School of Law, for example, established the Arthur Garfield Hays Civil Liberties Program in September 1958, to conduct research on human rights, provide technical assistance to civil rights groups, sponsor conferences and special projects in the field, and train civil rights lawyers. Under its director, Norman Dorsen, who later became head of the American Civil Liberties Union, the program brought numerous test cases challenging the constitutionality of statutes, ordinances, and administrative actions. This group looked increasingly to the courts for implementation of their objectives. According to Dorsen, civil rights litigation required constant follow-up to prevent backsliding by illegal police actions or by an indifferent public. When backsliding occurred and government enforcement was lacking, Dorsen argued, "the civil liberties lawyer [had] to force compliance, usually by instituting new suits."[36]

The impulse to seek changes in the social fabric through litigation was aided not only by the Court's decisions expanding the permissible substantive area of judicial review (e.g., legislative apportionment) but through a relaxation of the standards for initiating legal proceed-

[36] Norman Dorsen, *The Frontiers of Civil Liberties* (New York, 1968), p. xxi.

ings. In *National Association for the Advancement of Colored People v. Button* (1962), the Court held that litigation may be "the sole practicable avenue open to a minority to petition for redress of grievances."[37] The case involved an effort by the National Association for the Advancement of Colored People (NAACP) to enjoin the enforcement of a Virginia statute that made solicitation of legal business by lawyers not a party to a judicial proceeding or having "no pecuniary right or liability in it" a form of malpractice. Writing the majority opinion, Justice William Brennan argued that from the standpoint of the NAACP, litigation was not a technique for resolving private differences but "a means for achieving the lawful objectives of equality of treatment by all government, federal, state, and local, for the members of the Negro community in this country."[38] In effect, the Court endorsed litigation as a constitutionally protected right that organizations and groups such as the NAACP could adopt to secure reform and that states, under their authority to regulate the legal profession, might not prohibit. By permitting the NAACP to advise prospective litigants of their rights and need for legal assistance, the Court made a profound distinction between malicious solicitation for private gain and solicitation for the purpose of enforcing constitutional rights in the public interest. This distinction would have substantial implications in the future for how the legal profession structured its provision of legal services.

The Response to Judicial Activism

By the late sixties, the Warren Court decisions, civil rights movement, and Great Society legislation began to react against themselves and each other. Civil disorder, motivated both by racial injustice and by the United States's escalating role in the Vietnam conflict, frightened many Americans and led conservatives to seek restraints on liberals and liberal institutions, particularly the Supreme Court. Criticism of the Warren Court also emerged more prominently from within the Court and among respected legal scholars. Although it had always had its dissenting voices, such as Felix Frankfurter and John

---

[37] *National Association for the Advancement of Colored People v. Button*, 371 U.S., 415, 430 (1962).
[38] Ibid., p. 429.

Marshall Harlan, some change in the Court's liberal majority was evident when Hugo Black joined those who urged restraint. In *Griswold v. Connecticut* (1965), Black dissented from the Court's decision to overturn a Connecticut statute making it a crime to use, or advise the use of, contraceptives. Although he agreed that the law was silly, he did not believe it violated any of the fundamental rights of citizens. He expressed his fear that the Court was once again using the due process clause to strike down legislation it personally disagreed with, in a manner similar to the laissez-faire Court of the twenties and thirties. Moreover, he bitterly opposed the highly libertarian interpretation of the Ninth Amendment that Goldberg used, in a concurring opinion, to invalidate the law. Apparently, Black concluded that limits were needed to halt what he perceived to be an excess of democracy. In fact, Black's opinion seemed consistent with his belief that judicial activism was legitimate only in defense of constitutional absolutes. He saw no constitutional right to marital privacy.

Black's plea for restraint was echoed by a growing number of legal critics. In a series of three lectures at Harvard University in 1969, which *New York Times* correspondent Anthony Lewis termed, "one of those intellectual events whose reverberations generally disturb a widening circle,"[39] Yale Law School professor Alexander Bickel argued that the Warren Court's concept of the future, which consisted of such values as majoritarianism, egalitarianism, and judicial activism, were not necessarily desirable or rational policies. In a manner reminiscent of Justice Jackson's opinion in *West Virginia State Board of Education v. Barnette*, Bickel argued that the Court was trying to establish national standards of social intercourse when, in fact, the needs of the country were diverse and needed more careful expression. "It is diversity that the law will have to recognize as the essential value during the last third of the twentieth century," he stated. "A striving for diversity is not necessarily in express conflict with the goal of an egalitarian society, but it connotes a different order of priorities."[40] The legal process, Bickel argued, was based on accommodation and respect for established procedure. The pace of reform established by the Court had weakened the underpin-

---

[39] Anthony Lewis, "The Heavenly City of Professor Bickel," *New York Times*, October 10, 1969, p. 46.
[40] Alexander Bickel, *The Supreme Court and the Idea of Progress* (New York, 1970), pp. 112–113.

nings of the legal process, which necessarily needs time to absorb change.

These attitudes were shared by Harvard University sociologist and law professor David Riesman, who, like Bickel, thought reform was better achieved through the legislative process. In commenting on the work of activist lawyers, Riesman observed, "They see themselves as advocacy lawyers, persuading a judge or at most five judges of something and then not having to persuade the general population." Riesman held the litigious mentality responsible for promoting an atmosphere of confrontation. "Whether it concerns environment or race or other causes which are deemed populist but . . . are not popular, I am reminded of the New Deal lawyers. . . . I kept arguing with them that it was important to bring people . . . along by the political process, by conciliation and coalition, rather than coerce by litigation. The adversary process seems to me exactly wrong for deciding intricate issues of cost-benefit; and, in the American evangelical grain, it tends to moralize these issues."[41]

Defenders of the Court countered this criticism by suggesting that the Warren Court was only seeking to ensure that those without political power were not shut off from the avenues of representation. The Court, argued Skelly Wright, had touched only those "formal" levers of power. And since the American "political system operates largely through informal channels, . . . the Warren Court did not bring true democracy to America."[42] Courts, in Wright's opinion, had not supplanted the political process as the principal agency for social change. But as University of Chicago Law School professor Philip Kurland observed, defenders of the Court had always claimed it was a "nonpolitical, reasoning, objective, judicial body." This had been necessary, Kurland noted, because of the relative weakness of the judiciary to exert its power vis-à-vis the legislature and executive. Kurland pointed out that what had saved the Court from unpopular decisions in the past was either an appeal to its judicialness—that is, its objectivity—or a withdrawal from past positions. Kurland advised the Court to take more account of the practical difficulties its principled decisions created and consider whether means existed to accomplish its ends. He warned, "[T]here is certainly, at least, a

---

[41] David Riesman to Alexander Bickel, January 14, 1974, Alexander Bickel Papers, Yale University Library.
[42] Wright, "Professor Bickel," p. 793.

prima facie case to be made that the deficiencies of the opinions are approaching the danger point."[43]

By 1968, law and politics were once more converging to create the conditions for constitutional crisis. In June 1968, Warren announced his decision to retire, only a few months after President Johnson had decided not to seek reelection. To many, particularly the conservatives in Congress, it appeared Warren had timed his retirement to allow Johnson to name a liberal successor. Johnson did just that, by naming his longtime friend, Associate Justice Abe Fortas, as chief justice. However, with the prospect that Richard Nixon might be elected President in the upcoming fall election, Republicans rallied enough support to defeat the nomination. In the process, Fortas became the target for the frustration of those who opposed the Court's decisions, particularly those dealing with the rights of the criminally accused. He countered this hostility by arguing that as a judge, he merely applied constitutional principles and precedents to the case at hand. But as Kurland had warned, this explanation was tenable only when there was public support for the Court's decisions. Fortas resigned a year later in the face of allegations of judicial impropriety. Meanwhile, after serving another year, Warren retired and was replaced by United States Court of Appeals Judge Warren Burger. Although these developments seemed to presage a conservative backlash, in fact, the Supreme Court continued during the seventies to take a progressive and activist position on many social issues.

Modernizing Legal Practice in America

The legislative and judicial actions of the fifties and early sixties transformed the economic and social character of American society. But only a small portion of the legal profession had played an important role in designing and helping implement these social changes. By the late sixties, however, it appeared that the changes wrought in America's social structure were about to alter the character, organization, and attitudes of the organized bar as a

[43] Philip Kurland, "The Court Should Decide Less and Explain More," *New York Times Magazine*, June 9, 1968, p. 34.

whole. The civil rights movement and the war on poverty forced the legal community into a reevaluation of its public and professional responsibilities. The Court's decision in *Gideon*, ruling that states must provide counsel on behalf of indigent defendants at trial and on appeal, sharpened the issue of the relationship between access to legal services, and income and social standing. "That government hires lawyers to prosecute," Justice Black wrote, "and defendants who have the money hire lawyers to defend are the strongest indications of the widespread belief that lawyers . . . are necessities, not luxuries."[44] The decision contributed to the legal profession's willingness to examine the provision and consumption of its services. Leading observers of the profession's relationship to the public claimed that it had gone too long without reconstructing the economic basis of its services. The bar had been too preoccupied, as one law professor put it, with "improvement of the quality of services, instead of revision and expansion of methods by which the services may be brought to all in need of them."[45]

The first effort to tackle the question of providing better access to legal services was focused on the poor. Some sociologists and lawyers linked the provision of legal services to reconstruction of the economic and social life of the poor. Model programs, such as the Ford Foundation's Mobilization for Youth, were designed on the premise that adequate legal services were the only means of redress the poor had against the complexity and indifference of administrative bureaucracy. "In addition to exploring violations of the rights or entitlements of the poor under law," observed one expert, "the legal profession is now challenged by an even more difficult responsibility if it is to take its place in the war against poverty. It must explore and discover new methods and procedures so as to protect and safeguard the individual entitled to assistance from the dehumanization that all too often characterizes the governmental administration of 'benefits' under law."[46] Safeguarding these rights involved more than a casual concern on the part of the bar; it meant a substantial commitment by large numbers of lawyers for lengthy periods of time. Advocates of legal services to the poor urged the creation of a distinct corps of "poverty lawyers."

---

[44] *Gideon v. Wainwright*, 372 U.S., 335, 344, (1963).
[45] Elliott Evans Cheatham, *A Lawyer When Needed* (New York, 1963), p. 2.
[46] Justine Polier, "Problems Involving Family and Child," in *National Conference on Law and Poverty: Conference Proceedings* (Washington, D.C., 1965), p. 26.

Congress responded to the need for substantial financial and programmatic support by creating a Legal Services Office within the Office of Economic Opportunity in 1966. The program differed from traditional legal aid activities, which were not oriented toward making substantive changes in the economic and social structure, were privately supported, and were limited in the number of clients they served. The new public interest legal activities spawned by this new agency took an aggressive position in seeking to reform laws and practices unfavorable to the poor, were heavily supported through government grants, and sought to represent large numbers and groups of poor persons and minorities. "Advocacy of appropriate reforms in statutes, regulations, and administrative practices is a part of the traditional role of the lawyer," read one of the early guidelines of the National Advisory Committee of OEO Legal Services, "and should be among the services afforded by the program." This mandate included "judicial challenges to particular practices and regulations of governmental agencies, research into conflicting or discriminating applications of laws or administrative rules, and proposals for administrative and legislative changes."[47]

But the path of federally supported legal services over the next decade was anything but consistent. For one thing, there was uncertainty regarding the extent to which legal services could be fully integrated into the everyday activities of the organized bar. A number of political and legal developments exacerbated these concerns. Statutory restrictions imposed on the Legal Services Corporation (1974), the successor to the OEO Legal Services Office, precluded grants for legal services involving school desegregation, abortion, and postconviction procedures, thereby limiting the reform function of the agency. Internal Revenue Service rules preventing tax-exempt public interest groups from accepting fees for professional services reduced the ability of these groups to develop new clienteles. As a result, their efforts tended to be responsive rather than active. The same rules prevented these groups from lobbying. This restriction forced them to rely entirely on litigation, which many still thought was not the best way to make long-lasting changes in established practices. By the eighties, legal services for the poor had an uncertain future, in light of Reagan administration efforts to dismantle the agency or, failing this, to reduce its budget.

[47] Quoted in Earl Johnson, Jr., *Justice and Reform: The Formative Years of the OEO Legal Services Program* (New York, 1974), p. 116.

The "New" Consumer Movement

Provision of legal services for the poor represented a growing movement toward implementing, in fact and not just in theory, rights guaranteed by Warren Court decisions and congressional legislation. This concept, often referred to as "entitlement," led some judges to believe that their role involved not only preventing past and future discrimination, but molding remedial relief. In *Wyatt v. Stickney* (1972), for example, federal judge Frank Johnson, one of a small number of liberal southern jurists, ruled that the patients at an Alabama state mental facility were entitled, under the Constitution, "to receive individual treatment as will give each of them a realistic opportunity to be cured or to improve."[48] Johnson translated this right into concrete action by ordering the state legislature to appropriate sufficient funds to reconstruct and properly staff the facility. As he later said, "If we, as judges, have learned anything from *Brown v. Board of Education* and its progeny, it is that prohibitory relief alone affords but a hollow protection to the basic and fundamental rights of citizens under equal protection of the law."[49]

But it was not only the poor who began to make claims on traditional institutions. During the seventies, more and more Americans began to demand of government, business, and the professions greater accountability for their actions, more involvement in the decision making process, and better service generally. As in the past, consumers were concerned with the production, quality, and price of goods and services, and the conditions under which goods were manufactured and services rendered. The growth of conglomerates and multinational corporations led to a deepening sense of isolation from the sources of production and hence from a role in shaping market decisions. Congress broadened the authority of the Federal Trade Commission in 1974 (Magnuson-Moss Warranty/FTC Improvement Act) to enable the FTC to set standards to prohibit abusive business practices in an entire industry, rather than among individual wrongdoers. The FTC was so vigorous in seeking to break up monopolistic conditions and unfair trade practices that by the late

---

[48] *Wyatt v. Stickney*, 344 F. Supp. 374 (M.D. Ala. 1972).
[49] Frank M. Johnson, Jr. "Judicial Activism Is a Duty—Not an Intrusion," *Judges Journal*, 16 (Fall 1977), 6.

seventies, efforts were under way to curtail its authority through a congressional veto on its investigations.

In contrast, the Supreme Court held that individual consumers, not just businesses, could bring suit under the antitrust laws when they thought their "property" rights were interfered with by anticompetitive conduct. "The essence of the antitrust laws," Burger declared in *Reiter v. Sonotone Corporation*, "is to ensure fair price competition in an open market."[50] The case involved a class action brought by an individual on behalf of herself and all persons in the United States against several hearing aid manufacturers, alleging violation of the price-fixing provisions of the antitrust laws. Burger argued that the antitrust laws were designed to encourage private challenges to antitrust violations. "These private suits provide a significant supplement to the limited resources available to the Department of Justice for enforcing the antitrust laws and deterring violations."[51] Rather than discouraging them on the grounds that the courts might not be equipped to handle such a load, he suggested that Congress provide adequate judicial resources.

The trend toward individualism and private action was also evident in the efforts by Americans to win new personal rights and economic opportunities. Women, for example, became more aggressive in pressing claims of gender discrimination and seeking control of such intimate considerations as the decision to have an abortion. They won considerable power to do the latter as a result of the Supreme Court's decision in *Roe v. Wade* (1973), ruling state antiabortion laws unconstitutional. The case involved an action by an unmarried pregnant woman who wished to terminate her pregnancy by abortion. She sought a declaratory judgment that the Texas criminal abortion statutes, which prohibited abortion except with respect to those procured or attempted by medical advice for the purpose of saving the mother's life, were unconstitutional. The Court decided that prior reasons for the laws no longer seemed tenable, and that a woman's right to privacy, though not absolute, did include the abortion decision. It found reason for a state interest after the first trimester, when mortality resulting from abortion is greater than it is in the early months of pregnancy. Only after this period, the Court

---

[50] *Reiter v. Sonotone Corporation*, 442 U.S. 330, 342 (1979).
[51] Ibid., p. 344.

concluded, does the state's regulatory interest become greater than the individual's.

The decision had far-reaching social implications for family planning and sexual activity, and added to the developing constitutional concept of privacy. Although the Constitution did not explicitly mention a right of privacy, the Court argued that such a right existed. "Zones of privacy," as the Court characterized this right, have their roots in several of the provisions of the Constitution and in numerous decisions. "These decisions," Justice Blackmun wrote, "make it clear that only personal rights that can be deemed 'fundamental' or 'implicit in the concept of ordered liberty'. . . are included in this guarantee of personal privacy."[52] A stable, yet fluid, social order would be reached, in the Court's mind, by relieving the psychological and emotional distress associated with an unwanted child. The decision showed that on some social issues, the Court remained activist in spite of the presence of such ostensibly conservative jurists as Blackmun and Burger.

Challenges to established power were not confined solely to government and business; they were also directed at professional groups. With costs for professional services increasing, many Americans concluded that if professionals were more competitive, services would be better and prices fairer. Unlike business, which had come to grips with the problem of marketing during the early part of the century, the self-regulatory prerogatives and antitrust exemption of many professional groups, including lawyers, insulated them from having to deal with the provision of their services to the population as a whole. Past claims to craftsmanship and learnedness no longer provided a convincing justification for restricting broader access to professional services. Thus in *Goldfarb v. Virginia State Bar* (1975), the Court declared that publication of a minimum fee schedule by a county bar association and enforcement by a state bar created a rigid price floor for services and constituted a "classic illustration of price fixing" in violation of antitrust statutes.[53] And in *National Society of Professional Engineers v. United States* (1978), the Supreme Court found that the society's ban against competitive bidding, supposedly an ethical necessity, violated the Sherman Antitrust Act. Architects and accountants settled antitrust suits by agreeing to remove restric-

[52] *Roe v. Wade*, 410 U.S., 113, 152 (1973).
[53] *Goldfarb v. Virginia State Bar*, 421 U.S. 773, 783 (1975).

tions on competitive bidding from their codes. By 1980, it appeared the Court was also receptive to breaking up efforts by real estate brokers to fix prices through uniform commission rates on real estate transactions.

Democratization of professional services was also achieved through the Court's development of the concept of "commercial free speech." In *Virginia State Board of Pharmacy v. Virginia Citizens Consumer Council* (1976), the Court held a Virginia law prohibiting pharmacists from engaging in price advertising to be a violation of the First Amendment. And in *Bates v. State Bar of Arizona* (1977), the Court ruled that bar association codes against advertising violated First Amendment rights to commercial free speech. The Court ruled that no adverse effects on professional standards would result from lawyers' advertising their services. Bates and O'Steen had set up a legal clinic to provide low-cost legal services to individuals who did not qualify for government assistance. In order to sustain their profitability, they needed a large volume of business, which they determined was possible only through advertising. Advertising legal services had been prohibited by Arizona Supreme Court rules, enforced by the state bar association.

Bates signified not only an attempt to broaden consumer access to professional services but an effort by a younger and less established group of practitioners to challenge the authority and economic structure of an older, more established group, represented by the bar association. This intense generational and professional conflict, a characteristic of American social history since the early eighteenth century, was evident in Justice Blackmun's majority opinion. "[C]ynicism with regard to the profession," he observed, "may be created by the fact that it long has publicly eschewed advertising, while condoning the actions of the attorney who structures his social or civic associations so as to provide contacts with potential clients."[54] The decision inspired the creation of low-cost legal clinics throughout the country, some even in local department stores.

These decisions also prompted national, state, and local bar groups to undertake an extensive review of their structure, organization, and policies affecting the provision of legal services and the training of practitioners. Among the more promising developments was the American Bar Association's recognition that competition and

[54] *Bates v. State Bar of Arizona*, 433 U.S. 350, 370–371 (1977).

professionalism were not incompatible. To underwrite this philosophy, the association proposed new rules of professional responsibility
to allow for advertising. These rules also reduced the emphasis on
client caretaking in favor of a statement stressing the lawyer's
responsibility to society. Nevertheless, the proposed rules stopped
short of imposing an enforceable mandatory requirement on lawyers
to perform public interest work. Instead, the bar settled for admon-
ishment of those who did not contribute to such work. With this new
code, written as if it were a legislative document, the organized bar
hoped to retain its self-regulatory privileges.

The contours of legal reform in this century were shaped by the
Progressive-era generation of leaders, such men as Woodrow Wilson,
Louis Brandeis, Theodore Roosevelt, and Oliver Wendell Holmes,
who spoke of the need for order yet held firmly to a belief in liberty.
They encouraged regulation of business, not to limit its productive
capacity but to make the system more efficient and more fair. The
more recent generation of Progressive mandarins, such as Earl
Warren and Lyndon Johnson, sought similar goals. Realizing that
many Americans still lacked opportunity, they sought in their own
ways, to encourage efforts that would enlarge the scope of economic
and social freedom. Both generations sought to keep open the
channels of commerce and communication, to discourage discrimination, and to promote the idea of an American commonwealth.
Working through appropriate legal institutions, these social and legal
reformers helped blanket America with a network of rules and
regulations that affect every person from birth to death. How well
these laws function in the future, which among them survive, and
which new ones are added will require, as it always has, legal figures
capable of balancing personal interest and community needs. Moreover, it will need those leaders who understand what Woodrow
Wilson tried to suggest nearly a century ago, that the law is a liberal
discipline and must be taught and practiced as such.

Documents

Introduction to the Document Collection

The documents have been arranged in three groups or categories. The first consists of excerpts from the Constitution that reflect grants of and restrictions on Congressional and state power, together with pieces of legislation that have influenced the shape of American life. The second group comprises excerpts from the opinions of Supreme Court justices—again, in cases raising critical economic and social questions. The third group consists of statements by lawyers about the nature and function of the law and legal institutions. In all three categories, the focus of attention shifts from a concern for economic matters early in the century to social values in the latter half.

CONSTITUTION AND STATUTES

The excerpts reprinted here from the Constitution of the United States of America reflect some of the powers of and restrictions on the Congress and the state governments. They are particularly pertinent because they relate to issues discussed in the essay. For example, Section 10 concerns state compacts, such as the one used in the creation of the Port of New York Authority. The enforcement provision of the Fourteenth Amendment and the commerce clause figured in conflicting views by Justices Clark and Douglas on the constitutionality of the Civil Rights Act of 1964 (the Heart of Atlanta *case). A large part of the discussion of legal reform in America, then, concerns the exercise by Congress and state and local agencies of powers derived from the Constitution.*

As you read the statutes, consider how they reflect the periods in which they were enacted. To what degree do they represent an expansion of Congress's power under the commerce clause? In what way is legal process used to regulate economic and social activity? Pay particular attention to the procedures established in the Federal Trade Commission Act for regulating unfair business practices. Examine the statutes to find instances of both cooperative and regulatory approaches. Compare the FTC Act and the Civil Rights Act of 1964. How is the commerce power used to regulate, first, economic concerns and, later, social relations? In what ways do the statutes represent a trend toward the creation of an egalitarian society? From your knowledge of twentieth-century American history, how do these statutes exemplify changes in the attitudes of Americans toward business freedom and social justice? Bearing in mind that some of these statutes have been amended by subsequent legislation and one has been declared un-constitutional, do you think these statutes still are viable as organic statements of economic and social values? Do you think they need revision? If so, in what respect? Imagine a research project in which you have the opportunity to play the role of a legislative draftsperson. Analyze and discuss the extent to which the legislation is likely to meet the needs of society in the eighties.

*Constitution of the United States of America (1787)**

WE THE PEOPLE of the United States, in Order to form a more perfect Union, establish Justice, insure domestic Tranquility, provide for the common defence, promote the general Welfare, and secure the Blessings of Liberty to ourselves and our posterity, do ordain and establish this Constitution for the United States of America.

ARTICLE I.

SECTION 1. All legislative Powers herein granted shall be vested in a Congress of the United States, which shall consist of a Senate and House of Representatives. . . .

SECTION 8. The Congress shall have Power To lay and collect Taxes, Duties, Imposts and Excises, to pay the Debts and provide for the common Defence and general Welfare of the United States; but all Duties, Imposts and Excises shall be uniform throughout the United States; . . .

To regulate Commerce with foreign Nations, and among the several States, and with the Indian Tribes; . . .

To make all Laws which shall be necessary and proper for carrying into Execution the foregoing Powers, and all other Powers vested by this Constitution in the Government of the United States, or in any Department or Officer thereof.

SECTION 10.

No State shall, without the Consent of Congress, . . . enter into any Agreement or Compact with another State. . . .

* *United States Code*, 1976 ed., vol. 1, p. xlv.

ARTICLES IN ADDITION TO, AND AMENDMENT OF THE CONSTITUTION OF THE UNITED STATES OF AMERICA. . . .

ARTICLE [I.]

Congress shall make no law respecting an establishment of religion, or prohibiting the free exercise thereof; or abridging the freedom of speech, or of the press; or the right of the people peaceably to assemble, and to petition the Government for a redress of grievances.

ARTICLE [IV.]

The right of the people to be secure in their persons, houses, papers, and effects, against unreasonable searches and seizures, shall not be violated, and no warrants shall issue, but upon probable cause, supported by oath or affirmation, and particularly describing the place to be searched, and the persons or things to be seized.

ARTICLE [V.]

No person shall be . . . compelled in any criminal case to be a witness against himself, nor be deprived of life, liberty, or property, without due process of law; nor shall private property be taken for public use, without just compensation.

ARTICLE [VI.]

In all criminal prosecutions, the accused shall enjoy the right to a speedy and public trial, by an impartial jury of the State and district wherein the crime shall have been committed, . . . and to have the assistance of counsel for his defence.

ARTICLE [IX.]

The enumeration in the Constitution, of certain rights, shall not be construed to deny or disparage others retained by the people.

ARTICLE [X.]

The powers not delegated to the United States by the Constitution, nor prohibited by it to the States, are reserved to the States respectively, or to the people.

ARTICLE XIV.

SECTION 1. . . . No State shall make or enforce any law which shall abridge the privileges or immunities of citizens of the United States; nor shall any State deprive any person of life, liberty, or property, without due process of law; nor deny to any person within its jurisdiction the equal protection of the laws. . . .

SECTION 5. The Congress shall have power to enforce, by appropriate legislation, the provisions of this article.

Sherman Antitrust Act (1890)*

SEC. 1. Every contract, combination in the form of trust or otherwise, or conspiracy, in restraint of trade or commerce among the several States, or with foreign nations, is hereby declared to be illegal. Every person who shall make any such contract or engage in any such combination or conspiracy, shall be deemed guilty of a misdemeanor, and, on conviction thereof, shall be punished by fine not exceeding five thousand dollars, or by imprisonment not exceeding one year, or by both said punishments, in the discretion of the court.

SEC. 2. Every person who shall monopolize, or attempt to monopolize, or combine or conspire with any other person or persons, to monopolize any part of the trade or commerce among the several States, or with foreign nations, shall be deemed guilty of a misdemeanor, and, on conviction thereof, shall be punished by fine not exceeding five thousand dollars, or by imprisonment not exceeding one year, or by both said punishments, in the discretion of the court. . . .

SEC. 7. Any person who shall be injured in his business or property by any other person or corporation by reason of anything forbidden or declared to be unlawful by this act, may sue therefor in any circuit court of the United States in the district in which the defendant resides or is found, without respect to the amount in controversy, and shall recover threefold the damages by him sustained, and the costs of the suit, including a reasonable attorney's fee.

* U.S., *Statutes at Large*, Vol. XXVI, Ch. 647, July 2, 1890, 51st Cong., 1st Sess., p. 209.

SEC. 8. That the word "person" or "persons," wherever used in this act shall be deemed to include corporations and associations existing under or authorized by the laws of either the United States, the laws of any of the Territories, the laws of any State, or the laws of any foreign country.

Federal Trade Commission Act (1914)*

SEC. 5. That unfair methods of competition in commerce are hereby declared unlawful.

The commission is hereby empowered and directed to prevent persons, partnerships, or corporations, except banks, and common carriers subject to the Acts to regulate commerce, from using unfair methods of competition in commerce.

Whenever the commission shall have reason to believe that any such person, partnership, or corporation has been or is using any unfair method of competition in commerce, and if it shall appear to the commission that a proceeding by it in respect thereof would be to the interest of the public, it shall issue and serve upon such person, partnership, or corporation a complaint stating its charges in that respect, and containing a notice of a hearing upon a day and at a place therein fixed at least thirty days after the service of said complaint. The person, partnership, or corporation so complained of shall have the right to appear at the place and time so fixed and show cause why an order should not be entered by the commission requiring such person, partnership, or corporation to cease and desist from the violation of the law so charged in said complaint. Any person, partnership, or corporation may make application, and upon good cause shown may be allowed by the commission, to intervene and appear in said proceeding by counsel or in person. The testimony in any such proceeding shall be reduced to writing and filed in the office of the commission. If upon such hearing the commission shall be of the opinion that the method of competition in question is prohibited by this Act, it shall make a report in writing in which it shall state its findings as to the facts, and shall issue and cause to be served on such person, partnership, or corporation an order requiring

* U.S., *Statutes at Large, Two Parts*, Vol. XXXVIII, Pt. 1, Ch. 311, September 26, 1914, 63rd Cong., 2d Sess., p. 717.

such person, partnership, or corporation to cease and desist from using such method of competition. Until a transcript of the record in such hearing shall have been filed in a circuit court of appeals of the United States, as hereinafter provided, the commission may at any time, upon such notice and in such manner as it shall deem proper, modify or set aside, in whole or in part, any report or any order made or issued by it under this section.

If such person, partnership, or corporation fails or neglects to obey such order of the commission while the same is in effect, the commission may apply to the circuit court of appeals of the United States, within any circuit where the method of competition in question was used or where such person, partnership, or corporation resides or carries on business, for the enforcement of its order, and shall certify and file with its application a transcript of the entire record in the proceeding, including all the testimony taken and the report and order of the commission. Upon such filing of the application and transcript the court shall cause notice thereof to be served upon such person, partnership, or corporation and thereupon shall have jurisdiction of the proceeding and of the question determined therein, and shall have power to make and enter upon the pleadings, testimony, and proceedings set forth in such transcript a decree affirming, modifying, or setting aside the order of the commission. The findings of the commission as to the facts, if supported by testimony, shall be conclusive. If either party shall apply to the court for leave to adduce additional evidence, and shall show to the satisfaction of the court that such additional evidence is material and that there were reasonable grounds for the failure to adduce such evidence in the proceeding before the commission, the court may order such additional evidence to be taken before the commission and to be adduced upon the hearing in such manner and upon such terms and conditions as to the court may seem proper. The commission may modify its findings as to the facts, or make new findings, by reason of the additional evidence so taken and it shall file such modified or new findings, which, if supported by testimony, shall be conclusive, and its recommendation, if any, for the modification or setting aside of its original order, with the return of such additional evidence. The judgment and decree of the court shall be final, except that the same shall be subject to review by the Supreme Court upon certiorari as provided in section two hundred and forty of the Judicial Code.

Any party required by such order of the commission to cease and desist from using such method of competition may obtain a review of such order in said circuit court of appeals by filing in the court a written petition praying that the order of the commission be set aside. A copy of such petition shall be forthwith served upon the commission, and thereupon the commission forthwith shall certify and file in the court a transcript of the record as hereinbefore provided. Upon the filing of the transcript the court shall have the same jurisdiction to affirm, set aside, or modify the order of the commission as in the case of an application by the commission for the enforcement of its order, and the findings of the commission as to the facts, if supported by testimony, shall in like manner be conclusive.

The jurisdiction of the circuit court of appeals of the United States to enforce, set aside, or modify orders of the commission shall be exclusive.

Such proceedings in the circuit court of appeals shall be given precedence over other cases pending therein, and shall be in every way expedited. No order of the commission or judgment of the court to enforce the same shall in any wise relieve or absolve any person, partnership, or corporation from any liability under the antitrust Acts. . . .

SEC. 6. That the commission shall also have the power—

(a) To gather and compile information concerning, and to investigate from time to time the organization, business, conduct, practices, and management of any corporation engaged in commerce, excepting banks and common carriers subject to the Act to regulate commerce, and its relation to other corporations and to individuals, associations, and partnerships.

(b) To require, by general or special orders, corporations engaged in commerce, excepting banks, and common carriers subject to the Act to regulate commerce, or any class of them, or any of them, respectively, to file with the commission in such form as the commissison may prescribe annual or special, or both annual and special, reports or answers in writing to specific questions, furnishing to the commission such information as it may require as to the organization, business, conduct, practices, management, and relation to other corporations, partnerships, and individuals of the respective corporations filing such reports or answers in writing. . . .

(c) Whenever a final decree has been entered against any defendant corporation in any suit brought by the United States to prevent and restrain any violation of the antitrust Acts, to make investigation, upon its own initiative, of the manner in which the decree has been or is being carried out, and upon the application of the Attorney General it shall be its duty to make such investigation. It shall transmit to the Attorney General a report embodying its findings and recommendations as a result of any such investigation, and the report shall be made public in the discretion of the commission.

(d)   Upon the direction of the President or either house of Congress to investigate and report the facts relating to any alleged violations of the antitrust Acts by any corporation.

(e)   Upon the application of the Attorney General to investigate and make recommendations for the readjustment of the business of any corporation alleged to be violating the antitrust Acts in order that the corporation may thereafter maintain its organization, management, and conduct of business in accordance with law.

(f)   To make public from time to time such portions of the information obtained by it hereunder, except trade secrets and names of customers, as it shall deem expedient in the public interest; and to make annual and special reports to the Congress and to submit therewith recommendations for additional legislation; and to provide for the publication of its reports and decisions in such form and manner as may be best adapted for public information and use.

(g)   From time to time to classify corporations and to make rules and regulations for the purpose of carrying out the provisions of this Act.

(h)   To investigate, from time to time, trade conditions in and with foreign countries where associations, combinations, or practices of manufacturers, merchants, or traders, or other conditions, may affect the foreign trade of the United States, and to report to Congress thereon, with such recommendations as it deems advisable. . . .

Clayton Antitrust Act (1914)*

SEC. 2. That it shall be unlawful for any person engaged in commerce, in the course of such commerce, either directly or indirectly to discriminate in price between different purchasers of commodities, which commodities are sold for use, consumption, or resale within the United States or any Territory thereof or the

* U.S., *Statues at Large, Two Parts,* Vol. XXXVIII, Pt. 1, Ch. 323, October 15, 1914, 63rd Cong., 2d Sess., p. 730.

District of Columbia or any insular possession or other place under the jurisdiction of the United States, where the effect of such discrimination may be to substantially lessen competition or tend to create a monopoly in any line of commerce: *Provided*, That nothing herein contained shall prevent discrimination in price between purchasers of commodities on account of differences in the grade, quality, or quantity of the commodity sold, or that makes only due allowance for difference in the cost of selling or transportation, or discrimination in price in the same or different communities made in good faith to meet competition: *And provided further*, That nothing herein contained shall prevent persons engaged in selling goods, wares, or merchandise in commerce from selecting their own customers in bona fide transactions and not in restraint of trade. . . .

SEC. 6. That the labor of a human being is not a commodity or article of commerce. Nothing contained in the antitrust laws shall be construed to forbid the existence and operation of labor, agricultural, or horticultural organizations, instituted for the purposes of mutual help, and not having capital stock or conducted for profit, or to forbid or restrain individual members of such organizations from lawfully carrying out the legitimate objects thereof; nor shall such organizations, or the members thereof, be held or construed to be illegal combinations or conspiracies in restraint of trade, under the antitrust laws. . . .

SEC. 20. That no restraining order or injunction shall be granted by any court of the United States, or a judge or the judges thereof, in any case between an employer and employees, or between employers and employees, or between employees, involving, or growing out of, a dispute concerning terms or conditions of employment, unless necessary to prevent irreparable injury to property, or to a property right, of the party making the application, for which injury there is no adequate remedy at law, and such property or property right must be described with particularity in the application, which must be in writing and sworn to by the applicant or by his agent or attorney.

And no such restraining order or injunction shall prohibit any person or persons, whether singly or in concert, from terminating any relation of employment, or from ceasing to perform any work or labor, or from recommending, advising, or persuading others by peaceful means so to do; or from attending at any place where any such person or persons may lawfully be, for the purpose of peacefully obtaining or communicating information, or from peacefully persuading any person to work or to abstain from working; or from ceasing to patronize or to employ any party to such dispute, or from recommending, advising, or persuading others by peaceful and lawful means so to do; or from paying or giving to, or withholding from, any person engaged in such dispute, any strike benefits or other moneys or things of value; or from peaceably assembling in a lawful manner, and for lawful purposes; or from doing any act or thing which might lawfully be done in the absence of such dispute by any party thereto; nor shall any of the acts specified in this paragraph be considered or held to be violations of any law of the United States. . . .

National Industrial Recovery Act ===========
*(1933)**

TITLE I—INDUSTRIAL RECOVERY

DECLARATION OF POLICY

SEC. 1. A national emergency productive of widespread unemployment and disorganization of industry, which burdens interstate and foreign commerce, affects the public welfare, and undermines the standards of living of the American people, is hereby declared to exist. It is hereby declared to be the policy of Congress to remove obstructions to the free flow of interstate and foreign commerce which tend to diminish the amount thereof; and to provide for the general welfare by promoting the organization of industry for the purpose of cooperative action among trade groups, to induce and maintain united action of labor and management under adequate governmental sanctions and supervision, to eliminate unfair competitive practices, to promote the fullest possible utilization of the present productive capacity of industries, to avoid undue restriction of production (except as may be temporarily required), to increase the consumption of industrial and agricultural products by increasing purchasing power, to reduce and relieve unemployment, to improve standards of labor, and otherwise to rehabilitate industry and to conserve natural resources.

* U.S., *Statutes at Large, Two Parts*, Vol. XLVIII, Pt. 1, Ch. 90, June 16, 1933, 73rd Cong., 1st Sess., p. 195.

ADMINISTRATIVE AGENCIES

SEC. 2. (a) To effectuate the policy of this title, the President is hereby authorized to establish such agencies, to accept and utilize such voluntary and uncompensated services, to appoint, without regard to the provisions of the civil service laws, such officers and employees, and to utilize such Federal officers and employees, and, with the consent of the State, such State and local officers and employees, as he may find necessary, to prescribe their authorities, duties, responsibilities, and tenure, and, without regard to the Classification Act of 1923, as amended, to fix the compensation of any officers and employees so appointed.

(b) The President may delegate any of his functions and powers under this title to such officers, agents, and employees as he may designate or appoint, and may establish an industrial planning and research agency to aid in carrying out his functions under this title.

(c) This title shall cease to be in effect and any agencies established hereunder shall cease to exist at the expiration of two years after the date of enactment of this Act, or sooner if the President shall by proclamation or the Congress shall by joint resolution declare that the emergency recognized by section 1 has ended.

CODES OF FAIR COMPETITION

SEC. 3. (a) Upon the application to the President by one or more trade or industrial associations or groups, the President may approve a code or codes of fair competition for the trade or industry or subdivision thereof, represented by the applicant or applicants, if the President finds (1) that such associations or groups impose no inequitable restrictions on admission to membership therein and are truly representative of such trades or industries or subdivisions thereof, and (2) that such code or codes are not designed to promote monopolies or to eliminate or oppress small enterprises and will not operate to discriminate against them, and will tend to effectuate the policy of this title: *Provided*, That such code or codes shall not permit monopolies or monopolistic practices: *Provided further*, That where such code or codes affect the services and welfare of persons engaged in other steps of the economic process, nothing in this section shall deprive such persons of the right to be heard prior to approval by the President of such code or codes. The President may, as a condition of his approval of any such code, impose such conditions (including requirements for the making of reports and the keeping of accounts) for the protection of consumers, competitors, employees, and others, and in furtherance of the public interest, and may provide such exceptions to and exemptions from the provisions of such code, as the President in his discretion deems necessary to effectuate the policy herein declared.

(b)　After the President shall have approved any such code, the provisions of such code shall be the standards of fair competition for such trade or industry or subdivision thereof. Any violation of such standards in any transactions in or affecting interstate or foreign commerce shall be deemed an unfair method of competition in commerce within the meaning of the Federal Trade Commission Act, as amended; but nothing in this title shall be construed to impair the powers of the Federal Trade Commission under such Act, as amended.

(c)　The several district courts of the United States are hereby invested with jurisdiction to prevent and restrain violations of any code of fair competition approved under this title; and it shall be the duty of the several district attorneys of the United States, in their respective districts, under the direction of the Attorney General, to institute proceedings in equity to prevent and restrain such violations.

(d)　Upon his own motion, or if complaint is made to the President that abuses inimical to the public interest and contrary to the policy herein declared are prevalent in any trade or industry or subdivision thereof, and if no code of fair competition therefor has theretofore been approved by the President, the President, after such public notice and hearing as he shall specify, may prescribe and approve a code of fair competition for such trade or industry or subdivision thereof, which shall have the same effect as a code of fair competition approved by the President under subsection (a) of this section. . . .

(f)　When a code of fair competition has been approved or prescribed by the President under this title, any violation of any provision thereof in any transaction in or affecting interstate or foreign commerce shall be a misdemeanor and upon conviction thereof an offender shall be fined not more than $500 for each offense, and each day such violation continues shall be deemed a separate offense.

AGREEMENTS AND LICENSES

SEC. 4. (a) The President is authorized to enter into agreements with, and to approve voluntary agreements between and among, persons engaged in a trade or industry, labor organizations, and trade or industrial organizations, associations, or groups, relating to any trade or industry, if in his judgment such agreements will aid in effectuating the policy of this title with respect to transactions in or affecting interstate or foreign commerce, and will be consistent with the requirements of clause (2) of subsection (a) of section 3 for a code of fair competition. . . .

LIMITATIONS UPON APPLICATION OF TITLE

SEC. 6. (a) No trade or industrial association or group shall be eligible to receive the benefit of the provisions of this title until it files with the President a statement containing such information relating to the activities of the association or group as the President shall by regulation prescribe.

(b) The President is authorized to prescribe rules and regulations designed to insure that any organization availing itself of the benefits of this title shall be truly representative of the trade or industry or subdivision thereof represented by such organization. Any organization violating any such rule or regulation shall cease to be entitled to the benefits of this title.

SEC. 7. (a) Every code of fair competition, agreement, and license approved, prescribed, or issued under this title shall contain the following conditions: (1) That employees shall have the right to organize and bargain collectively through representatives of their own choosing, and shall be free from the interference, restraint, or coercion of employers of labor, or their agents, in the designation of such representatives or in self-organization or in other concerted activities for the purpose of collective bargaining or other mutual aid or protection; (2) that no employee and no one seeking employment shall be required as a condition of employment to join any company union or to refrain from joining, organizing, or assisting a labor organization of his own choosing; and (3) that employers shall comply with the maximum hours of labor, minimum rates of pay, and other conditions of employment, approved or prescribed by the President.

(b) The President shall, so far as practicable, afford every opportunity to employers and employees in any trade or industry or subdivision thereof with respect to which the conditions referred to in clauses (1) and (2) of subsection (a) prevail, to establish by mutual agreement, the standards as to the maximum hours of labor, minimum rates of pay, and such other conditions of employment as may be necessary in such trade or industry or subdivision thereof to effectuate the policy of this title; and the standards established in such agreements, when approved by the President, shall have the same effect as a code of fair competition, approved by the President under subsection (a) of section 3.

(c)   Where no such mutual agreement has been approved by the President he may investigate the labor practices, policies, wages, hours of labor, and conditions of employment in such trade or industry or subdivision thereof; and upon the basis of such investigations, and after such hearings as the President finds advisable, he is authorized to prescribe a limited code of fair competition fixing such maximum hours of labor, minimum rates of pay, and other conditions of employment in the trade or industry or subdivision thereof investigated as he finds to be necessary to effectuate the policy of this title, which shall have the same effect as a code of fair competition approved by the President under subsection (a) of section 3. The President may differentiate according to experience and skill of the employees affected and according to the locality of employment; but no attempt shall be made to introduce any classification according to the nature of the work involved which might tend to set a maximum as well as a minimum wage. . . .

National Labor Relations Act (1935)*

FINDINGS AND POLICY

SEC. 1. The denial by employers of the right of employees to organize and the refusal by employers to accept the procedure of collective bargaining lead to strikes and other forms of industrial strife or unrest, which have the intent or the necessary effect of burdening or obstructing commerce by (a) impairing the efficiency, safety, or operation of the instrumentalities of commerce; (b) occurring in the current of commerce; (c) materially affecting, re-

---

* U.S., *Statutes at Large, Two Parts*, Vol. XLIX, Pt. 1, Ch. 372, July 5, 1935, 74th Cong., 1st Sess., p. 449.

straining, or controlling the flow of raw materials or manufactured or processed goods from or into the channels of commerce, or the prices of such materials or goods in commerce; or (d) causing diminution of employment and wages in such volume as substantially to impair or disrupt the market for goods flowing from or into the channels of commerce.

The inequality of bargaining power between employees who do not possess full freedom of association or actual liberty of contract, and employers who are organized in the corporate or other forms of ownership association substantially burdens and affects the flow of commerce, and tends to aggravate recurrent business depressions, by depressing wage rates and the purchasing power of wage earners in industry and by preventing the stabilization of competitive wage rates and working conditions within and between industries.

Experience has proved that protection by law of the right of employees to organize and bargain collectively safeguards commerce from injury, impairment, or interruption, and promotes the flow of commerce by removing certain recognized sources of industrial strife and unrest, by encouraging practices fundamental to the friendly adjustment of industrial disputes arising out of differences as to wages, hours, or other working conditions, and by restoring equality of bargaining power between employers and employees.

It is hereby declared to be the policy of the United States to eliminate the causes of certain substantial obstructions to the free flow of commerce and to mitigate and eliminate these obstructions when they have occurred by encouraging the practice and procedure of collective bargaining and by protecting the exercise by workers of full freedom of association, self-organization, and designation of representatives of their own choosing, for the purpose of negotiating the terms and conditions of their employment or other mutual aid or protection. . . .

RIGHTS OF EMPLOYEES

SEC. 7. Employees shall have the right to self-organization, to form, join, or assist labor organizations, to bargain collectively through representatives of their own choosing, and to engage in concerted activities, for the purpose of collective bargaining or other mutual aid or protection.

SEC 8. It shall be an unfair labor practice for an employer—

(1) To interfere with, restrain, or coerce employees in the exercise of the rights guaranteed in section 7.

(2) To dominate or interfere with the formation or administration of any labor organization or contribute financial or other support to it. . . .

(3) By discrimination in regard to hire or tenure of employment of any term or condition of employment to encourage or discourage membership in any labor organization. . . .

(4) To discharge or otherwise discriminate against an employee because he has filed charges or given testimony under this Act.

(5) To refuse to bargain collectively with the representatives of his employees, subject to the provisions of section 9 (a).

REPRESENTATIVES AND ELECTIONS

SEC. 9. (a) Representatives designated or selected for the purposes of collective bargaining by the majority of the employees in a unit appropriate for such purposes, shall be the exclusive representatives of all the employees in such unit for the purposes of collective bargaining in respect to rates of pay, wages, hours of employment, or other conditions of employment: *Provided*, That any individual employee or a group of employees shall have the right at any time to present grievances to their employer.

(b) The Board shall decide in each case whether, in order to insure to employees the full benefit of their right to self-organization and to collective bargaining, and otherwise to effectuate the policies of this Act, the unit appropriate for the purposes of collective bargaining shall be the employer unit, craft unit, plant unit, or subdivision thereof.

(c) Whenever a question affecting commerce arises concerning the representation of employees, the Board may investigate such controversy and certify to the parties, in writing, the name or names of the representatives that have been designated or selected. In any such investigation, the Board shall provide for an appropriate hearing upon due notice, either in conjunction with a proceeding under section 10 or otherwise, and may take a secret ballot of employees, or utilize any other suitable method to ascertin [*sic*] such representatives.

PREVENTION OF UNFAIR LABOR PRACTICES

SEC. 10. (a) The Board is empowered, as hereinafter provided, to prevent any person from engaging in any unfair labor practice (listed in section 8) affecting commerce. This power shall be exclusive, and shall not be affected by any other means of adjustment or prevention that has been or may be established by agreement, code, law, or otherwise. . . .

Civil Rights Act of 1964*

TITLE II—INJUNCTIVE RELIEF AGAINST DISCRIMINATION IN PLACES OF PUBLIC ACCOMMODATION

SEC. 201. (a) All persons shall be entitled to the full and equal enjoyment of the goods, services, facilities, privileges, advantages, and accommodations of any place of public accommodation, as defined in this section, without discrimination or segregation on the ground of race, color, religion, or national origin.

(b) Each of the following establishments which serves the public is a place of public accommodation within the meaning of this title if its operations affect commerce, or if discrimination or segregation by it is supported by State action:

(1) any inn, hotel, motel, or other establishment which provides lodging to transient guests, other than an establishment located within a building which contains not more than five rooms for rent or hire and which is actually occupied by the proprietor of such establishment as his residence;

(2) any restaurant, cafeteria, lunchroom, lunch counter, soda fountain, or other facility principally engaged in selling food for consumption on the premises, including, but not limited to, any such facility located on the premises of any retail establishment; or any gasoline station;

(3) any motion picture house, theater, concert hall, sports arena, stadium or other place of exhibition or entertainment; and

(4) any establishment (A) (i) which is physically located within the premises of any establishment otherwise covered by this subsection, or (ii) within the premises of which is physically located any such covered establishment, and (B) which holds itself out as serving patrons of such covered establishment.

(c) The operations of an establishment affect commerce within

* U.S., *Statutes at Large, Two Parts*, Vol. LXXVIII, P.L. 88–352, July 2, 1964, 88th Cong., 2d Sess., p. 241.

the meaning of this title if (1) it is one of the establishments described in paragraph (1) of subsection (b); (2) in the case of an establishment described in paragraph (2) of subsection (b), it serves or offers to serve interstate travelers or a substantial portion of the food which it serves, or gasoline or other products which it sells, has moved in commerce; (3) in the case of an establishment described in paragraph (3) of subsection (b), it customarily presents films, performances, athletic teams, exhibitions, or other sources of entertainment which move in commerce; and (4) in the case of an establishment described in paragraph (4) of subsection (b), it is physically located within the premises of, or there is physically located within its premises, an establishment the operations of which affect commerce within the meaning of this subsection. For purposes of this section, "commerce" means travel, trade, traffic, commerce, transportation, or communication among the several States, or between any foreign country or any territory or possession and any State or the District of Columbia, or between points in the same State but through any other State or the District of Columbia or a foreign country.

(d)   Discrimination or segregation by an establishment is supported by State action within the meaning of this title if such discrimination or segregation (1) is carried on under color of any law, statute, ordinance, or regulation; or (2) is carried on under color of any custom or usage required or enforced by officials of the State or political subdivision thereof; or (3) is required by action of the State or political subdivision thereof.

(e)   The provisions of this title shall not apply to a private club or other establishment not in fact open to the public, except to the extent that the facilities of such establishment are made available to the customers or patrons of an establishment within the scope of subsection (b). . . .

TITLE V—COMMISSION ON CIVIL RIGHTS . . .

DUTIES OF THE COMMISSION

SEC. 104. (a)   The Commission shall—

(2)   study and collect information concerning legal developments constituting a denial of equal protection of the laws under the Constitution because of race, color, religion or national origin or in the administration of justice;

(3)   appraise the laws and policies of the Federal Government with respect to denials of equal protection of the laws under the Constitution because of race, color, religion or national origin or in the administration of justice;

(4)   serve as a national clearinghouse for information in respect to denials of equal protection of the laws because of race, color, religion or national origin, including but not limited to the fields of voting, education, housing, employment, the use of public facilities, and transportation, or in the administration of justice;

(5)   investigate allegations, made in writing and under oath or affirmation, that citizens of the United States are unlawfully being accorded or denied the right to vote, or to have their votes properly counted, in any election of presidential electors, Members of the United States Senate, or of the House of Representatives, as a result of any patterns or practice of fraud or discrimination in the conduct of such election; . . .

TITLE VII—EQUAL EMPLOYMENT OPPORTUNITY . . .

DISCRIMINATION BECAUSE OF RACE, COLOR, RELIGION, SEX, OR NATIONAL ORIGIN

SEC. 703.   (a)   It shall be an unlawful employment practice for an employer—

(1)   to fail or refuse to hire or to discharge any individual, or otherwise to discriminate against any individual with respect to his compensation, terms, conditions, or privileges of employment, because of such individual's race, color, religion, sex, or national origin; or

(2)   to limit, segregate, or classify his employees in any way which would deprive or tend to deprive any individual of employment opportunities or otherwise adversely affect his status as an employee, because of such individual's race, color, religion, sex, or national origin. . . .

(d)   It shall be an unlawful employment practice for any employer, labor organization, or joint labor–management committee controlling apprenticeship or other training or retraining, including on-the-job training programs to discriminate against any individual because of his race, color, religion, sex, or national origin in admission to, or employment in, any program established to provide apprenticeship or other training. . . .

(j)   Nothing contained in this title shall be interpreted to require any employer, employment agency, labor organization, or joint labor–management committee subject to this title to grant preferential treatment to any individual or to any group because of the race, color, religion, sex, or national origin of such individual or group on account of an imbalance which may exist with respect to the total number or percentage of persons of any race, color, religion, sex, or national origin employed by any employer, referred or classified for employment by any employment agency or labor organization, admitted to membership or classified by any labor organization, or admitted to, or employed in, any apprenticeship or other training program, in comparison with the total number or percentage of persons of such race, color, religion, sex, or national origin in any community, State, section, or other area, or in the available work force in any community, State, section or other area. . . .

EQUAL EMPLOYMENT OPPORTUNITY COMMISSION

SEC. 705. (a)   There is hereby created a Commission to be known as the Equal Employment Opportunity Commission, which shall be composed of five members, not more than three of who shall be members of the same political party, who shall be appointed by the President by and with the advice and consent of the Senate. . . .

PREVENTION OF UNLAWFUL EMPLOYMENT PRACTICES

SEC. 706. (a)   Whenever it is charged in writing under oath by a person claiming to be aggrieved, or a written charge has been filed by a member of the Commission where he has reasonable cause to believe a violation of this title has occurred (and such charge sets forth the facts upon which it is based) that an employer, employment agency, or labor organization has engaged in an unlawful employment practice, the Commission shall furnish such employer, employment agency, or labor organization (hereinafter referred to as the "respondent") with a copy of such charge and shall make an investigation of such charge, provided that such charge shall not be made public by the Commission. If the Commission shall determine, after such investigation, that there is reasonable cause to believe that the charge is true, the Commission shall endeavor to eliminate any such alleged unlawful employment practice by informal methods of conference, conciliation, and persuasion. . . .

(e)   If within thirty days after a charge is filed with the Commission . . ., the Commission has been unable to obtain voluntary compliance with this title, the Commission shall so notify the person aggrieved and a civil action may . . . be brought against respondent named in the charge. . . . [T]he court may, in its discretion, permit the Attorney General to intervene in such civil action if he certifies that the case is of general public importance. . . .

Legal Services Corporation Act (1974)*

STATEMENT OF FINDINGS AND DECLARATION OF PURPOSE

SEC. 1001. The Congress finds and declares that—
(1)   there is a need to provide equal access to the system of justice in our Nation for individuals who seek redress of grievances;
(2)   there is a need to provide high quality legal assistance to those who would be otherwise unable to afford adequate legal counsel and to continue the present vital legal services program;
(3)   providing legal assistance to those who face an economic barrier to adequate legal counsel will serve best the ends of justice;
(4)   for many of our citizens, the availability of legal services has reaffirmed faith in our government of laws;
(5)   to preserve its strength, the legal services program be kept free from the influence of or use by it of political pressures; and
(6)   attorneys providing legal assistance must have full freedom to protect the best interests of their clients in keeping with the Code of Professional Responsibility, the Canons of Ethics, and the high standards of the legal profession. . . .

ESTABLISHMENT OF CORPORATION

SEC. 1003. (a)   There is established in the District of Columbia a private nonmembership nonprofit corporation, which shall be known as the Legal Services Corporation, for the purpose of providing financial support for legal assistance in noncriminal proceedings or matters to persons financially unable to afford legal assistance. . . .

* U.S., *Statutes at Large, Two Parts*, Vol. LXXXVIII, Pt. 1, P.L. 93–355, July 25, 1974, 93rd Cong., 2d Sess., p. 378.

POWERS, DUTIES AND LIMITATIONS

SEC. 1006. (a) . . . [T]he corporation is authorized—

(1) (A) to provide financial assistance to qualified programs furnishing legal assistance to eligible clients, and to make grants to and contracts with—

(i) individuals, partnerships, firms, corporations, and nonprofit organizations, and

(ii) State and local governments. . . .

(3) to undertake directly and not by grant or contract, the following activities relating to the delivery of legal assistance—

(A) research

(B) training and technical assistance, and

(C) to serve as a clearinghouse for information. . . .

(b) (3) The Corporation shall not, under any provision of this title, interfere with any attorney in carrying out his professional responsibilities to his client as established in the Canons of Ethics and the Code of Professional Responsibility of the American Bar Association (referred to collectively in this title as 'professional responsibilities') or abrogate as to attorneys in programs assisted under this title the authority of a State or other jurisdiction to enforce the standards of professional responsibility generally applicable to attorneys in such jurisdiction. The Corporation shall ensure that activities under this title are carried out in a manner consistent with attorneys' professional responsibilities. . . .

(5) The Corporation shall insure that (A) no employee of the Corporation or of any recipient (except as permitted by law in connection with such employee's own employment situation), while carrying out legal assistance activities under this title, engage in, or encourage others to engage in, any public demonstration or picketing, boycott, or strike; and (B) no such employee shall, at any time, engage in, or encourage others to engage in, any of the following activities: (i) any rioting or civil disturbance, (ii) any activity which is in violation of an outstanding injunction of any court of competent jurisdiction, (iii) any other illegal activity, or (iv) any intentional identification of the Corporation or any recipient with any political activity prohibited by section 1007 (a) (6). . . .

(c) The Corporation shall not itself—

(1) participate in litigation on behalf of clients other than the Corporation; or

(2) undertake to influence the passage or defeat of any legislation by the Congress of the United States or by any State or local legislative bodies. . . .

(d) (3) Neither the Corporation nor any recipient shall contribute or make available corporate funds or program personnel or equipment to any political party or association, or the campaign of any candidate for public or party office. . . .

(5) No class action suit, class action appeal, or amicus curiae class action may be undertaken, directly or through others by a staff attorney, except with the express approval of a project director of a recipient in accordance with policies established by the governing body of such recipient. . . .

GRANTS AND CONTRACTS

SEC. 1007. (a) With respect to grants or contracts in connection with the provisions of legal assistance to eligible clients under this title, the Corporation shall—

(6) insure that all attorneys engaged in legal assistance activities supported in whole or in part by the Corporation refrain, while so engaged, from—

(A) any political activity, or

(B) any activity to provide voters or prospective voters with transportation to the polls or provide similar assistance in connection with an election (other than legal advice and representation); . . .

(7) require recipients to establish guidelines, consistent with regulations promulgated by the Corporation, for a system for review of appeals to insure the efficient utilization of resources and to avoid frivolous appeals (except that such guidelines or regulations shall in no way interfere with attorneys' professional responsibilities);

(8) insure that recipients solicit the recommendations of the organized bar in the community being served before filling staff attorney positions in any project funded pursuant to this title and give preference in filling such positions to qualified persons who reside in the community to be served; . . .

(10) insure that all attorneys, while engaged in legal assistance activities supported in whole or in part by the Corporation, refrain from the persistent incitement of litigation. . . .

(b) No funds made available by the Corporation under this title either by grant or contract, may be used— . . .

(7) to provide legal assistance with respect to any proceeding or litigation relating to the desegregation of any elementary or secondary school or school system;

(8) to provide legal assistance with respect to any proceeding or litigation which seeks to procure a nontherapeutic abortion or to compel any individual or institution to perform an abortion, or assist in the performance of an abortion, or provide facilities for the performance of an abortion, contrary to the religious beliefs or moral convictions of such individual or institution. . . .

B

CASES AND CONTROVERSIES

According to Article III, Section 1 of the United States Constitution, the judicial power of the United States is "vested in one supreme Court, and in such inferior courts as the Congress may from time to time ordain and establish." It goes on to clarify the kinds of cases and controversies to which the judicial power shall extend. It does not, however, describe the manner in which that power shall be exercised. That issue was addressed by Chief Justice John Marshall in Marbury v. Madison *(1803) when he observed, "It is emphatically the province and duty of the judicial department to say what the law is. Those who apply the rule to particular cases, must of necessity expound and interpret that rule. If two laws conflict with each other, the courts must decide on the operation of each." But what if the law conflicts with the Constitution; which would be controlling—statute or Constitution? Marshall had no doubt. Unless the Constitution were to be considered an ordinary act—a conclusion that "would subvert the very foundation of all written constitutions"—it, not the statute, was paramount. To hold otherwise, Marshall argued, "would be giving to the legislature a practical and real omnipotence, with the same breath which professes to restrict their powers within narrow limits [1 Cranch 137, 177]."*

Although Marshall firmly established the judiciary's right to review legislation, judges still faced the problem of determining when a legislature exceeded its authority under the Constitution. Some judges warned that this function was a very narrow one, to be used only in exceptional circumstances. They pointed out that legislation must be measured against constitutional power, not abstract standards such as natural rights. As James Iredell, an early Supreme Court justice, observed in Calder v. Bull, *1798:*

> *If any act of Congress, or of the Legislature of a state, violates those constitutional provisions, it is unquestionably void; though, I admit, that as the authority to declare it void is of a delicate and awful nature, the Court will never resort to that authority, but in a clear and urgent case. If, on the other hand, the Legislature of the Union, or the Legislature of any member of the Union, shall pass a law, within the general scope of their constitutional power, the Court cannot pronounce it to be void, merely because it is, in their judgment, contrary to the principles of natural justice. The ideas of natural justice are regulated by no fixed standard: the ablest and purest men have differed upon the subject; and all that the Court could properly say, in such an event, would be, that the Legislature (possessed of an equal right of opinion) had passed an act which, in the opinion of the judges, was inconsistent with the abstract principles of natural justice [3 Dallas 386, 399].*

In many of the cases that follow, one finds evidence of this tension between legislature and judiciary. Confronted by conflicts over the rights of Americans and the power of the legislature, judges have responded in different ways—often reflecting their attitude toward both the substantive issue and the role of the judiciary. When the issue concerned the constitutionality of economic regulatory legislation, some judges, such as Oliver Wendell Holmes, argued that the legislature should be accorded the freedom to exercise its broad authority, restrained only by the Constitution or by what an ordinary man or woman would think was unreasonable. Like Iredell, Holmes objected to judges who confused constitutionality with wisdom, and substituted their views about the latter under the guise of protecting natural rights. He made a very sharp distinction between constitutionality and wisdom.

As the issues that confronted the Court shifted from economic regulation to personal freedoms in the forties, judges adopted several approaches for exercising their roles. Some, such as William O. Douglas, argued that personal freedoms needed greater protection from legislative interference than property rights, and, therefore, more careful judicial scrutiny. In contrast, Felix Frankfurter maintained, as had Holmes, that judges should be wary of interfering with the legislative branch, whether the issue involved regulation of business or restriction of personal freedoms. Robert Jackson, on the other hand, adopted no fixed position and preferred to decide each case selectively. Finally, Hugo Black believed that only those personal freedoms protected by the Bill of Rights deserved judicial protection. He viewed with dismay the Court's tendency to erect new areas of protection (e.g., marital privacy)—what some of his colleagues called "penumbras" emanating from Bill of Rights freedoms. In this respect, he adhered to the position of Iredell and Holmes, chiding the Court for using natural law rather than the Constitution as its standard for judicial review. Was he correct?

Northern Securities Company v. United States (1904)*

The following case arose out of suit by the United States against the Northern Securities Company for violation of the Sherman Antitrust Act. The Northern Securities Company was a holding company formed in 1901 through the merger of two railroads, the Great Northern Railway Company and the Northern Pacific Railway Company. The Great Northern and the Northern Pacific had been parallel competing lines stretching from the Great Lakes to the Pacific across the northern tier of states. With an eye toward unifying control of their operations, the two companies in 1901 jointly purchased the capital stock of the Chicago, Burlington and Quincy Railway Company. The purchase had given both railroads a direct connection with Chicago and other major midwestern cities, and strengthened their ability to control freight transportation in the entire Middle West. The sponsors of the consolidation had seen it as a means of making freight shipment more efficient and less costly.

At about the same time, again with the intention of unifying their interests, the directors of the Great Northern (led by James J. Hill) and the Northern Pacific (led by J. Pierpont Morgan) had agreed to form a holding company (the Northern Securities Company) to hold the stock of both companies. In effect, through this stock manipulation, they were able to create a single company with a common directorate, pursuing, according to the government, "a policy which would promote the interests, not of one system at the expense of the other, but of both at the expense of the public, all inducement for competition between the two systems was to be removed, a virtual consolidation effected, and a monopoly of the interstate and foreign commerce formerly carried on by the two systems as independent competitors established" (Northern Securities v. United States, 193 U.S. 197, 207). *The government*

* 193 U.S. 197 (1904).

*claimed that if declared legal, such a combination would lead to the eventual
absorption of all transcontinental lines by holding corporations.*

*A majority of the Court agreed that the Northern Securities Company was
an illegal combination. As Justice John Harlan observed, "Those who were
stockholders of the Great Northern and Northern Pacific and became stockholders in the holding company are now interested in preventing all competition between the two lines, and as owners of stock or of certificates of stock in
the holding company, they will see to it that no competition is tolerated" (Ibid.,
327).*

*Coming only two years after his appointment to the Court, the following
dissent by Justice Holmes upset President Theodore Roosevelt, who was
establishing a reputation for his strong stand against trusts. In what way is
Holmes trying to take the question of monopoly out of the realm of popular
sentiment and view it as a practical legal and economic matter? What
distinction does he draw between business size and monopoly? What, in his
opinion, constitutes restraint of trade?*

MR. JUSTICE HOLMES, . . . , dissenting. . . .

Great cases like hard cases make bad law. For great cases are
called great, not by reason of their real importance in shaping the law
of the future, but because of some accident of immediate overwhelming interest which appeals to the feelings and distorts the judgment.
These immediate interests exercise a kind of hydraulic pressure which
makes what previously was clear seem doubtful, and before which
even well settled principles of law will bend. What we have to do in
this case is to find the meaning of some not very difficult words. We
must try, I have tried, to do it with the same freedom of natural and
spontaneous interpretation that one would be sure of if the same
question arose upon an indictment for a similar act which excited no
public attention, and was of importance only to a prisoner before the
court. Furthermore, while at times judges need for their work the
training of economists or statesmen, and must act in view of their
foresight of consequences, yet when their task is to interpret and
apply the words of a statute, their function is merely academic to
begin with—to read English intelligently—and a consideration of
consequences comes into play, if at all, only when the meaning of the
words used is open to reasonable doubt.

The question to be decided is whether, under the act of July 2,
1890, C. 647, 26 Stat. 209, it is unlawful, at any stage of the process, if
several men unite to form a corporation for the purpose of buying
more than half the stock of each of two competing interstate railroad
companies, if they form the corporation, and the corporation buys

the stock. I will suppose further that every step is taken, from the beginning, with the single intent of ending competition between the companies. I make this addition not because it may not be and is not disputed but because, as I shall try to show, it is totally unimportant under any part of the statute with which we have to deal.

The statute of which we have to find the meaning is a criminal statute. The two sections on which the Government relies both make certain acts crimes. That is their immediate purpose and that is what they say. It is vain to insist that this is not a criminal proceeding. The words cannot be read one way in a suit which is to end in fine and imprisonment and another way in one which seeks an injunction. The construction which is adopted in this case must be adopted in one of the other sort. I am no friend of artificial interpretations because a statute is of one kind rather than another, but all agree that before a statute is to be taken to punish that which always has been lawful it must express its intent in clear words. So I say we must read the words before us as if the question were whether two small exporting grocers should go to jail.

Again the statute is of a very sweeping and general character. It hits "every" contract or combination of the prohibited sort, great or small, and "every" person who shall monopolize or attempt to monopolize, in the sense of the act, "any part" of the trade or commerce among the several States. There is a natural inclination to assume that it was directed against certain great combinations and to read it in that light. It does not say so. On the contrary, it says "every," and "any part." Still less was it directed specially against railroads. There even was a reasonable doubt whether it included railroads until the point was decided by this court. . . .

This act is construed by the Government to affect the purchasers of shares in two railroad companies because of the effect it may have, or, if you like, is certain to have, upon the competition of these roads. If such a remote result of the exercise of an ordinary incident of property and personal freedom is enough to make that exercise unlawful, there is hardly any transaction concerning commerce between the States that may not be made a crime by the finding of a jury or a court. The personal ascendency [*sic*] of one man may be such that it would give to his advice the effect of a command, if he owned but a single share in each road. The tendency of his presence in the stockholders' meetings might be certain to prevent competition, and thus his advice, if not his mere existence, become a crime.

I state these general considerations as matters which I should have to take into account before I could agree to affirm the decree appealed from, but I do not need them for my own opinion, because when I read the act I cannot feel sufficient doubt as to the meaning of the words to need to fortify my conclusion by any generalities. Their meaning seems to me plain on their face.

The first section makes "Every contract, combination in the form of trust or otherwise, or conspiracy in restraint of trade or commerce among the several States, or with foreign nations" a misdemeanor, punishable by fine, imprisonment or both. Much trouble is made by substituting other phrases assumed to be equivalent, which then are reasoned from as if they were in the act. The court below argued as if maintaining competition were the expressed object of the act. The act says nothing about competition. I stick to the exact words used. The words hit two classes of cases, and only two—Contracts in restraint of trade and combinations or conspiracies in restraint of trade, and we have to consider what these respectively are. Contracts in restraint of trade are dealt with and defined by the common law. They are contracts with a stranger to the contractor's business (although in some cases carrying on a similar one,) which wholly or partially restrict the freedom of the contractor in carrying on that business as otherwise he would. The objection of the common law to them was primarily on the contractor's own account. The notion of monopoly did not come in unless the contract covered the whole of England. Of course this objection did not apply to partnerships or other forms, if there were any, of substituting a community of interest where there had been competition. There was no objection to such combinations merely as in restraint of trade, or otherwise unless they amounted to a monopoly. Contracts in restraint of trade, I repeat, were contracts with strangers to the contractor's business, and the trade restrained was the contractor's own.

Combinations or conspiracies in restraint of trade, on the other hand, were combinations to keep strangers to the agreement out of the business. The objection to them was not an objection to their effect upon the parties making the contract, the members of the combination or firm, but an objection to their intended effect upon strangers to the firm and their supposed consequent effect upon the public at large. In other words, they were regarded as contrary to public policy because they monopolized or attempted to monopolize some portion of the trade or commerce of the realm. See *United States v. E. C. Knight Co.*, 156 U.S.1. All that is added to the first section by § 2 is that like penalties are imposed upon every single person who, without combination, monopolizes or attempts to monopolize commerce among the States; and that the liability is extended to attempting to monopolize any part of such trade or commerce. It is more important as an aid to the construction of § 1 than it is on its own account. It shows that whatever is criminal when done by way of combination is equally criminal if done by a single man. That I am right in my interpretation of the words of § 1 is shown by the words "in the form of trust or otherwise." The prohibition was suggested by the trusts, the objection to which, as every one knows, was not the union of former competitors, but the sinister power exercised or supposed to be exercised by the combination in keeping rivals out of the business and ruining those who already were in. It was the ferocious extreme of competition with others, not the cessation of competition among the partners, that was the evil feared. Further proof is to be found in § 7, giving an action to any person injured in his business or property by the forbidden conduct. This cannot refer to the parties to the agreement and plainly means that outsiders who are injured in their attempt to compete with a trust or other similar combination may recover for it. How effective the section may be or how far it goes, is not material to my point. My general summary of the two classes of cases which the act affects is confirmed by the title, which is "An Act to protect Trade and Commerce against unlawful Restraints and Monopolies." . . .

If the statute applies to this case it must be because the parties, or some of them, have formed, or because the Northern Securities Company is, a combination in restraint of trade among the States, or, what comes to the same thing in my opinion, because the defendants, or some of them, are monopolizing or attempting to monopolize some part of the commerce between the States. But the mere reading of those words shows that they are used in a limited and accurate sense. According to popular speech, every concern monopolizes whatever business it does, and if that business is trade between two States it monopolizes a part of the trade among the States. Of course the statute does not forbid that. It does not mean that all business must cease. A single railroad down a narrow valley or through a mountain gorge monopolizes all the railroad transportation through that valley or gorge. Indeed every railroad monopolizes, in a popular sense, the trade of some area. Yet I suppose no one would say that the statute forbids a combination of men into a corporation to build and run such a railroad between the States.

I assume that the Minnesota charter of the Great Northern and the Wisconsin charter of the Northern Pacific both are valid. Suppose that, before either road was built, Minnesota, as part of a system of transportation between the States, had created a railroad company authorized singly to build all the lines in the States now actually built, owned or controlled by either of the two existing companies. I take it that that charter would have been just as good as the present one, even if the statutes which we are considering had been in force. In whatever sense it would have created a monopoly the present charter does. It would have been a large one, but the act of Congress makes no discrimination according to size. Size has nothing to do with the matter. A monopoly of "any part" of commerce among the States is unlawful. The supposed company would have owned lines that might have been competing—probably the present one does. But the act of Congress will not be construed to mean the universal disintegration of society into single men, each at war with all the rest, or even the prevention of all further combinations for a common end.

There is a natural feeling that somehow or other the statute meant to strike at combinations great enough to cause just anxiety on the part of those who love their country more than money, while it viewed such little ones as I have supposed with just indifference. This notion, it may be said, somehow breathes from the pores of the act, although it seems to be contradicted in every way by the words in detail. And it has occurred to me that it might be that when a combination reached a certain size it might have attributed to it more of the character of a monopoly merely by virtue of its size than would be attributed to a smaller one. I am quite clear that it is only in connection with monopolies that size could play any part. But my answer has been indicated already. In the first place size in the case of railroads is an inevitable incident and if it were an objection under the act, the Great Northern and the Northern Pacific already were too great and encountered the law. In the next place in the case of railroads it is evident that the size of the combination is reached for other ends than those which would make them monopolies. The combinations are not formed for the purpose of excluding others from the field. Finally, even a small railroad will have the same tendency to exclude others from its narrow area that great ones have to exclude others from a greater one, and the statute attacks the small monopolies as well as the great. The very words of the act make such a distinction impossible in this case and it has not been attempted in express terms.

If the charter which I have imagined above would have been good notwithstanding the monopoly, in a popular sense, which it created, one next is led to ask whether and why a combination or consolidation of existing roads, although in actual competition, into one company of exactly the same powers and extent, would be any more obnoxious to the law. Although it was decided in *Louisville & Nashville Railroad Co. v. Kentucky*, 161 U.S. 677, 701, that since the statute, as before, the States have the power to regulate the matter, it was said, in the argument, that such a consolidation would be unlawful, and it seems to me that the Attorney General was compelled to say so in order to maintain his case. But I think that logic would not let him stop there, or short of denying the power of a State at the present time to authorize one company to construct and own two parallel lines that might compete. The monopoly would be the same as if the roads were consolidated after they had begun to compete—and it is on the footing of monopoly that I now am supposing the objection made. But to meet the objection to the prevention of competition at the same time, I will suppose that three parties apply to a State for charters; one for each of two new and possibly competing lines respectively, and one for both of these lines, and that the charter is granted to the last. I think that charter would be good, and I think the whole argument to the contrary rests on a popular instead of an accurate and legal conception of what the word "monopolize" in the statute means. I repeat, that in my opinion there is no attempt to monopolize, and what, as I have said, in my judgment amounts to the same thing, that there is no combination in restraint of trade, until something is done with the intent to exclude strangers to the combination from competing with it in some part of the business which it carries on. . . .

*Truax v. Corrigan (1921)**

Taft's opinion in Truax v. Corrigan *reflects the Court's attitude toward the Fourteenth Amendment's due process and equal protection of the law clauses. The issue before the Court was the constitutionality of a 1913 Arizona statute that prohibited state courts from granting injunctions in cases involving labor disputes between employers and employees. More specifically, the statute prevented state judges from restraining any former employee "from recommending, advising, or persuading others by peaceful means" to cease working for the employer or patronizing his business. In the case, the plaintiffs, that is,*

---

* 257 U.S. 312 (1921).

Truax and others, were owners of a restaurant, which they claimed had lost substantial income because of the actions of the defendants, Corrigan and others, who were former cooks and waiters. The plaintiffs claimed that the statute deprived them of their right under the Arizona constitution to obtain equity relief from acts prejudicial to their business, solely because the defendants were former employees. How would you compare Taft's attitude toward legislative experimentation with that of Holmes and Brandeis?

MR. CHIEF JUSTICE TAFT delivered the opinion of the Court. . . .

Plaintiffs' business is a property right and free access for employees, owner and customers to his place of business is incident to such right. Intentional injury caused to either right or both by a conspiracy is a tort. Concert of action is a conspiracy if its object is unlawful or if the means used are unlawful. Intention to inflict the loss and the actual loss caused are clear. The real question here is, were the means used illegal? The above recital of what the defendants did, can leave no doubt of that. The libelous attacks upon the plaintiffs, their business, their employees, and their customers, and the abusive epithets applied to them were palpable wrongs. They were uttered in aid of the plan to induce plaintiffs' customers and would-be customers to refrain from patronizing the plaintiffs. The patrolling of defendants immediately in front of the restaurant on the main street and within five feet of plaintiffs' premises continuously during business hours, with the banners announcing plaintiffs' unfairness; the attendance by the picketers at the entrance to the restaurant and their insistent and loud appeals all day long, the constant circulation by them of the libels and epithets applied to employees, plaintiffs and customers, and the threats of injurious consequences to future customers, all linked together in a campaign, were an unlawful annoyance and a hurtful nuisance in respect of the free access to the plaintiffs' place of business. It was not lawful persuasion or inducing. It was not a mere appeal to the sympathetic aid of would-be customers by a simple statement of the fact of the strike and a request to withhold patronage. It was compelling every customer or would-be customer to run the gauntlet of most uncomfortable publicity, aggressive and annoying importunity, libelous attacks and fear of injurious consequences, illegally inflicted, to his reputation and standing in the community. No wonder that a business of $50,000 was reduced to only one-fourth of its former extent. Violence could not have been more effective. It was moral coercion by illegal annoyance and obstruction and it thus was plainly a conspiracy. . . .

A law which operates to make lawful such a wrong as is described in plaintiffs' complaint deprives the owner of the business and the premises of his property without due process, and can not be held valid under the Fourteenth Amendment. . . .

This brings us to consider the effect in this case of that provision of the Fourteenth Amendment which forbids any State to deny to any person the equal protection of the laws. The clause is associated in the Amendment with the due process clause and it is customary to consider them together. It may be that they overlap, that a violation of one may involve at times the violation of the other, but the spheres of the protection they offer are not coterminous. The due process clause, brought down from Magna Charta, was found in the early state constitutions, and later in the Fifth Amendment to the Federal Constitution as a limitation upon the executive, legislative and judicial powers of the Federal Government, while the equality clause does not appear in the Fifth Amendment and so does not apply to congressional legislation. The due process clause requires that every man shall have the protection of his day in court, and the benefit of the general law, a law which hears before it condemns, which proceeds not arbitrarily or capriciously but upon inquiry, and renders judgment only after trial, so that every citizen shall hold his life, liberty, property and immunities under the protection of the general rules which govern society. It, of course, tends to secure equality of law in the sense that it makes a required minimum of protection for every one's right of life, liberty and property, which the Congress or the legislature may not withhold. Our whole system of law is predicated on the general, fundamental principle of equality of application of the law. "All men are equal before the law," "This is a government of laws and not of men," "No man is above the law," are all maxims showing the spirit in which legislatures, executives and courts are expected to make, execute and apply laws. But the framers and adopters of this Amendment were not content to depend on a mere minimum secured by the due process clause, or upon the spirit of equality which might not be insisted on by local public opinion. They therefore embodied that spirit in a specific guaranty.

The guaranty was aimed at undue favor and individual or class privilege, on the one hand, and at hostile discrimination or the oppression of inequality, on the other. It sought an equality of treatment of all persons, even though all enjoyed the protection of due process. Mr. Justice Field, delivering the opinion of this court in *Barbier v. Connolly*, of the equality clause, said—"Class legislation, discriminating against some and favoring others, is prohibited, but legislation which, in carrying out a public purpose, is limited in its application, if within the sphere of its operation it affects alike all persons similarly situated, is not within the amendment." . . .

It is beside the point to say that plaintiffs had no vested right in equity relief and that taking it away does not deprive them of due process of law. If, as is asserted, the granting of equitable remedies falls within the police power and is a matter which the legislature may vary as its judgment and discretion shall dictate, this does not meet the objection under the equality clause which forbids the granting of equitable relief to one man and the denying of it to another under like circumstances and in the same territorial jurisdiction. . . .

To sustain the distinction here between the ex-employees and other tort feasors in the matter of remedies against them, it is contended that the legislature may establish a class of such ex-employees for special legislative treatment. In adjusting legislation to the need of the people of a State, the legislature has a wide discretion and it may be fully conceded that perfect uniformity of treatment of all persons is neither practical nor desirable, that classification of persons is constantly necessary and that questions of proper classification are not free from difficulty. But we venture to think that not in any of the cases in this court has classification of persons of sound mind and full responsibility, having no special relation to each other, in respect of remedial procedure for an admitted tort been sustained. Classification must be reasonable. . . . Classification is the most inveterate of our reasoning processes. We can scarcely think or speak without consciously or unconsciously exercising it. It must therefore obtain in and determine legislation; but it must regard real resemblances and real differences between things, and persons, and class them in accordance with their pertinence to the purpose in hand. Classification like the one with which we are here dealing is said to be the development of the philosophic thought of the world and is opening the door to legalized experiment. When fundamental rights are thus attempted to be taken away, however, we may well subject such experiment to attentive judgment. The Constitution was intended, its very purpose was, to prevent experimentation with the fundamental rights of the individual. . . .

It is urged that this court has frequently recognized the special classification of the relations of employees and employers as proper and necessary for the welfare of the community and requiring special treatment. This is undoubtedly true, but those cases, as we have already pointed out in discussing the due process clause, were cases of the responsibility of the employer for injuries sustained by employees in the course of their employment. The general end of such legislation is that the employer shall become the insurer of the employee against injuries from the employment without regard to the negligence, if any, through which it occurred, leaving to the employer to protect himself by insurance and to compensate himself for the additional cost of production by adding to the prices he charges for his products. It seems a far cry from classification on the basis of the relation of employer and employee in respect of injuries received in course of employment to classification based on the relation of an employer, not to an employee, but to one who has ceased to be so, in respect of torts thereafter committed by such ex-employee on the business and property right of the employer. It is really a little difficult to say, if such classification can be sustained, why special legislative treatment of assaults upon an employer or his employees by ex-employees may not be sustained with equal reason. It is said the State may deal separately with such disputes because such controversies are a frequent and characteristic outgrowth of disputes over terms and conditions of employment. Violence of ex-employees toward present employees is also a characteristic of such disputes. Would this justify a legislature in excepting ex-employees from criminal prosecution for such assaults and leaving the assaulted persons to suits for damages at common law? . . .

MR. JUSTICE HOLMES, dissenting.

The dangers of a delusive exactness in the application of the Fourteenth Amendment have been adverted to before now. Delusive exactness is a source of fallacy throughout the law. By calling a business "property" you make it seem like land, and lead up to the conclusion that a statute cannot substantially cut down the advantages of ownership existing before the statute was passed. An established business no doubt may have pecuniary value and commonly is protected by law against various unjustified injuries. But you cannot give it definiteness of contour by calling it a thing. It is a course of conduct and like other conduct is subject to substantial modification according to time and circumstances both in itself and in regard to what shall justify doing it a harm. I cannot understand the notion that it would be unconstitutional to authorize boycotts and the like in aid of the employees' or employers' interest by statute when the same result has been reached constitutionally without statute by Courts with whom I agree. . . .

I think further that the selection of the class of employers and employees for special treatment, dealing with both sides alike, is beyond criticism on principles often asserted by this Court. And especially I think that without legalizing the conduct complained of the extraordinary relief by injunction may be denied to the class. Legislation may begin where an evil begins. If, as many intelligent people believe, there is more danger that the injunction will be abused in labor cases than elsewhere I can feel no doubt of the power of the legislature to deny it in such cases. . . .

I must add one general consideration. There is nothing that I more deprecate than the use of the Fourteenth Amendment beyond the absolute compulsion of its words to prevent the making of social experiments that an important part of the community desires, in the insulated chambers afforded by the several States, even though the experiments may seem futile or even noxious to me and to those whose judgment I most respect. . . .

New State Ice Company v. Liebmann (1932)*

Louis Brandeis's dissenting opinion in New State Ice Company v. Liebmann *in 1932 is a classic statement of the liberal philosophy regarding the constitutional authority of state government to regulate private enterprise.*

The case concerned the constitutionality of a 1925 Oklahoma law that declared the manufacture of ice for sale and distribution a "public business," and conferred upon an administrative board the power to issue licenses (known as certificates of public convenience and necessity) to engage in the ice business.

The New State Ice Company had been in the business of manufacturing, selling and distributing ice for several years prior to the passage of the law. Liebmann, on the other hand, began an ice business after passage of the act, without applying for or securing the proper license. New State sued Liebmann to enjoin him from engaging in his ice business. Liebmann claimed that the ice business was private, and preventing him from engaging in it deprived him of his liberty and property without due process of law as provided by the Fourteenth Amendment.

A majority of the Supreme Court agreed with this claim and declared the Oklahoma law unconstitutional. Brandeis, long an advocate of allowing experimentation in social and economic areas, examined the motivations for the law, the role of judicial power in reviewing such legislation, and the

* 285 U.S. 262 (1932).

importance of state experimentation, particularly during periods of severe economic depression and scarcity.

What values seem preeminent in Brandeis's statement? At what stages in his argument do law and policy converge? What does the excerpt tell us about the use of law in times of economic disruption? In what way is the certificate of public convenience an example of cooperative economic policy?

MR. JUSTICE BRANDEIS dissenting. . . .

Oklahoma declared the business of manufacturing ice for sale and distribution a "public business," that is, a public utility. So far as appears, it was the first state to do so. Of course, a legislature cannot by mere legislative fiat convert a business into a public utility. . . . But the conception of a public utility is not static. The welfare of the community may require that the business of supplying ice be made a public utility, as well as the business of supplying water or any other necessary commodity or service. If the business is, or can be made, a public utility, it must be possible to make the issue of a certificate a prerequisite to engaging in it.

Whether the local conditions are such as to justify converting a private business into a public one is a matter primarily for the determination of the state legislature. Its determination is subject to judicial review; but the usual presumption of validity attends the enactment. The action of the state must be held valid unless clearly arbitrary, capricious, or unreasonable. . . . A decision that the Legislature's belief of evils was arbitrary, capricious, and unreasonable may not be made without inquiry into the facts with reference to which it acted. . . .

Liebmann rests his defense upon the broad claim that the Federal Constitution gives him the right to enter the business of manufacturing ice for sale even if his doing so be found by the properly constituted authority to be inconsistent with the public welfare. He claims that, whatever the local conditions may demand, to confer upon the Commission power to deny that right is an unreasonable, arbitrary, and capricious restraint upon his liberty.

The function of the Court is primarily to detemine whether the conditions in Oklahoma are such that the Legislature could not reasonably conclude (1) that the public welfare required treating the manufacture of ice for sale and distribution as a "public business;" and (2) in order to ensure to the inhabitants of some communities an adequate supply of ice at reasonable rates, it was necessary to give the Commission power to exclude the establishment of an additional ice plant in places where the community was already well served. Unless the Court can say that the Federal Constitution confers an absolute right to engage anywhere in the business of manufacturing ice for sale, it cannot properly decide that the legislators acted unreasonably without first ascertaining what was the experience of Oklahoma in respect to the ice business. . . .

In Oklahoma a regular supply of ice may reasonably be considered a necessary of life, comparable to that of water, gas, and electricity. The climate, which heightens the need of ice for comfortable and wholesome living, precludes resort to the natural product. . . . Ice has come to be regarded as a household necessity, indispensable to the preservation of food and so to economical household management and the maintenance of health. Its commercial uses are extensive. . . . It appears from the record that in certain parts of Oklahoma a large trade in dairy and other products has been built up as a result of rulings of the Corporation Commission under the Act of 1925, compelling licensed manufacturers to serve agricultural communities; and that this trade would be destroyed if the supply of ice were withdrawn. We cannot say that the legislature of Oklahoma acted arbitrarily in declaring that ice is an article of primary necessity, in industry and agriculture as well as in the household, partaking of the fundamental character of electricity, gas, water, transportation and communication.

Nor can the Court properly take judicial notice that, in Oklahoma, the means of manufacturing ice for private use are within the reach of all persons who are dependent upon it. Certainly it has not been so. In 1925 domestic mechanical refrigeration had scarcely emerged from the experimental stage. Since that time, the production and consumption of ice manufactured for sale, far from diminishing, has steadily increased. . . .

The business of supplying ice is not only a necessity, like that of supplying food or clothing or shelter, but the legislature could also consider that it is one which lends itself peculiarly to monopoly. Characteristically the business is conducted in local plants with a market narrowly limited in area, and this for the reason that ice manufactured at a distance cannot effectively compete with a plant on the ground. In small towns and rural communities the duplication of plants, and in larger communities the duplication of delivery service, is wasteful and ultimately burdensome to consumers. At the same time the relative ease and cheapness with which an ice plant may be constructed exposes the industry to destructive and frequently ruinous competition. Competition in the industry tends to be destructive because ice plants have a determinate capacity, and inflexible fixed charges and operating costs, and because in a market of limited area the volume of sales is not readily expanded. Thus, the erection of a new plant in a locality already adequately served often causes managers to go to extremes in cutting prices in order to secure business. Trade journals and reports of association meetings of ice manufacturers bear ample witness to the hostility of the industry to such competition, and to its unremitting efforts, through trade associations, informal agreements, combination of delivery systems, and in particular through the consolidation of plants, to protect markets and prices against competition of any character. . . .

Can it be said in the light of these facts that it was not an appropriate exercise of legislative discretion to authorize the Commission to deny a license to enter the business in localities where necessity for another plant did not exist? The need of some remedy for the evil of destructive competition, where competition existed, had been and was widely felt. Where competition did not exist, the propriety of public regulation had been proven. Many communities were not supplied with ice at all. The particular remedy adopted was not enacted hastily. The statute was based upon a long-established state policy recognizing the public importance of the ice business, and upon 17 years' legislative and administrative experience in the regulation of it. . . . The measure bore a substantial relation to the evils found to exist. Under these circumstances, to hold the Act void as being unreasonable would, in my opinion involve the exercise not of the function of judicial review, but the function of a super-legislature. If the Act is to be stricken down, it must be on the ground that the Federal Constitution guarantees to the individual the absolute right to enter the ice business, however, detrimental the exercise of that right may be to the public welfare. Such, indeed, appears to be the contention made.

The claim is that manufacturing ice for sale and distribution is a business inherently private, and, in effect, that no state of facts can justify denial of the right to engage in it. To supply one's self with water, electricity, gas, ice or any other article, is inherently a matter of private concern. So also may be the business of supplying the same articles to others for compensation. But the business of supplying to others, for compensation, any article or service whatsoever may become a matter of public concern. Whether it is, or is not, depends upon the conditions existing in the community affected. If it is a matter of public concern, it may be regulated, whatever the business. . . . Where this is true, it is common to speak of the business as being a "public" one, although it is privately owned. . . .

. . . Whatever the nature of the business, whatever the scope or character of the regulation applied, the source of the power invoked is the same. And likewise the constitutional limitation upon that power. The source is the police power. The limitation is that set by the due process clause, which, as construed, requires that the regulation shall be not unreasonable, arbitrary or capricious; and that the means of regulation selected shall have a real or substantial relation to the object sought to be obtained. . . . In my opinion, the true principle is that the State's power extends to every regulation of any business reasonably required and appropriate for the public protection. I find in the due process clause no other limitation upon the character or the scope of regulation permissible. . . .

It is settled that the police power commonly invoked in aid of health, safety and morals, extends equally to the promotion of the public welfare. . . . [W]hile, ordinarily, free competition in the common callings has been encouraged, the public welfare may at other times demand that monopolies be created. Upon this principle is based our whole modern practice of public utility regulation. It is no objection to the validity of the statute here assailed that it fosters monopoly. That, indeed, is its design. The certificate of public convenience and invention is a device—a recent social-economic invention—through which the monopoly is kept under effective control by vesting in a commission the power to terminate it whenever that course is required in the public interest. To grant any monopoly to any person as a favor is forbidden even if terminable. But where, as here, there is reasonable ground for the legislative conclusion that in order to secure a necessary service at reasonable rates, it may be necessary to curtail the right to enter the calling, it is, in my opinion, consistent with the due process clause to do so, whatever the nature of the business. The existence of such power in the legislature seems indispensable in our ever-changing society. . . .

The people of the United States are now confronted with an emergency more serious than war. Misery is wide-spread, in a time, not of scarcity, but of over-abundance. The long-continued depression has brought unprecedented unemployment, a catastrophic fall in commodity prices and a volume of economic losses which threatens our financial institutions. Some people believe that the existing conditions threaten even the stability of the capitalistic system. Economists are searching for the causes of this disorder and are reexamining the basis of our industrial structure. Business men are seeking possible remedies. Most of them realize that failure to distribute widely the profits of industry has been a prime cause of our present plight. But rightly or wrongly, many persons think that one of the major contributing causes has been unbridled competition. Increasingly, doubt is expressed whether it is economically wise, or morally right, that men should be permitted to add to the producing facilities of an industry which is already suffering from over-capacity. In justification of that doubt, men point to the excess-capacity of our productive facilities resulting from their vast expansion without corresponding increase in the consumptive capacity of the people. They assert that through improved methods of manufacture, made possible by advances in science and invention and vast accumulation of capital, our industries had become capable of producing from thirty to one hundred per cent. more than was consumed even in days of vaunted prosperity; and that the present capacity will, for a long time, exceed the needs of business. All agree that irregularity in employment—the greatest of our evils—cannot be overcome unless production and consumption are more nearly balanced. Many insist there must be some form of economic control. There are plans for proration. There are many proposals for stabilization. And some thoughtful men of wide business experience insist that all projects for stabilization and proration must prove futile unless, in some way, the equivalent of the certificate of public convenience and necessity is made a prerequisite to embarking new capital in an industry in which the capacity already exceeds the production schedules.

Whether that view is sound nobody knows. The objections to the proposal are obvious and grave. The remedy might bring evils worse than the present disease. The obstacles to success seem insuperable. The economic and social sciences are largely uncharted seas. We have been none too successful in the modest essays in economic control already entered upon. The new proposal involves a vast extension of the area of control. Merely to acquire the knowledge essential as a basis for the exercise of this multitude of judgments would be a formidable task; and each of the thousands of these judgments would call for some measure of prophecy. Even more serious are the obstacles to success inherent in the demands which execution of the project would make upon human intelligence and upon the character of men. Man is weak and his judgment is at best fallible.

Yet the advances in the exact sciences and the achievements in invention remind us that the seemingly impossible sometimes happens. There are many men now living who were in the habit of using the age-old expression: "It is as impossible as flying." The discoveries in physical science, the triumphs in invention, attest the value of the process of trial and error. In large measure, these advances have been due to experimentation. In those fields experimentation has, for two centuries, been not only free but encouraged. Some people assert that our present plight is due, in part, to the limitations set by courts upon experimentation in the fields of social and economic science; and to the discouragement to which proposals for betterment there have been subjected otherwise. There must be power in the States and the Nation to remould, through experimentation, our economic practices and institutions to meet changing social and economic needs. I cannot believe that the framers of the Fourteenth Amendment, or the States which ratified it, intended to deprive us of the power to correct the evils of technological unemployment and excess productive capacity which have attended progress in the useful arts.

To stay experimentation in things social and economic is a grave responsibility. Denial of the right to experiment may be fraught with serious consequences to the Nation. It is one of the happy incidents of the federal system that a single courageous State may, if its citizens choose, serve as a laboratory; and try novel social and economic experiments without risk to the rest of the country. This Court has the power to prevent an experiment. We may strike down the statute which embodies it on the ground that, in our opinion, the measure is arbitrary, capricious or unreasonable. We have power to do this, because the due process clause has been held by the Court applicable to matters of substantive law as well as to matters of procedure. But in the exercise of this high power, we must be ever on our guard, lest we erect our prejudices into legal principles. If we would guide by the light of reason, we must let our minds be bold.

Schechter Poultry Corporation v. United States (1935)*

The Schechter brothers, operators of wholesale poultry slaughterhouse markets in New York City, were charged with violating several provisions of the Live Poultry Code, including those setting the minimum wage at fifty cents per hour and maximum hours at fifty per week. The code was enacted under authority of paragraph 3 of the National Industrial Recovery Act.

In the following excerpt, Chief Justice Charles Evans Hughes, delivering the opinion of the Court, discusses Congress's power under the commerce clause. In a remarkable statement, Hughes relies on a nineteenth-century interpretation of the commerce power. He defines commerce as intercourse or as a flow of trade, and he states that it succeeds to manufacturing rather than being a part of it. Furthermore, he views transactions involving production, except where they directly affect interstate commerce, as matters to be left to the states to regulate.

Hughes applies these two tests in Schechter *to determine the constitutionality of the code and, hence, of the NIRA. First, he examines whether the Schechters' business is a stream of commerce. Proving it is not, he seeks to determine whether violating the hours and wage provisions directly affects interstate commerce. Here, too, he finds no evidence to justify federal regulation. He concludes that the act is unconstitutional—both as a violation of the commerce power and, as was discussed in the essay, as an unwarranted delegation of legislative power. How did New Deal planners expect regulation of wages and hours to relieve economic depression? Compare Hughes's philosophy about government experimentation with Brandeis's in the* New State Ice Company *case.*

MR. CHIEF JUSTICE HUGHES delivered the opinion of the Court. . . .

. . . We are told that the provision of the statute authorizing the adoption of codes must be viewed in the light of the grave national crisis with which Congress was confronted. Undoubtedly, the conditions to which power is addressed are always to be considered when the exercise of power is challenged. Extraordinary conditions may call for extraordinary remedies. But the argument necessarily stops short of an attempt to justify action which lies outside the sphere of constitutional authority. Extraordinary conditions do not create or enlarge constitutional power. The Constitution established a national

* 295 U.S. 495 (1935).

government with powers deemed to be adequate, as they have proved to be both in war and peace, but these powers of the national government are limited by the constitutional grants. Those who act under these grants are not at liberty to transcend the imposed limits because they believe that more or different power is necessary. . . .

. . . Although the validity of the codes (apart from the question of delegation) rests upon the commerce clause of the Constitution, § 3 (a) is not in terms limited to interstate and foreign commerce. From the generality of its terms, and from the argument of the Government at the bar, it would appear that § 3 (a) was designed to authorize codes without that limitation. But under § 3 (f) penalties are confined to violations of a code provision "in any transaction in or affecting interstate or foreign commerce." This aspect of the case presents the question whether the particular provisions of the Live Poultry Code, which the defendants were convicted for violating and for having conspired to violate, were within the regulating power of Congress.

These provisions relate to the hours and wages of those employed by defendants in their slaughterhouses in Brooklyn and to the sales there made to retail dealers and butchers.

(1) Were these transactions "*in*" interstate commerce? Much is made of the fact that almost all the poultry coming to New York is sent there from other States. But the code provisions, as here applied, do not concern the transportation of the poultry from other States to New York, or the transactions of the commission men or others to whom it is consigned, or the sales made by such consignees to defendants. When defendants had made their purchases, whether at the West Washington Market in New York City or at the railroad terminals serving the City, or elsewhere, the poultry was trucked to their slaughterhouses in Brooklyn for local disposition. The interstate transactions in relation to that poultry then ended. Defendants held the poultry at their slaughterhouse markets for slaughter and local sale to retail dealers and butchers who in turn sold directly to consumers. Neither the slaughtering nor the sales by defendants were transactions in interstate commerce.

The undisputed facts thus afford no warrant for the argument that the poultry handled by defendants at their slaughterhouse markets was in a "*current*" or "*flow*" of interstate commerce and was thus subject to congressional regulation. The mere fact that there may be a constant flow of commodities into a State does not mean that the flow continues after the property has arrived and has become commingled with the mass of property within the State and is there held solely for local disposition and use. So far as the poultry here in question is concerned, the flow in interstate commerce had ceased. The poultry had come to a permanent rest within the State. It was not held, used, or sold by defendants in relation to any further transactions in interstate commerce and was not destined for transportation to other States. Hence, decisions which deal with a stream of interstate commerce—where goods come to rest within a State temporarily and are later to go forward in interstate commerce—and with the regulations of transactions involved in that practical continuity of movement, are not applicable here.

(2) Did the defendants' transactions directly *"affect"* interstate commerce so as to be subject to federal regulation? The power of Congress extends not only to the regulation of transactions which are part of interstate commerce, but to the protection of that commerce from injury. It matters not that the injury may be due to the conduct of those engaged in intrastate operations. Thus, Congress may protect the safety of those employed in interstate transportation "no matter what may be the source of the dangers which threaten it." We said in *Second Employers' Liability Cases*, that it is the "effect upon interstate commerce," not "the source of the injury," which is "the criterion of congressional power." We have held that, in dealing with common carriers engaged in both interstate and intrastate commerce, the dominant authority of Congress necessarily embraces the right to control their intrastate operations in all matters having such a close and substantial relation to interstate traffic that the control is essential or appropriate to secure the freedom of that traffic from interference or unjust discrimination and to promote the efficiency of the interstate service. And combinations and conspiracies to restrain interstate commerce, or to monopolize any part of it, are none the less within the reach of the Anti-Trust Act because the conspirators seek to attain their end by means of intrastate activities.

We recently had occasion to apply this principle in connection with the live poultry industry. That was a suit to enjoin a conspiracy to restrain and monopolize interstate commerce in violation of the Anti-Trust Act. It was shown that marketmen, teamsters and slaughterers (shochtim) had conspired to burden the free movement of live poultry into the metropolitan area in and about New York City. Marketmen had organized an association, had allocated retailers among themselves, and had agreed to increase prices. To accomplish their objects, large amounts of money were raised by levies upon poultry sold, men were hired to obstruct the business of dealers who resisted, wholesalers and retailers were spied upon and by violence and other forms of intimidation were prevented from freely purchasing live poultry. Teamsters refused to handle poultry for recalcitrant marketmen and members of the shochtim union refused to slaughter. In view of the proof of that conspiracy, we said that it was unnecessary to decide when interstate commerce ended and when intrastate commerce began. We found that the proved interference by the conspirators "with the unloading, the transportation, the sales by marketmen to retailers, the prices charged and the amount of profits exacted" operated "substantially and directly to restrain and burden the untrammeled shipment and movement of the poultry" while unquestionably it was in interstate commerce. The intrastate acts of the conspirators were included in the injunction because that was found to be necessary for the protection of interstate commerce against the attempted and illegal restraint.

The instant case is not of that sort. This is not a prosecution for a conspiracy to restrain or monopolize interstate commerce in violation of the Anti-Trust Act. Defendants have been convicted, not upon direct charges of injury to interstate commerce or of interference with persons engaged in that commerce, but of violations of certain provisions of the Live Poultry Code and of conspiracy to commit these violations. Interstate commerce is brought in only upon the charge that violations of these provisions—as to hours and wages of employees and local sales—"*affected*" interstate commerce.

In determining how far the federal government may go in controlling intrastate transactions upon the ground that they "affect" interstate commerce, there is a necessary and well-established distinction between direct and indirect effects. The precise line can be drawn only as individual cases arise, but the distinction is clear in principle. Direct effects are illustrated by the railroad cases we have cited, as *e.g.*, the effect of failure to use prescribed safety appliances on railroads which are the highways of both interstate and intrastate commerce, injury to an employee engaged in interstate transportation by the negligence of an employee engaged in an intrastate movement, the fixing of rates for intrastate transportation which unjustly discriminate against interstate commerce. But where the effect of intrastate transactions upon interstate commerce is merely indirect, such transactions remain within the domain of state power. If the commerce clause were construed to reach all enterprises and transactions which could be said to have an indirect effect upon interstate commerce, the federal authority would embrace practically all the activities of the people and the authority of the State over its domestic concerns would exist only by sufferance of the federal government. . . .

The question of chief importance relates to the provisions of the Code as to the hours and wages of those employed in defendants' slaughterhouse markets. It is plain that these requirements are imposed in order to govern the details of defendants' management of their local business. The persons employed in slaughtering and selling in local trade are not employed in interstate commerce. Their hours and wages have no direct relation to interstate commerce. The question of how many hours these employees should work and what they should be paid differs in no essential respect from similar questions in other local businesses which handle commodities brought into a State and there dealt in as a part of its internal commerce. This appears from an examination of the considerations urged by the Government with respect to conditions in the poultry trade. Thus, the Government argues that hours and wages affect prices; that slaughterhouse men sell at a small margin above operating costs; that labor represents 50 to 60 per cent. of these costs; that a slaughterhouse operator paying lower wages or reducing his cost by exacting long hours of work, translates his saving into lower prices; that this results in demands for a cheaper grade of goods; and that the cutting of prices brings about a demoralization of the price structure. Similar conditions may be adduced in relation to other businesses. The argument of the Government proves too much. If the federal government may determine the wages and hours of employees in the internal commerce of a State, because of their relation to cost and prices and their indirect effect upon interstate commerce, it would seem that a similar control might be exerted over other elements of cost, also affecting prices, such as the number of employees, rents, advertising, methods of doing business, etc. All the processes of production and distribution that enter into cost could likewise be controlled. If the cost of doing an intrastate business is in itself the permitted object of federal control, the extent of the regulation of cost would be a question of discretion and not of power.

The Government also makes the point that efforts to enact state legislation establishing high labor standards have been impeded by the belief that unless similar action is taken generally, commerce will be diverted from the States adopting such standards, and that this fear of diversion has led to demands for federal legislation on the subject of wages and hours. The apparent implication is that the federal authority under the commerce clause should be deemed to extend to the establishment of rules to govern wages and hours in intrastate trade and industry generally throughout the country, thus overriding the authority of the States to deal with domestic problems arising from labor conditions in their internal commerce.

It is not the province of the Court to consider the economic advantages or disadvantages of such a centralized system. It is sufficient to say that the Federal Constitution does not provide for it. Our growth and development have called for wide use of the commerce power of the federal government in its control over the expanded activities of interstate commerce, and in protecting that commerce from burdens, interferences, and conspiracies to restrain and monopolize it. But the authority of the federal government may not be pushed to such an extreme as to destroy the distinction, which the commerce clause itself establishes, between commerce "among the several States" and the internal concerns of a State. The same answer must be made to the contention that is based upon the serious economic situation which led to the passage of the Recovery Act,—the fall in prices, the decline in wages and employment, and the curtailment of the market for commodities. Stress is laid upon the great importance of maintaining wage distributions which would provide the necessary stimulus in starting "the cumulative forces making for expanding commercial activity." Without in any way disparaging this motive, it is enough to say that the recuperative efforts of the federal government must be made in a manner consistent with the authority granted by the Constitution.

We are of the opinion that the attempt through the provisions of the Code to fix the hours and wages of employees of defendants in their intrastate business was not a valid exercise of federal power. . . .

*National Labor Relations Board v. Jones & Laughlin Steel Corporation (1937)**

Two years after the Schechter *case, Chief Justice Hughes reversed his position on the commerce power. In* National Labor Relations Board v. Jones

* 301 U.S. 1 (1937).

& Laughlin Steel Corporation, *Hughes upheld the constitutionality of the Wagner Act, which, though it differed from the NIRA in the use of federal power, also sought to extend federal control to labor and industrial relations. In Jones & Laughlin, Hughes admits that manufacturing is commerce and that labor conditions at a plant, particularly if it is organized on a national scale, can have a direct effect on interstate commerce. He puts aside "stream of commerce" as a handy, though not exclusive, test of whether a business is engaged in interstate commerce: "The congressional authority to protect interstate commerce from burdens and obstructions is not limited to transactions which can be deemed to be an essential part of a 'flow' of interstate or foreign commerce. Burdens and obstructions may be due to injurious action springing from other sources." Now, the test is the degree of harm that may result from the source (labor strife) rather than the nature of the source itself. Constitutional scholars call this distinction a shift from degree to kind. To the student, it may appear to be a case of splitting of hairs. Nevertheless, the Jones & Laughlin opinion and others that followed, upholding what is commonly referred to as "second New Deal" legislation, revised the commerce clause and made it a source of congressional power over economic affairs and later, in the sixties, over civil rights. In the excerpt from Jones & Laughlin that follows, compare and contrast Hughes's position on commerce with his opinion in* Schechter.

MR. CHIEF JUSTICE HUGHES delivered the opinion of the Court.

In a proceeding under the National Labor Relations Act of 1935, the National Labor Relations Board found that the respondent, Jones & Laughlin Steel Corporation, had violated the Act by engaging in unfair labor practices affecting commerce. The proceeding was instituted by the Beaver Valley Lodge No. 200, affiliated with the Amalgamated Association of Iron, Steel and Tin Workers of America, a labor organization. The unfair labor practices charged were that the corporation was discriminating against members of the union with regard to hire and tenure of employment, and was coercing and intimidating its employees in order to interfere with their self-organization. The discriminatory and coercive action alleged was the discharge of certain employees. . . .

We think it clear that the National Labor Relations Act may be construed so as to operate within the sphere of constitutional authority. The jurisdiction conferred upon the Board, and invoked in this instance, is found in § 10 (a) . . .

The critical words of this provision, prescribing the limits of the Board's authority in dealing with the labor practices, are "affecting commerce." . . .

This definition is one of exclusion as well as inclusion. The grant of authority to the Board does not purport to extend to the relationship between all industrial employees and employers. Its terms do not impose collective bargaining upon all industry regardless of effects upon interstate or foreign commerce. It purports to reach only what may be deemed to burden or obstruct that commerce and, thus qualified, it must be construed as contemplating the exercise of control within constitutional bounds. It is a familiar principle that acts which directly burden or obstruct interstate or foreign commerce, or its free flow, are within the reach of the congressional power. Acts having that effect are not rendered immune because they grow out of labor disputes. It is the effect upon commerce, not the source of the injury, which is the criterion. Whether or not particular action does affect commerce in such a close and intimate fashion as to be subject to federal control, and hence to lie within the authority conferred upon the Board, is left by the statute to be determined as individual cases arise. We are thus to inquire whether in the instant case the constitutional boundary has been passed. . . .

. . . Respondent says that whatever may be said of employees engaged in interstate commerce, the industrial relations and activities in the manufacturing department of respondent's enterprise are not subject to federal regulation. The argument rests upon the proposition that manufacturing in itself is not commerce.

The Government distinguishes these cases. The various parts of respondent's enterprise are described as interdependent and as thus involving "a great movement of iron ore, coal and limestone along well-defined paths to the steel mills, thence through them, and thence in the form of steel products into the consuming centers of the country—a definite and well-understood course of business." It is urged that these activities constitute a "stream" or "flow" of commerce, of which the Aliquippa manufacturing plant is the focal point, and that industrial strife at that point would cripple the entire movement. Reference is made to our decision sustaining the Packers and Stockyards Act. *Stafford* v. *Wallace*, 258 U.S. 495. The Court found that the stockyards were but a "throat" through which the current of commerce flowed and the transactions which there occurred could not be separated from that movement. Hence the sales at the stockyards were not regarded as merely local transactions, for while they created "a local change of title" they did not "stop the flow," but merely changed the private interests in the subject of the current. Distinguishing the cases which upheld the power of the State to impose a non-discriminatory tax upon property which the owner intended to transport to another State, but which was not in actual transit and was held within the State subject to the disposition of the owner, the Court remarked: "The question, it should be observed, is not with respect to the extent of the power of Congress to regulate interstate commerce, but whether a particular exercise of state power in view of its nature and operation must be deemed to be in conflict with this paramount authority." Applying the doctrine of *Stafford* v. *Wallace*, the Court sustained the Grain Futures Act of 1922 with respect to transactions on the Chicago Board of Trade, although these transactions were "not in and of themselves interstate commerce." Congress had found that they had become "a constantly recurring burden and obstruction to that commerce."

Respondent contends that the instant case presents material distinctions. Respondent says that the Aliquippa plant is extensive in size and represents a large investment in buildings, machinery and equipment. The raw materials which are brought to the plant are delayed for long periods and, after being subjected to manufacturing processes, "are changed substantially as to character, utility and value." The finished products which emerge "are to a large extent manufactured without reference to pre-existing orders and contracts and are entirely different from the raw materials which enter at the other end." Hence respondent argues that "If importation and exportation in interstate commerce do not singly transfer purely local activities into the field of congressional regulation, it should follow that their combination would not alter the local situation."

We do not find it necessary to determine whether these features of defendant's business dispose of the asserted analogy to the "stream of commerce" cases. The instances in which that metaphor has been used are but particular, and not exclusive, illustrations of the protective power which the Government invokes in support of the present Act. The congressional authority to protect interstate commerce from burdens and obstructions is not limited to transactions which can be deemed to be an essential part of a "flow" of interstate or foreign commerce. Burdens and obstructions may be due to injurious action springing from other sources. The fundamental principle is that the power to regulate commerce is the power to enact "all appropriate legislation" for "its protection and advancement"; to adopt measures "to promote its growth and insure its safety"; "to foster, protect, control and restrain." That power is plenary and may be exerted to protect interstate commerce "no matter what the source of the dangers which threaten it." Although activities may be intrastate in character when separately considered, if they have such a close and substantial relation to interstate commerce that their control is essential or appropriate to protect that commerce from burdens and obstructions, Congress cannot be denied the power to exercise that control. *Schechter Corp.* v. *United States.* Undoubtedly the scope of this power must be considered in the light of our dual system of government and may not be extended so as to embrace effects upon interstate commerce so indirect and remote that to embrace them, in view of our complex society, would effectually obliterate the distinction between what is national and what is local and create a completely centralized government. The question is necessarily one of degree. . . .

The close and intimate effect which brings the subject within the reach of federal power may be due to activities in relation to productive industry although the industry when separately viewed is local. . . .

It is thus apparent that the fact that the employees here concerned were engaged in production is not determinative. The question remains as to the effect upon interstate commerce of the labor practice involved. In the *Schechter* case, we found that the effect there was so remote as to be beyond the federal power. To find "immediacy or directness" there was to find it "almost everywhere," a result inconsistent with the maintenance of our federal system. . . .

. . . Giving full weight to respondent's contention with respect to a break in the complete continuity of the "stream of commerce" by reason of respondent's manufacturing operations, the fact remains that the stoppage of those operations by industrial strife would have a most serious effect upon interstate commerce. In view of respondent's far-flung activities, it is idle to say that the effect would be indirect or remote. It is obvious that it would be immediate and might be catastrophic. We are asked to shut our eyes to the plainest facts of our national life and to deal with the question of direct and indirect effects in an intellectual vacuum. Because there may be but indirect and remote effects upon interstate commerce in connection with a host of local enterprises throughout the country, it does not follow that other industrial activities do not have such a close and intimate relation to interstate commerce as to make the presence of industrial strife a matter of the most urgent national concern. When industries organize themselves on a national scale, making their relation to interstate commerce the dominant factor in their activities, how can it be maintained that their industrial labor relations constitute a forbidden field into which Congress may not enter when it is necessary to protect interstate commerce from the paralyzing consequences of industrial war? We have often said that interstate commerce itself is a practical conception. It is equally true that interferences with that commerce must be appraised by a judgment that does not ignore actual experience.

Experience has abundantly demonstrated that the recognition of the right of employees to self-organization and to have representatives of their own choosing for the purpose of collective bargaining is often an essential condition of industrial peace. Refusal to confer and negotiate has been one of the most prolific causes of strife. This is such an outstanding fact in the history of labor disturbances that it is a proper subject of judicial notice and requires no citation of instances. . . .

West Virginia State Board of Education v. Barnette (1943)*

In West Virginia State Board of Education v. Barnette, *the Supreme Court faced the issue of whether a West Virginia statute requiring all state schools to conduct courses that would foster the ideals of patriotism and a subsequent State Board of Education resolution requiring a mandatory flag salute were constitutional. The Jehovah's Witnesses, a religious group that taught allegiance to God over government, brought a suit asking for an injunction to restrain enforcement of these laws and regulations. Reversing a three-year-old precedent* (Minersville School District v. Gobitis 310 U.S. 586), *a majority of the Court held that the flag salute and pledge violated the First Amendment's protection against state interference with one's intellect and spirit.*

Felix Frankfurter's dissent is a representative statement of the philosophy of judicial restraint. Unlike Brandeis's dissenting opinion in New State, *which also was an example of judicial restraint, Frankfurter's opinion achieves a different result. Brandeis would uphold the constitutionality of a law that a majority of the citizens of Oklahoma, acting through their legislative representatives, considered necessary to preserve economic order. Frankfurter's de-*

* 319 U.S. 624 (1943).

*fense of a law that would compel allegiance to the American flag by a religious
sect opposed to such expressions has the appearance of being antiliberal. Yet
in Frankfurter's opinion, such allegiance was critical to social order. He would
make no distinction between the right of the legislature to regulate in a
reasonable manner the economy and its right to regulate speech and religion,
in defense of the welfare of the community and in the absence of specific
language in the Constitution to the contrary. Do you agree?*

*Is it the proper role of the judiciary to invalidate laws passed by a legislative
body in proper fashion? Are there dangers in such authority? Can advantages
be gained by such a practice? What does Frankfurter mean when he says
Americans are too preoccupied with the constitutionality of legislation rather
than its wisdom?*

MR. JUSTICE FELIX FRANKFURTER, dissenting. . . .

The admonition that judicial self-restraint alone limits arbitrary
exercise of our authority is relevant every time we are asked to nullify
legislation. The Constitution does not give us greater veto power
when dealing with one phase of "liberty" than with another. . . . Judicial self-restraint is equally necessary whenever an exercise of
political or legislative power is challenged. There is no warrant in the
constitutional basis of this Court's authority for attributing different
roles to it depending upon the nature of the challenge to the
legislation. Our power does not vary according to the particular
provision of the Bill of Rights which is invoked. The right not to have
property taken without just compensation has, so far as the scope of
judicial power is concerned, the same constitutional dignity as the
right to be protected against unreasonable searches and seizures, and
the latter has no less claim than freedom of the press or freedom of
speech or religious freedom. In no instance is this Court the primary
protector of the particular liberty that is invoked. This Court has
recognized, what hardly could be denied, that all the provisions of the
first ten Amendments are "specific" prohibitions. But each specific
Amendment, in so far as embraced within the Fourteenth Amendment, must be equally respected, and the function of this Court does
not differ in passing on the constitutionality of legislation challenged
under different Amendments.

When Mr. Justice Holmes, speaking for this Court, wrote that "it
must be remembered that legislatures are ultimate guardians of the
liberties and welfare of the people in quite as great a degree as the
courts," he went to the very essence of our constitutional system and
the democratic conception of our society. He did not mean that for

only some phases of civil government this Court was not to supplant legislatures and sit in judgment upon the right or wrong of a challenged measure. He was stating the comprehensive judicial duty and role of this court in our constitutional scheme whenever legislation is sought to be nullified on any ground, namely, that responsibility for legislation lies with legislatures, answerable as they are directly to the people, and this Court's only and very narrow function is to determine whether within the broad grant of authority vested in legislatures they have exercised a judgment for which reasonable justification can be offered. . . .

The reason why from the beginning even the narrow judicial authority to nullify legislation has been viewed with a jealous eye is that it serves to prevent the full play of the democratic process. The fact that it may be an undemocratic aspect of our scheme of government does not call for its rejection or its disuse. But it is the best of reasons, as this Court has frequently recognized, for the greatest caution in its use.

The precise scope of the question before us defines the limits of the constitutional power that is in issue. The State of West Virginia requires all pupils to share in the salute to the flag as part of school training in citizenship. The present action is one to enjoin the enforcement of this requirement by those in school attendance. We have not before us any attempt by the State to punish disobedient children or visit penal consequences on their parents. All that is in question is the right of the State to compel participation in this exercise by those who choose to attend the public schools.

We are not reviewing merely the action of a local school board. The flag salute requirement in this case comes before us with the full authority of the State of West Virginia. We are in fact passing judgment on "the power of the State as a whole." Practically we are passing upon the political power of each of the forty-eight states. Moreover, since the First Amendment has been read into the Fourteenth, our problem is precisely the same as it would be if we had before us an Act of Congress for the District of Columbia. To suggest that we are here concerned with the heedless action of some village tyrants is to distort the augustness of the constitutional issue and the reach of the consequences of our decision.

Under our constitutional system the legislature is charged solely with civil concerns of society. If the avowed or intrinsic legislative purpose is either to promote or to discourage some religious community or creed, it is clearly within the constitutional restrictions imposed on legislatures and cannot stand. But it by no means follows that legislative power is wanting whenever a general non-discriminatory civil regulation in fact touches conscientious scruples or religious beliefs of an individual or a group. Regard for such scruples or beliefs undoubtedly presents one of the most reasonable claims for the exertion of legislative accommodation. It is, of course, beyond our power to rewrite the State's requirement, by providing exemptions for those who do not wish to participate in the flag salute or by making some other accommodations to meet their scruples. That wisdom might suggest the making of such accommodations and that school administration would not find it too difficult to make them and yet maintain the ceremony for those not refusing to conform, is outside our province to suggest. Tact, respect, and generosity toward variant views will always commend themselves to those charged with the duties of legislation so as to achieve a maximum of good will and to require a minimum of unwilling submission to a general law. But the real question is, who is to make such accommodations, the courts or the legislature?

This is no dry, technical matter. It cuts deep into one's conception of the democratic process—it concerns no less the practical differences between the means for making these accommodations that are open to courts and to legislatures. A court can only strike down. It can only say "This or that law is void." It cannot modify or qualify, it cannot make exceptions to a general requirement. And it strikes down not merely for a day. At least the finding of unconstitutionality ought not to have ephemeral significance unless the Constitution is to be reduced to the fugitive importance of mere legislation. . . .

The prohibition against any religious establishment by the government placed denominations on an equal footing—it assured freedom from support by the government to any mode of worship and the freedom of individuals to support any mode of worship. Any person may therefore believe or disbelieve what he pleases. He may practice what he will in his own house of worship or publicly within the limits of public order. But the lawmaking authority is not circumscribed by the variety of religious beliefs, otherwise the constitutional guaranty would be not a protection of the free exercise of religion but a denial of the exercise of legislation. . . .

An act compelling profession of allegiance to a religion, no matter how subtly or tenuously promoted, is bad. But an act promoting good citizenship and national allegiance is within the domain of governmental authority and is therefore to be judged by the same considerations of power and of constitutionality as those involved in the many claims of immunity from civil obedience because of religious scruples.

That claims are pressed on behalf of sincere religious convictions does not of itself establish their constitutional validity. Nor does waving the banner of religious freedom relieve us from examining into the power we are asked to deny the states. Otherwise the doctrine of separation of church and state, so cardinal in the history of this nation and for the liberty of our people, would mean not the disestablishment of a state church but the establishment of all churches and of all religious groups.

The subjection of dissidents to the general requirement of saluting the flag, as a measure conducive to the training of children in good citizenship, is very far from being the first instance of exacting obedience to general laws that have offended deep religious scruples. Compulsory vaccination, food inspection regulations, the obligation to bear arms, testimonial duties, compulsory medical treatment,—these are but illustrations of conduct that has often been compelled in the enforcement of legislation of general applicability even though the religious consciences of particular individuals rebelled at the exaction.

Law is concerned with external behavior and not with the inner life of man. It rests in large measure upon compulsion. Socrates lives in history partly because he gave his life for the conviction that duty of obedience to secular law does not presuppose consent to its enactment or belief in its virtue. The consent upon which free government rests is the consent that comes from sharing in the process of making and unmaking laws. The state is not shut out from a domain because the individual conscience may deny the state's claim. The individual conscience may profess what faith it chooses. It may affirm and promote that faith—in the language of the Constitution, it may "exercise" it freely—but it cannot thereby restrict community action through political organs in matters of community concern, so long as the action is not asserted in a discriminatory way either openly or by stealth. One may have the right to practice one's religion and at the same time owe the duty of formal obedience to laws that run counter to one's beliefs. Compelling belief implies denial of opportunity to combat it and to assert dissident views. Such compulsion is one thing. Quite another matter is submission to

conformity of action while denying its wisdom or virtue and with
ample opportunity for seeking its change or abrogation. . . .

One's conception of the Constitution cannot be severed from
one's conception of a judge's function in applying it. The Court has
no reason for existence if it merely reflects the pressures of the day.
Our system is built on the faith that men set apart for this special
function, freed from the influences of immediacy and from the deflec-
tions of worldly ambition, will become able to take a view of longer
range than the period of responsibility entrusted to Congress and
legislatures. We are dealing with matters as to which legislators and
voters have conflicting views. Are we as judges to impose our strong
convictions on where wisdom lies? . . .

The uncontrollable power wielded by this Court brings it very
close to the most sensitive areas of public affairs. As appeal from
legislation to adjudication becomes more frequent, and its consequences more far-reaching, judicial self-restraint becomes more and
not less important, lest we unwarrantably enter social and political
domains wholly outside our concern. I think I appreciate fully the
objections to the law before us. But to deny that it presents a
question upon which men might reasonably differ appears to me to be
intolerance. And since men may so reasonably differ, I deem it
beyond my constitutional power to assert my view of the wisdom of
this law against the view of the State of West Virginia. . . .

Of course patriotism can not be enforced by the flag salute. But
neither can the liberal spirit be enforced by judicial invalidation of
illiberal legislation. Our constant preoccupation with the constitutionality of legislation rather than with its wisdom tends to preoccupation of the American mind with a false value. The tendency of
focusing attention on constitutionality is to make constitutionality
synonymous with wisdom, to regard a law as all right if it is constitutional. Such an attitude is a great enemy of liberalism. Particularly in legislation affecting freedom of thought and freedom of
speech much which should offend a free-spirited society is constitutional. Reliance for the most precious interests of civilization,
therefore, must be found outside of their vindication in courts
of law. Only a persistent positive translation of the faith of a free
society into the convictions and habits and actions of a community
is the ultimate reliance against unabated temptations to fetter the
human spirit.

Griswold v. Connecticut (1965)*

Griswold v. Connecticut *involved the constitutionality of a Connecticut statute that made both the use of contraceptives and the counseling of such use illegal. The executive director of the Planned Parenthood League of Connecticut and its medical director were convicted of giving persons information and medical advice on contraception and of prescribing contraceptive devices. The case posed the issue of the constitutional rights of married persons. It provides an opportunity to explore contrasting interpretations of the Bill of Rights by three of the Court's most prominent libertarians. Douglas construes marital privacy as a right emanating from several constitutional guarantees. Goldberg, though not disagreeing, finds a broader basis for justifying the sanctity of marital privacy, the little-used Ninth Amendment. Finally, Black argues that the Court is imposing its views of social order to invalidate a law for which there is no specific provision in the Constitution prohibiting the legislature from enacting. In short, he views this sort of substantive evaluation of legislation analogous to the invalidation of economic legislation by early twentieth-century jurists.*

To what extent do you think the background and predilections of judges play a role in their decision making? To what extent are judges influenced by popular feeling, the political climate, and by their own sense of shaping policy? Trace the careers of Douglas, Black, and Goldberg to see if they shed any light on these questions.

MR. JUSTICE DOUGLAS delivered the opinion of the Court. . . .

Coming to the merits, we are met with a wide range of questions that implicate the Due Process Clause of the Fourteenth Amendment. Overtones of some arguments suggest that *Lochner v. New York*, should be our guide. But we decline that invitation as we did in *West Coast Hotel Co. v. Parrish*. We do not sit as a super-legislature to determine the wisdom, need, and propriety of laws that touch economic problems, business affairs, or social conditions. This law, however, operates directly on an intimate relation of husband and wife and their physician's role in one aspect of that relation.

The association of people is not mentioned in the Constitution nor in the Bill of Rights. The right to educate a child in a school of the parent's choice—whether public or private or parochial—is also not mentioned. Nor is the right to study any particular subject or any

*381 U.S. 479 (1965).

foreign language. Yet the First Amendment has been construed to include certain of those rights.

By *Pierce v. Society of Sisters* the right to educate one's children as one chooses is made applicable to the States by the force of the First and Fourteenth Amendments. By *Meyer v. Nebraska* the same dignity is given the right to study the German language in a private school. In other words, the State may not, consistently with the spirit of the First Amendment, contract the spectrum of available knowledge. The right of freedom of speech and press includes not only the right to utter or to print, but the right to distribute, the right to receive, the right to read and freedom of inquiry, freedom of thought and freedom to teach—indeed the freedom of the entire university community. Without those peripheral rights the specific rights would be less secure. And so we reaffirm the principle of the *Pierce* and the *Meyer* cases. . . .

The foregoing cases suggest that specific guarantees in the Bill of Rights have penumbras, formed by emanations from those guarantees that help give them life and substance. Various guarantees create zones of privacy. The right of association contained in the penumbra of the First Amendment is one, as we have seen. The Third Amendment in its prohibition against the quartering of soldiers "in any house" in time of peace without the consent of the owner is another facet of that privacy. The Fourth Amendment explicitly affirms the "right of the people to be secure in their persons, houses, papers, and effects, against unreasonable searches and seizures." The Fifth Amendment in its Self-Incrimination Clause enables the citizen to create a zone of privacy which government may not force him to surrender to his detriment. The Ninth Amendment provides: "The enumeration in the Constitution, of certain rights, shall not be construed to deny or disparage others retained by the people." . . .

The present case, then, concerns a relationship lying within the zone of privacy created by several fundamental constitutional guarantees. And it concerns a law which, in forbidding the *use* of contraceptives rather than regulating their manufacture or sale, seeks to achieve its goals by means having a maximum destructive impact upon that relationship. Such a law cannot stand in light of the familiar principle, so often applied by this Court, that a "governmental purpose to control or prevent activities constitutionally subject to state regulation may not be achieved by means which sweep unnecessarily broadly and thereby invade the area of protected freedoms."

Would we allow the police to search the sacred precincts of marital bedrooms for telltale signs of the use of contraceptives? The very idea is repulsive to the notions of privacy surrounding the marriage relationship.

We deal with a right of privacy older than the Bill of Rights— older than our political parties, older than our school system. Marriage is a coming together for better or for worse, hopefully enduring, and intimate to the degree of being sacred. It is an association that promotes a way of life, not causes; a harmony in living, not political faiths; a bilateral loyalty, not commercial or social projects. Yet it is an association for as noble a purpose as any involved in our prior decisions.

MR. JUSTICE GOLDBERG, whom THE CHIEF JUSTICE and MR. JUSTICE BRENNAN join, concurring.

I agree with the Court that Connecticut's birth-control law unconstitutionally intrudes upon the right of marital privacy, and I join in its opinion and judgment. Although I have not accepted the view that "due process" as used in the Fourteenth Amendment incorporates all of the first eight Amendments, I do agree that the concept of liberty protects those personal rights that are fundamental, and is not confined to the specific terms of the Bill of Rights. My conclusion that the concept of liberty is not so restricted and that it embraces the right of marital privacy though that right is not mentioned explicitly in the Constitution is supported both by numerous decisions of this Court, referred to in the Court's opinion, and by the language and history of the Ninth Amendment. In reaching the conclusion that the right of marital privacy is protected, as being within the protected penumbra of specific guarantees of the Bill of Rights, the Court refers to the Ninth Amendment. I add these words to emphasize the relevance of that Amendment to the Court's holding. . . .

This Court, in a series of decisions, has held that the Fourteenth Amendment absorbs and applies to the States those specifics of the first eight amendments which express fundamental personal rights. The language and history of the Ninth Amendment reveal that the Framers of the Constitution believed that there are additional fundamental rights, protected from governmental infringement, which exist alongside those fundamental rights specifically mentioned in the first eight constitutional amendments. . . .

. . . The Ninth Amendment to the Constitution may be regarded by some as a recent discovery and may be forgotten by others, but since 1791 it has been a basic part of the Constitution which we are sworn to uphold. To hold that a right so basic and fundamental and so deep-rooted in our society as the right of privacy in marriage may be infringed because that right is not guaranteed in so many words by the first eight amendments to the Constitution is to ignore the Ninth Amendment and to give it no effect whatsoever. Moreover, a judicial construction that this fundamental right is not protected by the Constitution because it is not mentioned in explicit terms by one of the first eight amendments or elsewhere in the Constitution would violate the Ninth Amendment, which specifically states that "[t]he enumeration in the Constitution, of certain rights, shall not be *construed* to deny or disparage others retained by the people." (Emphasis added.)

A dissenting opinion suggests that my interpretation of the Ninth Amendment somehow "broaden[s] the powers of the Court." With all due respect, I believe that it misses the import of what I am saying. I do not take the position of my Brother BLACK in his dissent in *Adamson v. California*, that the entire Bill of Rights is incorporated in the Fourteenth Amendment, and I do not mean to imply that the Ninth Amendment is applied against the States by the Fourteenth. Nor do I mean to state that the Ninth Amendment constitutes an independent source of rights protected from infringement by either the States or the Federal Government. Rather, the Ninth Amendment shows a belief of the Constitution's authors that fundamental rights exist that are not expressly enumerated in the first eight amendments and an intent that the list of rights included there not be deemed exhaustive. As any student of this Court's opinions knows, this Court has held, often unanimously, that the Fifth and Fourteenth Amendments protect certain fundamental personal liberties from abridgment by the Federal Government or the States. The Ninth Amendment simply shows the intent of the Constitution's authors that other fundamental personal rights should not be denied such protection or disparaged in any other way simply because they are not specifically listed in the first eight constitutional amendments. I do not see how this broadens the authority of the Court; rather it serves to support what this Court has been doing in protecting fundamental rights. . . .

MR. JUSTICE BLACK, with whom MR. JUSTICE STEWART joins, dissenting. . . .

My Brother GOLDBERG has adopted the recent discovery that the Ninth Amendment as well as the Due Process Clause can be used by this Court as authority to strike down all state legislation which this Court thinks violates "fundamental principles of liberty and justice," or is contrary to the "traditions and [collective] conscience of our people." He also states, without proof satisfactory to me, that in making decisions on this basis judges will not consider "their personal and private notions." One may ask how they can avoid considering them. Our Court certainly has no machinery with which to take a Gallup Poll. And the scientific miracles of this age have not yet produced a gadget which the Court can use to determine what traditions are rooted in the "[collective] conscience of our people." Moreover, one would certainly have to look far beyond the language of the Ninth Amendment to find that the Framers vested in this Court any such awesome veto powers over lawmaking, either by the States or by the Congress. Nor does anything in the history of the Amendment offer any support for such a shocking doctrine. The whole history of the adoption of the Constitution and Bill of Rights points the other way, and the very material quoted by my Brother GOLDBERG shows that the Ninth Amendment was intended to protect against the idea that "by enumerating particular exceptions to the grant of power" to the Federal Government, "those rights which were not singled out, were intended to be assigned into the hands of the General Government [the United States], and were consequently insecure." That Amendment was passed, not to broaden the powers of this Court or any other department of "the General Government," but, as every student of history knows, to assure the people that the Constitution in all its provisions was intended to limit the Federal Government to the powers granted expressly or by necessary implication. If any broad, unlimited power to hold laws unconstitutional because they offend what this Court conceives to be the "[collective] conscience of our people" is vested in this Court by the Ninth Amendment, the Fourteenth Amendment, or any other provision of the Constitution, it was not given by the Framers, but rather has been bestowed on the Court by the Court. This fact is perhaps responsible for the peculiar phenomenon that for a period of a century and a half no serious suggestion was ever made that the Ninth Amendment, enacted to protect state powers against federal invasion, could be used as a weapon of federal power to prevent state legislatures from passing laws they consider appropriate to govern local affairs. Use of any such broad, unbounded judicial authority would make of this Court's members a day-to-day constitutional convention.

I repeat so as not to be misunderstood that this Court does have power, which it should exercise, to hold laws unconstitutional where they are forbidden by the Federal Constitution. My point is that there is no provision of the Constitution which either expressly or impliedly vests power in this Court to sit as a supervisory agency over acts of duly constituted legislative bodies and set aside their laws because of the Court's belief that the legislative policies adopted are unreasonable, unwise, arbitrary, capricious or irrational. The adoption of such a loose, flexible, uncontrolled standard for holding laws unconstitutional, if ever it is finally achieved, will amount to a great unconstitutional shift of power to the courts which I believe and am constrained to say will be bad for the courts and worse for the country. Subjecting federal and state laws to such an unrestrained and unrestrainable judicial control as to the wisdom of legislative enactments would, I fear, jeopardize the separation of governmental powers that the Framers set up and at the same time threaten to take away much of the power of States to govern themselves which the Constitution plainly intended them to have.

I realize that many good and able men have eloquently spoken and written, sometimes in rhapsodical strains, about the duty of this Court to keep the Constitution in tune with the times. The idea is that the Constitution must be changed from time to time and that this Court is charged with a duty to make those changes. For myself, I must with all deference reject that philosophy. The Constitution makers knew the need for change and provided for it. Amendments suggested by the people's elected representatives can be submitted to the people or their selected agents for ratification. That method of change was good for our Fathers, and being somewhat old-fashioned I must add it is good enough for me. And so, I cannot rely on the Due Process Clause or the Ninth Amendment or any mysterious and uncertain natural law concept as a reason for striking down this state law. The Due Process Clause with an "arbitrary and capricious" or "shocking to the conscience" formula was liberally used by this Court to strike down economic legislation in the early decades of this century, threatening, many people thought, the tranquility [*sic*] and stability of the Nation. See, e.g., *Lochner v. New York*. That formula, based on subjective considerations of "natural justice," is no less dangerous when used to enforce this Court's views about personal rights than those about economic rights. I had thought that we had laid that formula, as a means for striking down state legislation, to rest once and for all in cases like *West Coast Hotel Co. v. Parrish.* . . .

. . . Apparently my Brethren have less quarrel with state economic regulations than former Justices of their persuasion had. But any limitation upon their using the natural law due process philosophy to strike down any state law, dealing with any activity whatever, will obviously be only self-imposed. . . .

The late Judge Learned Hand, after emphasizing his view that judges should not use the due process formula suggested in the concurring opinions today or any other formula like it to invalidate legislation offensive to their "personal preferences," made the statement, with which I fully agree, that:

> "For myself it would be most irksome to be ruled by a bevy of Platonic Guardians, even if I knew how to choose them, which I assuredly do not."

So far as I am concerned, Connecticut's law as applied here is not forbidden by any provision of the Federal Constitution as that Constitution was written, and I would therefore affirm.

*Roe v. Wade (1973)**

Roe v. Wade raised questions not only about constitutional and judicial authority, but also about deeply felt social and moral values. The case involved a class action suit brought by a pregnant woman (Jane Roe—a pseudonym) challenging the constitutionality of the Texas criminal abortion laws that prohibit abortions except when the life of the mother is at stake. Does the decision affirm the worst fears of judges such as Frankfurter and Black that the Court has become a superlegislature? In what way does Blackmun's use of history help to strengthen his case for invalidating the Texas laws against abortion? As a separate research project, consider examining the sociological impact of the decision on family planning. How has the decision served to inspire political controversy? What would be the effect of a constitutional amendment banning abortion?

**410 U.S. 113, (1973)

MR. JUSTICE BLACKMUN delivered the opinion of the Court. . . .

The principal thrust of appellant's attack on the Texas statutes is that they improperly invade a right, said to be possessed by the pregnant woman, to choose to terminate her pregnancy. Appellant would discover this right in the concept of personal "liberty" embodied in the Fourteenth Amendment's Due Process Clause; or in personal, marital, familial, and sexual privacy said to be protected by the Bill of Rights or its penumbras, or among those rights reserved to the people by the Ninth Amendment. Before addressing this claim, we feel it desirable briefly to survey, in several aspects, the history of abortion, for such insight as that history may afford us, and then to examine the state purposes and interests behind the criminal abortion laws.

It perhaps is not generally appreciated that the restrictive criminal abortion laws in effect in a majority of States today are of relatively recent vintage. Those laws, generally proscribing abortion or its attempt at any time during pregnancy except when necessary to preserve the pregnant woman's life, are not of ancient or even of common-law origin. Instead, they derive from statutory changes effected, for the most part, in the latter half of the 19th century. . . .

3. *The common law.* It is undisputed that at common law, abortion performed before "quickening"—the first recognizable movement of the fetus *in utero*, appearing usually from the 16th to the 18th week of pregnancy—was not an indictable offense. The absence of a common-law crime for pre-quickening abortion appears to have developed from a confluence of earlier philosophical, theological, and civil and canon law concepts of when life begins. These disciplines variously approached the question in terms of the point at which the embryo or fetus became "formed" or recognizably human, or in terms of when a "person" came into being, that is, infused with a "soul" or "animated." A loose consensus evolved in early English law that these events occurred at some point between conception and live birth. This was "mediate animation." . . .

5. *The American law.* In this country, the law in effect in all but a few States until mid-19th century was the pre-existing English common law. Connecticut, the first State to enact abortion legislation, adopted in 1821 that part of Lord Ellenborough's Act that related to a woman "quick with child." The death penalty was not imposed. Abortion before quickening was made a crime in that State only in 1860. In 1828, New York enacted legislation that, in two

respects, was to serve as a model for early anti-abortion statutes. First, while barring destruction of an unquickened fetus as well as a quick fetus, it made the former only a misdemeanor, but the latter second-degree manslaughter. Second, it incorporated a concept of therapeutic abortion by providing that an abortion was excused if it "shall have been necessary to preserve the life of such mother, or shall have been advised by two physicians to be necessary for such purpose." By 1840, when Texas had received the common law, only eight American States had statutes dealing with abortion. It was not until after the War Between the States that legislation began generally to replace the common law. Most of these initial statutes dealt severely with abortion after quickening but were lenient with it before quickening. Most punished attempts equally with completed abortions. While many statutes included the exception for an abortion thought by one or more physicians to be necessary to save the mother's life, that provision soon disappeared and the typical law required that the procedure actually be necessary for that purpose.

Gradually, in the middle and late 19th century the quickening distinction disappeared from the statutory law of most States and the degree of the offense and the penalties were increased. By the end of the 1950s, a large majority of the jurisdictions banned abortion, however and whenever performed, unless done to save or preserve the life of the mother. . . . In the past several years, however, a trend toward liberalization of abortion statutes has resulted in adoption, by about one-third of the States, of less stringent laws. . . .

It is thus apparent that at common law, at the time of the adoption of our Constitution, and throughout the major portion of the 19th century, abortion was viewed with less disfavor than under most American statutes currently in effect. Phrasing it another way, a woman enjoyed a substantially broader right to terminate a pregnancy than she does in most States today. At least with respect to the early stage of pregnancy, and very possibly without such a limitation, the opportunity to make this choice was present in this country well into the 19th century. Even later, the law continued for some time to treat less punitively an abortion procured in early pregnancy. . . .

Three reasons have been advanced to explain historically the enactment of criminal abortion laws in the 19th century and to justify their continued existence.

It has been argued occasionally that these laws were the product of a Victorian social concern to discourage illicit sexual conduct.

Texas, however, does not advance this justification in the present case, and it appears that no court or commentator has taken the argument seriously. . . .

A second reason is concerned with abortion as a medical procedure. When most criminal abortion laws were first enacted, the procedure was a hazardous one for the woman. This was particularly true prior to the development of antisepsis. Antiseptic techniques, of course, were based on discoveries by Lister, Pasteur, and others first announced in 1867, but were not generally accepted and employed until about the turn of the century. Abortion mortality was high. Even after 1900, and perhaps until as late as the development of antibiotics in the 1940s, standard modern techniques such as dilation and curettage were not nearly so safe as they are today. Thus, it has been argued that a State's real concern in enacting a criminal abortion law was to protect the pregnant woman, that is, to restrain her from submitting to a procedure that placed her life in serious jeopardy.

Modern medical techniques have altered this situation. Appellants and various *amici* refer to medical data indicating that abortion in early pregnancy, that is, prior to the end of the first trimester, although not without its risk, is now relatively safe. Mortality rates for women undergoing early abortions, where the procedure is legal, appear to be as low as or lower than the rates for normal childbirth. Consequently, any interest of the State in protecting the woman from an inherently hazardous procedure, except when it would be equally dangerous for her to forgo it, has largely disappeared. Of course, important state interests in the area of health and medical standards do remain.

The State has a legitimate interest in seeing to it that abortion, like any other medical procedure, is performed under circumstances that insure maximum safety for the patient. This interest obviously extends at least to the performing physician and his staff, to the facilities involved, to the availability of after-care, and to adequate provision for any complication or emergency that might arise. This prevalence of high mortality rates at illegal "abortion mills" strengthens, rather than weakens, the State's interest in regulating the conditions under which abortions are performed. Moreover, the risk to the woman increases as her pregnancy continues. Thus, the State retains a definite interest in protecting the woman's own health and safety when an abortion is proposed at a late stage of pregnancy.

The third reason is the State's interest—some phrase it in terms of duty—in protecting prenatal life. Some of the argument for this justification rests on the theory that a new human life is present from the moment of conception. The State's interest and general obligation to protect life then extends, it is argued, to prenatal life. Only when the life of the pregnant mother herself is at stake, balanced against the life she carries within her, should the interest of the embryo or fetus not prevail. Logically, of course, a legitimate state interest in this area need not stand or fall on acceptance of the belief that life begins at conception or at some other point prior to live birth. In assessing the State's interest, recognition may be given to the less rigid claim that as long as at least *potential* life is involved, the State may assert interests beyond the protection of the pregnant woman alone.

Parties challenging state abortion laws have sharply disputed in some courts the contention that a purpose of these laws, when enacted, was to protect prenatal life. Pointing to the absence of legislative history to support the contention, they claim that most state laws were designed solely to protect the woman. Because medical advances have lessened this concern, at least with respect to abortion in early pregnancy, they argue that with respect to such abortions the laws can no longer be justified by any state interest. There is some scholarly support for this view of original purpose. The few state courts called upon to interpret their laws in the late 19th and early 20th centuries did focus on the State's interest in protecting the woman's health rather than in preserving the embryo and fetus. Proponents of this view point out that in many States, including Texas, by statute or judicial interpretation, the pregnant woman herself could not be prosecuted for self-abortion or for cooperating in an abortion performed upon her by another. They claim that adoption of the "quickening" distinction through received common law and state statutes tacitly recognizes the greater health hazards inherent in late abortion and impliedly repudiates the theory that life begins at conception.

It is with these interests, and the weight to be attached to them, that this case is concerned.

The Constitution does not explicitly mention any right of privacy. In a line of decisions, . . . the Court has recognized that a right of personal privacy, or a guarantee of certain areas or zones of privacy, does exist under the Constitution. In varying contexts, the Court or individual Justices have, indeed, found at least the roots of the right in the First Amendment, in the Fourth and Fifth Amendments, in the penumbras of the Bill of Rights, in the Ninth Amendment, or in the concept of liberty guaranteed by the first section of the Fourteenth Amendment. These decisions make it clear that only personal rights that can be deemed "fundamental" or "implicit in the concept of ordered liberty," are included in this guarantee of personal privacy. They also make it clear that the right has some extension to activities relating to marriage, procreation, contraception, family relationships, and child rearing and education.

This right of privacy, whether it be founded in the Fourteenth Amendment's concept of personal liberty and restrictions upon state action as we feel it is, or, . . . in the Ninth Amendment's reservation of rights to the people, is broad enough to encompass a woman's decision whether or not to terminate her pregnancy. The detriment that the State would impose upon the pregnant woman by denying this choice altogether is apparent. Specific and direct harm medically diagnosable even in early pregnancy may be involved. Maternity, or additional offspring, may force upon the woman a distressful life and future. Psychological harm may be imminent. Mental and physical health may be taxed by child care. There is also the distress, for all concerned, associated with the unwanted child, and there is the problem of bringing a child into a family already unable, psychologically and otherwise, to care for it. In other cases, as in this one, the additional difficulties and continuing stigma of unwed motherhood may be involved. All these are factors the woman and her responsible physician necessarily will consider in consultation.

On the basis of elements such as these, appellant and some *amici* argue that the woman's right is absolute and that she is entitled to terminate her pregnancy at whatever time, in whatever way, and for whatever reason she alone chooses. With this we do not agree. . . .
The Court's decisions recognizing a right of privacy also acknowledge that some state regulation in areas protected by that right is appropriate. As noted above, a State may properly assert important interests in safeguarding health, in maintaining medical standards, and in protecting potential life. At some point in pregnancy, these respective interests become sufficiently compelling to sustain regulation of the factors that govern the abortion decision. The privacy right involved, therefore, cannot be said to be absolute. In fact, it is not clear to us that the claim asserted by some *amici* that one has an

unlimited right to do with one's body as one pleases bears a close relationship to the right of privacy previously articulated in the Court's decisions. The Court has refused to recognize an unlimited right of this kind in the past.

We, therefore, conclude that the right of personal privacy includes the abortion decision, but that this right is not unqualified and must be considered against important state interests in regulation. . . .

The pregnant woman cannot be isolated in her privacy. She carries an embryo and, later, a fetus, if one accepts the medical definitions of the developing young in the human uterus. The situation therefore is inherently different from marital intimacy, or bedroom possession of obscene material, or marriage, or procreation, or education. . . . As we have intimated above, it is reasonable and appropriate for a State to decide that at some point in time another interest, that of health of the mother or that of potential human life, becomes significantly involved. The woman's privacy is no longer sole and any right of privacy she possesses must be measured accordingly. . . .

With respect to the State's important and legitimate interest in the health of the mother, the "compelling" point, in the light of present medical knowledge, is at approximately the end of the first trimester. This is so because of the now-established medical fact, . . . that until the end of the first trimester mortality in abortion may be less than mortality in normal childbirth. It follows that, from and after this point, a State may regulate the abortion procedure to the extent that the regulation reasonably relates to the preservation and protection of maternal health. . . .

This means, on the other hand, that, for the period of pregnancy prior to this "compelling" point, the attending physician, in consultation with his patient, is free to determine, without regulation by the State, that, in his medical judgment, the patient's pregnancy should be terminated. If that decision is reached, the judgment may be effected by an abortion free of interference by the State. . . .

C

COMMENTARIES ON THE LAW AND THE LEGAL PROFESSION

The commentaries are by three figures who had different, yet intimate, acquaintance with the law and legal institutions: Woodrow Wilson was a lawyer, university president, governor, and President of the United States; Harlan Fiske Stone was a lawyer, law professor, law school dean, attorney-general, Supreme Court justice, and finally, chief justice; and Alexander Bickel was a lawyer, law school professor and author. The excerpts from the Wilson and Stone speeches reflect the nation's overriding concern during the first half of the century with adjusting legal rules to control corporate activities and with defining the role of lawyers in this process. Both speeches deal with the government's role as well. The speech by Alexander Bickel, written against the background of the Watergate scandal, highlights the dangers that occur when legal process is superseded by emotion and by visionary ideals of fairness. In effect, all three are talking about the need for law as a way of ordering our society. All three figures are confronting the question of liberty versus social control—a theme that also dominates the statutes and judicial opinions contained in the earlier parts of this document collection.

Woodrow Wilson: The Lawyer and the Community (1910)*

The following excerpt from a 1910 speech by Woodrow Wilson, then Princeton University president, to the American Bar Association in Tennessee is a classic statement of the Progressive-era indictment of the legal profession, and a strong statement of Progressive-era attitudes toward the relationship of law and corporate organization. Does Wilson's statement complement Holmes's dissent in Northern Securities? *To what extent does Wilson lay the groundwork for the Clayton and Federal Trade Commission Acts?*

We are lawyers. This is the field of our knowledge. We are servants of society, officers of the courts of justice. Our duty is a much larger thing than the mere advice of private clients. In every deliberate struggle for law we ought to be the guides, not too critical and unwilling, not too tenacious of the familiar technicalities in which we have been schooled, not too much in love with precedents and the easy maxims which have saved us the trouble of thinking, but ready to give expert and disinterested advice to those who purpose progress and the readjustment of the frontiers of justice.

You cannot but have marked the recent changes in the relation of lawyers to affairs in this country; and, if you feel as I do about the great profession to which we belong, you cannot but have been made uneasy by the change. Lawyers constructed the fabric of our state governments and of the government of the United States, and throughout the earlier periods of our national development presided over all the larger processes of politics. Our political conscience as a nation was embedded in our written fundamental law. Every question of public policy seemed sooner or later to become a question of law, upon which trained lawyers must be consulted. In all our legislative halls debate thundered in the phrases of the written enactments under which our legislators and our governors exercised authority. Public life was a lawyer's forum. Laymen lent their invaluable counsel, but lawyers guided, and lawyers framed the law. . . .

But they are gone. You have only to recall the many extraordinary interpretations of the interstate commerce clause of the constitution upon which serious debate has been wasted in Congress in recent years to be convinced of it. Our lawyers themselves are not carefully

* Woodrow Wilson. *The Public Papers of Woodrow Wilson: College and State*, vol. 2, ed. Ray Stannard Baker and William E. Dodd (New York: Harper, 1925), pp. 245–268. Copyright 1925 by Edith Bolling Wilson. Reprinted by permission of Harper & Row.

trained as they used to be in the principles of our constitutional law. It does not stand in the foreground of their study or practice, but in the background, very vague and general, a thing to be resorted to only upon rare occasion. Our legislatures now listen to debates upon constitutional questions with ill-concealed impatience, as tedious and academic. The nation has grown keen after certain practical objects and will not willingly brook the impediments set up by constitutions. The temper of the age is very nearly summed up in a feeling which you may put into words like these: "There are certain things we must do. Our life as a nation must be rectified in certain all-important particulars. If there be no law for the change, it must be found or made. We will not be argued into impotency by lawyers. We are not interested in the structure of our governments so much as in the exigencies of our life."

There are many reasons why this change of temper and of point of view has occurred. I will venture to mention one or two of the more obvious. It is not by chance that statesmanship has grown bigger than the bounds of mere legal precedent.

In the first place, the debates and constitutional struggles of the first seventy years of our political history settled most of the fundamental questions of our constitutional law. Solid lines of decided cases carry the definite outlines of the structure and make clear the methods of its action. We seemed after the Civil War to be released from the demands of formal definition. The life of the nation, running upon normal lines, has grown infinitely varied. It does not center now upon questions of governmental structure or of the distribution of governmental powers. It centers upon economic questions, questions of the very structure and operation of society itself, of which government is only the instrument. . . . We have been engaged in enterprises which the law as we formerly looked at it was clearly not meant to prevent or embarrass. We pushed them forward, therefore, without thinking of the effect they might have upon older conceptions of our legal processes. They seemed to spring out of the normal and necessary uses of the great continent whose riches we have been exploiting. We did not think of the legal consequences one way or the other, and therefore did not need or seek the advice of constitutional lawyers.

Constitutional lawyers have fallen into the background. We have relegated them to the Supreme Court, without asking ourselves where we are to find them when vacancies occur in that great tribunal. A new type of lawyer has been created; and that new type has come to be the prevailing type. Lawyers have been sucked into the maelstrom of the new business system of the country. That system is highly technical and highly specialized. It is divided into distinct sections and provinces, each with particular legal problems of its own. Lawyers, therefore, everywhere that business has thickened and had a large development, have become experts in some special technical field. They do not practise law. They do not handle the general, miscellaneous interests of society. They are not general counsellors of right and obligation. They do not bear the relation to the business of their neighborhoods that the family doctor bears to the health of the community in which he lives. They do not concern themselves with the universal aspects of society. . . .

And so society has lost something, or is losing it—something which it is very serious to lose in an age of law, when society depends more than ever before upon the law-giver and the courts for its structural steel, the harmony and coordination of its parts, its convenience, its permanency, and its facility. In gaining new functions, in being drawn into modern business instead of standing outside of it, in becoming identified with particular interests instead of holding aloof and impartially advising all interests, the lawyer has lost his old function, is looked askance at in politics, must disavow special engagements if he would have his counsel heeded in matters of common concern. Society has suffered a corresponding loss,—at least American society has. It has lost its one-time feeling for law as the basis of its peace, its progress, its prosperity. Lawyers are not now regarded as the mediators of progress. Society was always ready to be prejudiced against them; now it finds its prejudice confirmed.

Meanwhile, look what legal questions are to be settled, how stupendous they are, how far-reaching, and how impossible it will be to settle them without the advice of learned and experienced lawyers! The country must find lawyers of the right sort and of the old spirit to advise it, or it must stumble through a very chaos of blind experiment. It never needed lawyers who are also statesmen more than it needs them now,—needs them in its courts, in its legislatures, in its seats of executive authority,—lawyers who can think in the terms of society itself, mediate between interests, accommodate right to right, establish equity, and bring the peace that will come with genuine and hearty cooperation, and will come in no other way.

The specialization of business and the extraordinary development of corporate organization and administration have led to consequences well worth the lawyer's consideration. Everyone else is considering them, and considering them with deep concern. We have witnessed in modern business the submergence of the individual within the organization, and yet the increase to an extraordinary degree of the power of the individual,—of the individual who happens to control the organization. Most men are individuals no longer so far as their business, its activities or its moralities, is concerned. They are not units, but fractions; with their individuality and independence or choice in matters of business they have lost also their individual choice within the field of morals. They must do what they are told to do, or lose their connection with modern affairs. They are not at liberty to ask whether what they are told to do is right or wrong. They cannot get at the men who ordered it,—have no access to them. They have no voice of counsel or of protest. They are mere cogs in a machine which has men for its parts. And yet there are men here and there with whom the whole choice lies. There are men who control the machine as a whole and the men who compose it. There are men who use it with an imperial freedom of design, whose power and whose individuality overtop whole communities. There is more individual power than ever, but those who exercise it are few and formidable, and the mass of men are mere pawns in the game.

The present task of the law is nothing less than to rehabilitate the individual,—not to make the subordinate independent of the superior, not to turn corporations into debating societies, not to disintegrate what we have been at such pains to piece together in the organization of modern industrial enterprise, but to undo enough of what we have done in the development of our law of corporations to give the law direct access again to the individual,—to every individual in all his functions.

Corporations do not do wrong. Individuals do wrong, the individuals who direct and use them for selfish and illegitimate purposes, to the injury of society and the serious curtailment of private rights. Guilt, as has been very truly said, is always personal. You cannot punish corporations. Fines fall upon the wrong persons, more heavily upon the innocent than upon the guilty, as much upon those who knew nothing whatever of the transactions for which the fine is imposed as upon those who originated and carried them through, —upon the stockholders and the customers rather than upon the men who direct the policy of the business. If you dissolve the offending corporation, you throw great undertakings out of gear. You merely drive what you are seeking to check into other forms or temporarily disorganize some important business altogether, to the infinite loss of thousands of entirely innocent persons and to the great inconvenience of society as a whole. Law can never accomplish its objects in that way. It can never bring peace or command respect by such futilities.

I regard the corporation as indispensable to modern business enterprise. I am not jealous of its size or might, if you will but abandon at the right points the fatuous, antiquated, and quite unnecessary fiction which treats it as a legal person; if you will but cease to deal with it by means of your law as if it were a single individual not only but also,—what every child may perceive it is not,—a responsible individual. Such fictions and analogies were innocent and convenient enough so long as corporations were comparatively small and only one of many quite as important instrumentalities used in business, only a minor item in the economic order of society. But it is another matter now. They span society, and the responsibilities involved in their complex organization and action must be analyzed by the law as the responsibilities of society itself, in all its other aspects, have been. . . .

A modern corporation is an economic society, a little economic state,—and not always little, even as compared with states. Many modern corporations wield revenues and command resources which no ancient state possessed, and which some modern bodies politic show no approach to in their budgets. . . . In some instances even the functions are not separated. Railroad companies have been known to buy coal mines. Manufacturing combinations have been observed to develop a score of subsidiary industries, to spread a network of organization over related enterprises, and sometimes even over enterprises whose relation to their main undertakings it is difficult for the lay mind to perceive. Society, in short, has discovered a new way of massing its resources and its power of enterprise, is building up bodies economic outside its bodies politic which may, if we do not find the means to prevent them, the means of disclosing the responsibilities of the men who compose them, dominate bodies politic themselves. . . .

I would not have you think that I am speaking with a feeling of hostility towards the men who have in our day given the nation its extraordinary material power and prosperity by an exercise of genius such as in days gone by was used, in each great age, to build empires and alter the boundaries of states. . . . I am simply trying to analyze the existing constitution of business in blunt words of truth, without animus or passion of any kind, and with a single, clear purpose.

That purpose is to recall you to the service of the nation as a whole, from which you have been drifting away; to remind you that, no matter what the exactions of modern legal business, no matter what or how great the necessity for specialization in your practice of the law, you are not the servants of special interests, the mere expert counsellors of this, that, or the other group of business men; but guardians of the general peace, the guides of those who seek to realize by some best accomodation the rights of men. With that purpose in view, I am asking you to look again at the corporation. . . .

I call your attention to the fact, therefore, that it is perfectly possible to have corporations and serve all the necessities and conveniences of modern society by means of the great combinations of wealth and energy which we have found to be so excellent, and yet dispense with a large part of the quite outworn and now in many respects deeply demoralizing fiction that a corporation is an indivisible person. Of course we must continue to regard it as an artificial person so far as is necessary to enable it to hold such property as may be proper for the execution of its charter purposes, to sue and be sued, and to conduct its business through officers who speak for it as a whole, and whose signatures and orders are, under its by-laws and resolutions, binding upon it. It must act and live as a person, and must be capable of enjoying, what individuals cannot enjoy, a certain perpetuity of power and authority, though individual men within it come and go, live, die, resign, or are translated. But there its unity should stop.

In respect of the responsibility which the law imposes in order to protect society itself, in order to protect men and communities against wrongs which are not breaches of contract but offenses against the public interest, the common welfare, it is imperative that we should regard corporations as merely groups of individuals, from which it may, perhaps, be harder to pick out particular persons for punishment than it is to pick them out of the general body of unassociated men, but from which it is, nevertheless, possible to pick them out,—possible not only, but absolutely necessary if business is ever again to be moralized. Corporations must continue to be used as a convenience in the transaction of business, but they must cease to be used as a covert for wrong-doers.

The managers of corporations themselves always know the men who originated the acts charged against them as done in contravention of the law; is there no means by which their names may be disclosed to the officers of justice? Every act, every policy in the conduct of the affairs of a corporation originates with some particular officer, committee, or board. The officer, the committee, the board which orders an act or originates a policy contrary to the law of the land or intended to neutralize or contravene it is an insurgent against society: the man or men who originate any such act or policy should be punished, and they alone. It is not necessary that the corporation should be broken up. It is not fair that the stockholders should be mulcted in damages. If there are damages to be paid they should be paid out of the private means of the persons who are really guilty. An analysis of the guilt is perfectly feasible. It is the duty of lawyers, of all lawyers, to assist the makers of law and the reformers of abuses by pointing out the best and most effective way to make it. . . .

I know that the matter is not as simple as it sounds. I know that some corporations are in fact controlled from the outside, not from the inside: that it often happens that some man or some small group of men who are not even in its directorate dictate its policy, its individual acts, its attitude towards law and society, and that the men who act within it are little better than automata. But are they really beyond discovery? On the contrary, is it not generally a matter of common knowledge who they are? Would it take extraordinary acumen and intelligence to devise laws which would reach them also? What we are after, of course, is to obtain laws which will prevent the use of corporations to the public hurt and disadvantage. . . . Our processes of evidence may have to be considerably altered, but we can alter them; our formal conception of parties in interest may have to be extended, but it is easy to extend it; our make-believe that we can see nobody in the transaction but those who are avowed and formal members of the organization may have to be discarded, but that ought to be a relief to our consciences. We have allowed ourselves to be ridiculously limited and embarrassed by the theory that a corporation is an indivisible person not only, but that nobody outside of it, no matter how intimate his use and control, may be brought into the suit by any genteel lawyer bred in the orthodox schools of law. A corporation is merely a convenient instrument of business and we may regulate its use as we please, and those who use it. . . .

You are not a mere body of expert business advisers in the field of civil law or a mere body of expert advocates for those who get entangled in the meshes of the criminal law. You are servants of the public, of the state itself. You are under bonds to serve the general interest, the integrity and enlightenment of law itself, in the advice you give individuals. It is your duty also to advise those who make the laws,—to advise them in the general interest, with a view to the amelioration of every undesirable condition that the law can reach, the removal of every obstacle to progress and fair dealing that the law can remove, the lightening of every burden the law can lift and the righting of every wrong the law can rectify. The services of the lawyer are indispensable not only in the application of the accepted processes of the law, the interpretation of existing rules in the daily operations of life and business. His services are indispensable also in keeping, and in making, the law clear with regard to responsibility, to organization, to liability, and, above all, to the relation of private rights to the public interest. . . .

For there never was a time, in fact, when his advice, his disinterested and earnest advice, was more needed than it is now in the exigent processes of reform, in the busy processes of legislation through which we are passing, with so singular a mixture of hope and apprehension. I hear a great many lawyers join the cry of the business men, that it is time legislators left business alone, allowed it to recover from the confusion and distraction of regulative statutes, altered tariffs, and supervising commissions, find its natural methods again, and go forward upon a way of prosperity which will not be beset by fear and uncertainty. But the cry is futile, the impatience which gives rise to it is selfish and ignorant. Nothing is settled or can be let alone when it is known to be wrong until it is set right. We have settled nothing in our recent reform legislation. That is the reason it is so unsatisfactory, and why some prudent and thoughtful men grow tired of it. But that is only another reason for seeking out and finding what will be the happy and successful way of setting our economic interests in order. There has been no satisfactory settlement, but there must be one. Public opinion is wider awake about these matters than it has been within the memory of any man living, and it is not going to turn away from them until satisfactory reforms of the law are found. There will be no peace until a happy and honorable basis of

peace has been hit upon. Lawyers may come into the settlement or
stay out of it, as they please, but a settlement there must be. For one,
I hope that they will not stay out. I fear that it would be disastrous for
them to do so,—disastrous to them and to society. I covet for them
their old and honorable leadership in public counsel. . . .

Our reforms must be legal reforms. It is a pity they should go
forward without the aid of those who have studied the law in its habit
as it lives, those who know what is practicable and what is not, those
who know, or should know, if anybody does, the history of liberty. . . .

Harlan Fiske Stone: The Public Influence of the Bar (1934)*

*In an address delivered at the dedication of the Law Quadrangle of the
University of Michigan, Justice Harlan Fiske Stone took the occasion to
examine the role of the legal profession in the midst of the depression of the
1930s. This excerpt from Stone's speech draws us closer to several themes
outlined in the essay, including (1) the lawyer's relationship to business; (2) the
need that he or she take a larger role in shaping public policy; and (3) the
growing role of law teachers in studying and helping to solve legal problems
affecting social and economic relations. In what way has Stone's attitude about
legal reform changed from his position in 1915? (See p. 17.)*

We meet at a time when, as never before in the history of the
country, our most cherished ideals and traditions are being subjected
to searching criticism. The towering edifice of business and industry,
which had become the dominating feature of the American social
structure, has been shaken to its foundations by forces, the full
significance of which we still can see but dimly. What had seemed the
impregnable fortress of a boasted civilization has developed unsus-
pected weaknesses and in consequence we are now engaged in the
altogether wholesome task of critical reexamination of what our
hands have reared. . . .

No tradition of our profession is more cherished by lawyers than
that of its leadership in public affairs. . . .

. . . Yet candor would compel even those of us who have the
most abiding faith in our profession, and the firmest belief in its

---

* *Harvard Law Review*, 48, (1934), 1–14. Copyright © 1934 by The Harvard Law
Review Association. Reprinted by permission.

capacity for future usefulness, to admit that in our own time the Bar has not maintained its traditional position of public influence and leadership. Although it tends to prove the point, it is not of the first importance that there are fewer lawyers of standing serving in the halls of legislatures or in executive or administrative posts than in earlier days. Public office is not the only avenue to public influence. Representatives of other professions in public position have always been comparatively few, but wherever questions of professional concern to them touch the public interest, they are nevertheless profoundly influential. In matters of sanitation and public health, in great public undertakings involving engineering knowledge and skill, we place ourselves unreservedly in their hands. But it is not without its lesson for us that most laymen, at least, would deny that there is today a comparable leadership on the part of lawyers, or a disposition of the public to place reliance upon their leadership where the problems of government touch the law.

We cannot brush aside this lay dissatisfaction with lawyers with the comforting assurance that it is nothing more than the chronic distrust of the lawyer class which the literature of every age has portrayed. . . . [I]n the struggle, unique in our history, to determine whether the giant economic forces which our industrial and financial world have created shall be brought under some larger measure of control and, if so, what legal devices can and should be selected to accomplish that end, it is a matter of public comment that the practicing lawyer has been but a minor participant. . . .

In appraising the present-day relationship of the lawyer to his community, we cannot leave out of account either the altered character of public questions or the change in the function which the lawyers, as a class, are called upon to perform. . . . Public problems are no longer exclusively questions of individual right. They involve an understanding of the new and complex economic forces we have created, their relationship to the lives of individuals in widely separated communities engaged in widely differing activities, and the adaptation to those forces of old conceptions of law developed in a different environment to meet different needs.

The American Bar, like most other elements in the life of the nation, was ill prepared for a change so swift and sweeping. From the beginning of the commercial expansion in England almost to our own day, the problems of the law were those of an intensely individualistic society. An adequate technique, and skill in using it, engaged the attention of its practitioners. Its historical background and moral content, and more or less abortive attempts to reform its procedure, were the chief considerations of its philosophers.

When the universities, but a little more than a generation ago, found place for the study of the law, its expositors were at first mainly concerned with its precedents and its technique. There was a persistent delving into its past, an assiduous analysis of what courts had done and the manner of their doing it, but little reflection upon the relationship of law to the social and economic forces which produce it or contemplation of its function as a means of social control rather than as an end in itself. There was still less perception of the significance of the rise of new forces in American life which, with constantly accelerated speed, were reconstructing society upon a new economic basis, with an ever increasing interdependence of its every group and part upon every other.

The changed character of the lawyer's work has made it difficult for him to contemplate his function in its new setting, to see himself and his occupation in proper perspective. No longer does his list of clients represent a cross section of society; no longer do his contacts make him the typical representative and interpreter of his community. The demands of practice are more continuous and exacting. He has less time for reflection upon other than immediate professional undertakings. He is more the man of action, less the philosopher and less the student of history, economics, and government.

The rise of big business has produced an inevitable specialization of the Bar. The successful lawyer of our day more often than not is the proprietor or general manager of a new type of factory, whose legal product is increasingly the result of mass production methods. More and more the amount of his income is the measure of professional success. More and more he must look for his rewards to the material satisfactions derived from profits as from a successfully conducted business, rather than to the intangible and indubitably more durable satisfactions which are to be found in a professional service more consciously directed toward the advancement of the public interest. Steadily the best skill and capacity of the profession has been drawn into the exacting and highly specialized service of business and finance. At its best the changed system has brought to the command of the business world loyalty and a superb proficiency and technical skill. At its worst it has made the learned profession of an earlier day the obsequious servant of business, and tainted it with the morals and manners of the market place in its most anti-social manifestations. In any case we must concede that it has given us a Bar whose leaders, like its rank and file, are on the whole less likely to be well rounded professional men than their predecessors, whose energy and talent for public service and for bringing the law into harmony with changed conditions have been largely absorbed in the advancement of the interests of clients. . . .

. . . Like most other elements of the community, we are in a sense the victims of changes, of whose nature and effect we are still not wholly aware. Hence it is that the Bar needs to know and to focus its attention upon the facts, not in the form of assumptions or generalizations, nor yet on the details of petty misconduct in its disreputable outer fringes, but upon data patiently assembled and organized so as to show with the powerful impact of revealed truth the extent to which devotion to private interests has obscured our vision of the public welfare. . . .

I venture to assert that when the history of the financial era which has just drawn to a close comes to be written, most of its mistakes and its major faults will be ascribed to the failure to observe the fiduciary principle, the precept as old as holy writ, that "a man cannot serve two masters." More than a century ago equity gave a hospitable reception to that principle and the common law was not slow to follow in giving it recognition. No thinking man can believe that an economy built upon a business foundation can permanently endure without some loyalty to that principle. The separation of ownership from management, the development of the corporate structure so as to vest in small groups control over the resources of great numbers of small and uninformed investors, make imperative a fresh and active devotion to that principle if the modern world of business is to perform its proper function. Yet those who serve nominally as trustees, but relieved, by clever legal devices, from the obligation to protect those whose interests they purport to represent, corporate officers and directors who award to themselves huge bonuses from corporate funds without the assent or even the knowledge of their stockholders, reorganization committees created to serve interests of others than those whose securities they control, financial institutions which, in the infinite variety of their operations, consider only last, if at all, the interests of those whose funds they command, suggest how far we have ignored the necessary implications of that principle. The loss and suffering inflicted on individuals, the harm done to a social order founded upon business and dependent upon its integrity, are incalculable. There is little to suggest that the Bar has yet recognized that it must bear some burden of responsibility for these evils. But when we know and face the facts we shall have to acknowledge that such departures from the fiduciary principle do not usually occur without the active assistance of some member of our profession, and that their increasing recurrence would have been impossible but for the complaisance of a Bar, too absorbed in the workaday care of private interests to take account of these events of profound import or to sound the warning that the profession looks askance upon these, as things that "are not done". . . .

If you think I have sketched too dark a picture of the difficulties which beset us, I hasten to assure you that it is not from any counsel of despair. I would only point out that in the new order which has been forced upon us, we cannot expect the Bar to function as it did in other days and under other conditions. Before it can function at all as the guardian of public interests committed to its care, there must be appraisal and comprehension of the new conditions and the changed relationships of the lawyer to his clients, to his professional brethren and to the public. That appraisal must pass beyond the petty details of form and manners which have been so largely the subject of our codes of ethics, to more fundamental consideration of the way in which our professional activities affect the welfare of society as a whole. Our canons of ethics for the most part are generalizations designed for an earlier era. However undesirable the practices condemned, they do not profoundly affect the social order outside our own group. We must not permit our attention to the relatively inconsequential to divert us from preparing to set appropriate standards for those who design the legal patterns for business practices of far more consequence to society than any with which our grievance committees have been preoccupied.

Apart from the procedure of formulating new methods of discipline and new specifications of condemned practices, we must give more thoughtful consideration to squaring our own ethical conceptions with the traditional ethics and ideals of the community at large. The problems to which the machine and the corporation give rise have outstripped the ideology and values of an earlier day. The future demands that we undergo a corresponding moral readjustment. Just as the lawyers of 1790 to 1840 took a leading part in fashioning the country's ideals to suit political change, so we must now shoulder the task of relating them to business and economic change.

All this cannot be done in those occasional and brief intervals when the busy lawyer secures some respite from the pressing demands of clients to participate in the festivities of bar association meetings. It requires study and investigation, the painstaking gathering of data and their portrayal in such fashion that we may know the facts and, knowing them, develop a consciousness of their implications for our profession.

With so much to be done we must look to those elements in the profession best qualified for doing it. A generation ago that search must have begun and ended with practicing lawyers. But paralleling the development of the practicing bar has come, in the past fifty years, the steady growth in public esteem and influence of a new force in American legal life, that of the rapidly increasing group of university law teachers, devoting their lives to the task of advancing the cause of legal science for which they have been specially selected and trained. Members of the Bar, they nevertheless make up a distinct professional group within the Bar. More detached than is the barrister from the absorbing demands of clients and from those pressures of the new economic order which have so profoundly affected their practicing brethren, their approach to legal problems has been that of the disinterested scientist. For a generation they contented themselves with the necessary work of analysis, clarification and statement of legal doctrine. More recently, with penetrating insight, they have expanded their inquiries to embrace the relation of law to the social forces which create it, and which in turn it is designed to control. Today they are beginning to turn their attention to the Bar as an institution, seeking to gain an informed understanding of its problems, to appraise the performance of its public functions and to find ways of stimulating a more adequate performance of them. In all this they have rendered and are rendering a public service of a high order.

With the ever increasing demands on the time and energy of the practicing lawyer, it was but natural that it should fall to the lot of the law-school men to take the lead in discharging the public duties which rest on the profession as a whole. It is they who have taken the initiative in the most important reforms undertaken by the Bar in the past twenty years. They originated and have chiefly guided the movements espoused by the Bar for the enactment of uniform laws, the restatement of the law, the improvement in standards of admission to the Bar, and the reform of civil and criminal procedure. It is they who today represent the most cohesive, disinterested and potent single force operating within the profession to establish its public relationships on a higher plane. . . .

And so I turn to the part which our university law schools may take in the study and promotion of the highest interests of the Bar. The functioning of the Bar as an essential institution in present-day American life is worthy of research and exposition for the enlightenment of the Bar and the public, such as only the law schools can make. Their detachment, their scholarly resources, their growing influence with the Bar, all indicate plainly enough that it is they who must take the more active part in solving the problems which weigh upon our profession perhaps as never before. They, as can no others, may assemble and portray the facts which reveal, so that all may see, the manner in which the Bar is performing its functions and, portraying them, stir the latent idealism of lawyers to carry on.

It is equally true that the Bar cannot sit by and leave the burden entirely upon the law schools. In the light of information which they may make available the Bar must assume the responsibility of consciously bringing its conduct to conform to new standards fitting the times in which we live. And unless history reverses itself the cooperation and support of leaders of the Bar will not be wanting. There could be no more reassuring example of the possibility of drawing upon the reserves of wisdom, patriotism, and idealism of our profession in a cooperative effort to advance the public interest than that afforded by the Institute of Law. For more than ten years the judges, the leading practitioners of the country, and the representatives of our great schools of law have united in the sustained, self-sacrificing, harmonious effort of the Institute to bring order out of the chaos of some six centuries' accumulation of judicial precedent. One cannot doubt that a profession capable of such a demonstration of its capacity for united and disinterested public service can meet and solve these new and difficult problems. . . .

There is opportunity, too, for a new emphasis in the training of the young men who, thronging the lecture rooms of the law schools today, will give character and direction to our profession tomorrow. From the beginning the law schools have steadily raised their intellectual standards. It is not too much to say that they have worshiped the proficiency which they have sought and attained to a remarkable degree. But there is grave danger to the public if this proficiency be directed wholly to private ends without thought of the social consequences, and we may well pause to consider whether the professional school has done well to neglect so completely the inculcation of some knowledge of the social responsibility which rests upon a public profession. I do not refer to the teaching of professional ethics. I have no thought that men are made moral by the mere formulation of rules of conduct, no matter how solemnly bar associations may pronounce them, or that they may be made good by mere exhortation. But men serve causes because of their devotion to them. The zeal of the student for proficiency in the law, like that of his elder brother at the Bar, comes from a higher source than selfishness. It is devotion to his conception of a useful and worthy institution. But that conception is a distorted one if it envisages only the cultivation of skill without thought of how and to what end it is to be used, and the question what the law schools have done and can do to make that conception truer is one to be pondered and to be answered. It is not beyond the power of institutions which have so successfully mastered the art of penetrating all the intricacies of legal doctrine to impart a truer understanding of the functions of those who are to be its servants. That understanding will come, not from platitudinous exhortation, but from knowledge of the consequences of the failure of a profession to bear its social responsibilities, and what it is doing and may do to meet them. . . .

Alexander Bickel: Watergate and the Legal Order (1974)*

In an address delivered to the American Academy of Arts and Sciences and later published in revised form in Commentary *magazine, Yale Law School professor Alexander Bickel uses the Watergate incident to describe a more fundamental problem affecting the law and legal institutions. From the excerpt that follows, what conclusion can be drawn about the relationship between law and morality? Do you agree with Bickel's vision of the future?*

Months ago, when the scandals of the Nixon administration were fewer and relatively simpler, there was some self-serving talk of a commonalty of error among the Watergate perpetrators, as the arresting officers might have called them, and the radical Left of the 1960s. Too much zeal, that had been the sin of his people, the President himself suggested in one of his Watergate speeches in the

* *Commentary*, January 1974, pp. 19–25. Reprinted by permission of Joanne Bickel, Copyright holder.

spring; it was a sin and inexcusable, but also venial. Like the zealots of the Left, these people had put their cause above the law. They had been led into their error by the toleration that much liberal opinion had shown for the zealotry of the Left, for draft-dodgers and demonstrators of all sorts. The lesson to be drawn was that the law is sacred, rising above all causes, and no violation of it is excusable, none. A rededication to law and order on all sides, by all factions, was called for. The President indeed had been long calling for it. Watergate, we were left to infer, was actually a vindication of the President's long-held position, and a reproach to that large body of liberal opinion which had tolerated lawlessness, and ended by infecting even the righteous with it. . . .

It is not remarkable that self-righteousness and ideological fixation should be wedded to authoritarian attitudes, and that the temptation to abuse power should arise. What is interesting, what makes the point of contact a significant starting point for inquiry, what is interesting even about the vulgar—because wholly indiscriminate—attempt to turn Watergate into a reproach to liberal opinion, is that Watergate is evidence of a weakened capacity of our legal order to serve as a self-executing safeguard against this sort of abuse of power. The checks and balances of the government, the contrivance, in the words of the 51st *Federalist*, of "the interior structure of the government," so that "its several constituent parts may, by their mutual relations, be the means of keeping each other in their proper places"—this contrivance is working reasonably well. The inner structure was meant to insure accountability, and it is doing so. But it is accountability by crisis, accountability by trauma, accountability tending to shade into retribution. One would have expected that the legal order would have operated to prevent what we now know to have occurred. It is a first line of defense that has generally held: not always against plain theft, but effectively enough against self-righteous abuse of executive power in the service of ideological or moral ends. It has held in the past in this respect, making it unnecessary to reach the battlements and entrenchments of the constitutional checks and balances. It did not hold this time. . . .

In order to identify those aspects of recent history which I think came to a point of contact with Watergate, I must draw some distinctions concerning the position of conscientious objection and of civil disobedience in our legal order, as I see it. Our law has traditionally recognized a certain autonomy of conscience, and has therefore allowed certain conscientious objections, particularly to war, although not to war alone, as became happily evident when the Supreme Court in 1972 upheld the constitutional right of the Amish not to submit their young to organized education past the eighth grade. . . .

Much depends on the kind of law that is in question, the demands it makes of the individual, the foundation it has in shared values, and the kind of disobedience to it and its source. Frequently, however, the unlawfulness of disobedience to law on sincerely held grounds of conscience is not taken as conclusive against the legitimacy of disobedience. We often consider, rather, that disobedience raises a question about the law at which it is directed, a question not only about its effectiveness—that is obvious—but about its rightness, or at least its utility.

In what I just said I have blurred a distinction, useful for many purposes, between conscientious objection and civil disobedience. Conscientious objection, as has been pointed out by many writers, among them notably Hannah Arendt and Ernest van den Haag, demands nothing more than exemption from a legal obligation. No further or broader challenge to a law inheres in conscientious objection. But as Hannah Arendt has written and as I have just implied, "conscientious objection can become politically significant when a number of consciences happen to coincide and the conscientious objectors decide to enter the marketplace and make their voices heard in public." There is then necessarily implicit a challenge to the law objected to, or at least the legal order perceives such a widespread manifestation of conscientious objection as a challenge to the law, and the objectors are assimilated to the ranks of civil disobedients. . . .

A general definition of civil disobedience, applicable to our legal order, would be the following: Civil disobedience is the act of disobeying formally binding general law on grounds of moral or political principle without challenging the validity of the law; or the incidental disobedience of general law which is itself neither challenged as invalid nor disapproved of in the course of agitating for change in public policies, actions or social conditions which are regarded as bad on grounds of moral or political principle—all in circumstances where the legal order makes no allowance for the disobedience. This last qualification has to be added because the First Amendment is construed as making some allowance for the sort of incidental disobedience referred to in the second half of the definition.

In purpose if not in effect, civil disobedience differs greatly from conscientious objection. The effect of the coincidence of multiple consciences objecting to a law and the effect of civil disobedience may be the same. But conscientious objection is a withdrawal. Civil disobedience is ineluctably an attempt to coerce the legal order, an exercise of power in the sense in which Burke defined it: "Liberty, when men act in bodies, is *power*." And it is not easy to make room for it, although I shall argue that our legal order does so. Thus not only the Hobbesian but the contractarian view of the nature and foundation of society can tolerate no civil disobedience at all. The contractarian view legitimates government as a compact among citizens, embodying the agreement of each to abide the judgment of all. The ends of government are substantially predetermined in the contractarian view, in that they are limited by timeless principles, the rights of man. Government is allowed some margin of error, but the premise is that it will normally act only in plausible pursuit of predetermined ends. If it should not, says Locke, the remedy is revolution, and there is a right to use force against the government. Short of the right of revolution, there is an absolute duty to obey. Rousseau held that the people, expressing themselves through universal suffrage, give voice to the general will, although he allowed that they might also not. The general will is the highest good, and when the people by majority vote give it voice, the individual owes absolute obedience, even unto death. If at times a minority has hold of the true general will it follows that absolute obedience is equally owed to it. This in fact, said Rousseau, only forces the individual to be free.

The latest contribution to contractarian theory, by Professor John Rawls, in his *A Theory of Justice*, is somewhat curious. It defines the general will—called justice as fairness—in more detail than Rousseau, and commits government to its effectuation. Like Rousseau, it then insists on popular sovereignty, modified only by some power in the judges to keep government within the limits dictated by the general will. And it posits a duty to obey. But it makes allowance, one may think inconsistently, for civil disobedience, defined as above, with the proviso that it be public and willing to accept punishment. Civil disobedience is allowed because, it turns out, justice as fairness—the general will—is not always readily ascertainable, the majority and the judges may be wrong, or less right than a protesting minority, and civil disobedience can play its role in helping the entire society decide what is right. In that event, it would seem, there is less to the prior detailed definition of justice as fairness than met the eye.

In the actual American legal order, ends are less permanently predetermined than by contractarian theory, faith in majoritarianism is less enthusiastic than Rousseau's, readiness to have recourse to revolution is not as great as Locke's, and there is little willingness to accept the righteous dictates of a minority possessed of the true general will. What is above all important is consent—not a presumed theoretical consent, but a continuous actual one, born of continual responsiveness. There is popular sovereignty, and there are votes in which majorities or pluralities prevail, but that is not nearly all. Majorities are in large part fictions. They exist only on election day and they can be registered on very few issues. To be responsive and to enjoy consent, government must register numerous expressions of need and interest by numerous groups, and it must register relative intensities of need and interest. Neither the vote nor speech—the latter, after all, an elite exercise—sufficiently differentiates needs and interests, or expresses intensity. Civil disobedience can often effectively do so. Hence it is that civil disobedience has accompanied so many of the most fruitful reform movements in American history. Hence it is that its legitimacy must be recognized.

But there must be limits, both to conscientious objection and to civil disobedience, limits to be stated not as positive law imposed by the enforcement machinery of the legal order, but as a moral obligation, a duty to obey. For use of the enforcement machinery of the legal order denotes the point at which it has broken down. The test of a legal order is its self-executing capacity, its moral authority. In an extraordinarily sustained experience of civil disobedience and conscientious objection on the part of at least three distinct, sizable groups in the society over a period of some fifteen years, which perhaps no other society could have endured without a change of regime—in this sustained experience, I shall suggest, the limits were often transgressed. The experience started with white Southerners in the mid-50s; it was followed and overlapped by the civil-rights movement; and it ended with and was overlapped by the white-middle-class movement against the war, which bade fair for a while to take permanent shape as a movement addressing numerous other issues as well, from ecology up, down, and sideways to gay liberation.

The limits, as I say, were transgressed, and in some measure, I am willing to suggest, Watergate is a replica of the transgressions. . . .

. . . It is because on most issues we command no definite answers grounded in solid and generally shared values that we value an open, responsive, varied, and continual process of law-formation and provide numerous stages of decision-making, most of them provisional, and numerous opportunities for revision and resistance, including civil disobedience. But not only do the outcomes of the law-formation process, however provisional, count for something; what is more important, in the middle distance, and if also provisionally then over a much longer term, so that for a time they have a relatively enduring aspect, we do as a legal order hold some values, some principles, by which we judge the process and even some of its outcomes. Unless these are defended against coercive political action, there is no legal order, or at any rate, there is not this one. Therefore, the use of civil disobedience, not to redress grievances on the assumption of the continued operation of the system and by plausible appeal to its own principles, but against it, ought not be tolerated. Civil disobedience is one thing, revolutionary activity quite another, and the difference between them is told not only by their manner, but also by their objectives.

The distinction is rigorously drawn by Mr. Rawls in his *A Theory of Justice*, to which I referred earlier. The distinction was not drawn with anything like Mr. Rawls's rigor in the 60s. Much of the disobedience of the late 60s was aimed not at the government of the day, but at the system, and it opposed the system, not as flawed and perfectible, but as evil and abominable. The rhetoric was loud and it was reckless and vicious. It abandoned all pretense of allegiance, it acknowledged no restraint and no bounds. Yet it was often tolerated and even echoed by seemingly responsible opinion in the press, in the universities, and among political leaders. Cries of repression and of fascism, for example, were raised almost as soon as Mr. Nixon took office, and they were irresponsible and unfounded at the time, no matter how plausible they may now seem in retrospect. At the time, they were bound to have an effect on administration morale. Men who are loudly charged with repression before they have done anything to substantiate the charge are apt to proceed to substantiate it.

In a larger sense, toleration of this rhetoric and of disobedience with such aims undermined the moral authority of the liberal tradition in this country, which as Louis Hartz pointed out years ago is at once also the American conservative tradition, or at least the tradition that conserves the liberal American legal and political order. Hartz quoted the distinguished insight of Gunnar Myrdal, as he called it: "America is . . . conservative. . . . But the principles conserved are liberal and some, indeed, are radical.". . . It has historically been successful in coopting all but the revolutionary Left, moving far enough toward it to draw its sympathizers and outriders, but generally not so far as to be itself coopted rather than coopting. To move too far is to lose moral authority, and that rather than numbers is the source of the liberal ascendancy in American politics, which safeguards the norms of the American legal order against the lawlessness and ultimate authoritarianism of radical movements. Liberalism embraced too much of the Left in the 40s, and the result was the triumph for a moment of the radicalism of Joseph R. McCarthy. It embraced inexcusably much in the late 60s. In this sense Watergate is to American liberalism as McCarthyism was.

Still another necessary limit of civil disobedience was transgressed. Like law itself, civil disobedience is habit-forming, and the habit it forms is destructive of the legal order. Disobedience, even if legitimate in every other way, must not be allowed to become epidemic. Individuals are under a duty to ration themselves, to assess occasions in terms of their relative as well as absolute importance. For disobedience is attended by the overhanging threat of anarchy. We did not ration ourselves, and those in authority in the universities in the late 60s imposed no rationing. Coming as the third wave of massive disobedience movements in fifteen years, the demonstrations of the late 60s including the most peaceable and legitimate ones of all, carried the clear and present danger of anarchy. And their objectives were of course not restricted to stopping the war. They went on to ecology and to numberless other social and economic objectives. . . .

The legal order, after all, is an accommodation. It cannot sustain the continuous assault of moral imperatives, not even the moral imperative of "law-and-order," which as a moral imperative has only a verbal resemblance to the ends of the legal order. No legal order can sustain such a bombardment, and the less so a federal constitutional order of separated and diffused powers. It is the premise of our legal order that its own complicated arrangements, although subject to evolutionary change, are more important than any momentary objective. This premise must give way at times, of course, to accommodate inevitable change. And change which is significant, as Justice Brandeis once wrote, manifests itself more "in intellectual and moral conceptions than in material things." But our legal order cannot endure too rapid a pace of change in moral conceptions, and its fundamental premise is that its own stability is itself a high moral value, in most circumstances the highest. The legal order must be given time to absorb change, to accommodate it to itself as well as itself to it. If the pace is forced, there can be no law.

The assault upon the legal order by moral imperatives wasn't only or perhaps even the most effectively an assault from the outside. It came as well from within, in the Supreme Court headed for fifteen years by Earl Warren. The judicial hallmark of Chief Justice Warren was that when some lawyer would be standing before him arguing his side of a case on the basis of some legal doctrine or other, or making a procedural point, or contending that the Constitution allocated competence over a given issue to another branch of government than the Supreme Court or to the states rather than to the federal government, the Chief Justice would shake him off saying, "Yes, yes, yes, but is it [whatever the case exemplified about law or about the society] is it *right*? Is it *good*?" More than once, and in some of its most important actions, the Warren Court got over doctrinal difficulties or issues of the allocation of competences among various institutions by asking what it viewed as a decisive practical question: If the Court did not take a certain action which was *right* and *good*, would other institutions do so, given political realities? The Warren Court took the greatest pride in cutting through legal technicalities, in piercing through procedure to substance. But legal technicalities are the stuff of law, and piercing through a particular substance to get to procedures suitable to many substances is in fact what the task of law most often is.

From within and from without, then, the legal order was bombarded by moral imperatives, and was reduced to submission time and again. The derogators of procedure and of technicalities, and other anti-institutional forces, rode high, on the bench as well as off. These were the armies of conscience and of ideology. If it is parodoxical that they were also the armies of a new populism, it is not a paradox to wonder at, for it has occurred often before, not least of all in Rousseau, who may be counted the patron philosopher of the time. The paradox, of course, is that the people whom the populist exalts may well, will frequently, not vote for the results that conscience and ideology dictate. But then one can always hope, or identify the general will with the people despite their votes, and let the Supreme Court bespeak the people's general will when the vote comes out wrong.

It has been a time of populism to the Left and populism to the Right, strongly encouraged by the Supreme Court. There was a powerful strain of populism in the rhetoric by which the Court supported its one-man, one-vote doctrine, and after promulgating it the Court strove mightily to strike down all barriers, not only the poll tax, but duration of residence, all manner of special qualifications, and even in some measure, age, to the enlargement and true universalization of the franchise. In this the Court led successfully. It became irresistible dogma that no qualification for voting made any sense. It didn't matter that you were a transient—the election is a snapshot, and wherever it catches you, you vote with no questions asked. No connection to place is relevant, there is no room for balancing interests and places, no need to structure institutions so that they might rest on different electoral foundations and in the aggregate be better able to generate consent. Every impediment, every distortion, including the electoral college, must go. All that matters is the people, told by the head.

Here the connection with attitudes that at least contributed to Watergate is direct. It was utterly inevitable that such a populist fixation should tend toward the concentration of power in that single institution which has the most immediate link to the largest constituency. Naturally the consequence was a Gaullist Presidency, making war, making peace, spending, saving, being secret, being open, doing what is necessary, and needing no excuse for aggregating power to itself beside the excuse that it could do more effectively what other institutions, particularly Congress, did not do very rapidly or very well, or under particular political circumstances would not do at all. This was a leaf from the Warren Court's book, but the Presidency could undertake to act anti-institutionally in this fashion with more justification because, unlike the Court, it could claim not only a constituency, but the largest one. This Presidency acknowledged accountability only at quadrennial plebiscites, but not to other, less plebiscitary institutions, and certainly not to irresponsible private ones, or to something called "public opinion," which is led and formed in mysterious ways, rather than being told by the head.

The accumulation of power in the Presidency did not begin with Richard M. Nixon, of course, but it reached heights made possible by the populism of the day. There was a time there, soon after the election of 1972, when Mr. Nixon gave the impression that he thought the American political process had taken place, so to speak, that it was over for a while, and that he could simply rule. We know again now that an election is the beginning as well as the culmination of a political process, and that the President, separate, independent, and critically important as he is, is part of the process, not its ruler. We were being led to forget, however, and had it not been for Watergate, conceivably we might have forgotten.

The Presidency of inherent powers, futurism, populism, and certainly moral urgency—these have too often been the vestments of liberalism in this century, though worn for the most part with a certain modesty. In the 60s, the liberals, or large segments of them, consented to share these vestments, all but the first, with the radical Left, which adding several dashes of outrageous color, wore them immodestly. Diffusion of power, pragmatism, the relativism of values, gradualism, institutionalism, process, procedure, legality, technicalities—these were allowed to become the cloak of conservatism, indeed of reaction, and were not wanted on the voyage. Well, this cloak was not wanted in the White House either, we have learned. I don't know when Mr. Nixon caught the liberals bathing, but he did walk off with their clothes, and stood forth wearing the plebiscitary Presidency, his own futurism, and his own moral imperatives. We are all liberals, we are all conservatives, Mr. Nixon might have said, as for Jefferson we were all Republicans and all Federalists in 1800.

Watergate is the latest assault, the only one which was at once vicious and powerful, although other powerful ones were damaging, albeit not vicious—the latest assault in an age of assaultive politics. We cannot survive a politics of moral attack. I don't know how near a thing Watergate was, but perhaps it will be said that it was too near. We must resume the politics of what Burke called the "computing principle: adding, subtracting, multiplying, and dividing." The denominations to be computed are very often moral, to be sure. But few if any are absolute, few if any imperative. And the highest morality almost always is the morality of process, what Professor Paul Freund, speaking of Justice Brandeis's approach to issues, called "morality of mind."

Bibliographic Essay

The study of law in American history is generally conceded to be an area rich in untapped resources and ready for investigation by historians. Although legal history has gained considerable prominence over the last two decades, it remains a subject divided from the mainstream of historical study. This situation stems, in part, from the fact that historians not trained in the law are reluctant to investigate a subject suffused with technicalities and nuances that lawyers claim only the initiated can comprehend. There is no doubt that without some legal education the historical investigation of the law is difficult. But it is not impossible. Historians need not be lawyers to write about the law, in the same way that they need not be bankers to write about finance, or politicians to write about politics. The historian is a generalist, who draws on his or her imagination to re-create events and experiences. This role is no less the case when the personalities involved are lawyers and the events legal. Moreover, the historian brings to his or her reading of legal materials (e.g., cases; statutes) an understanding of the social context—an invaluable background for interpretation.

The effort here has been to relate law and history from a social and cultural standpoint. The process by which this has been done is reflected in the following bibliographic essay. Although by no means exhaustive, it is a fair statement of the sources that helped shape my judgment regarding the interaction of law and history in twentieth-century America. The essay is arranged topically to correspond with the chronology of the text.

1. The Nineteenth-Century Lawyer

For insights into the lawyer as participant in public and private affairs, and the growing difficulty some lawyers encountered in filling this role during the mid-nineteenth century, see R. Kent Newmyer, "Daniel Webster as Tocqueville's Lawyer: The *Dartmouth College* Case Again," *American Journal of Legal History*, 12 (January 1967), 127; Robert T. Swaine, *The Cravath Firm and Its Predecessors, vol. 1* (New York, 1946); and Charles Warren, *A History of the American Bar* (Boston, 1911). Another figure who encountered the problem was William Seward. Frederick Bancroft's biography *The Life of William Henry Seward* (New York, 1900) discusses this issue. The contrast to Webster was Samual Carter Tate Dodd, Rockefeller's lawyer, who bragged that he did his best to stay clear of politics. See *Memoirs of S. C. T. Dodd: Written for his Children and Friends, 1837–1907* (New York, 1907). For a discussion of the decline of the late-nineteenth-century lawyer from an idealized past of public service, see John R. Dos Passos, *The American Lawyer: As He Was—As He Is—As He Can Be* (New York, 1907).

2. Conservative Jurisprudence

The relationship between Social Darwinism and laissez-faire jurisprudence is examined in two valuable secondary accounts: Arnold Paul, *Conservative Crisis and the Rule of Law: Attitudes of Bar and Bench, 1887–1895* (Ithaca, N.Y., 1960), and Robert McCloskey, *American Conservatism in the Age of Enterprise 1865–1910* (New York, 1964). Primary literature on this subject includes William Guthrie, *Lectures on the Fourteenth Article of Amendment to the Constitution of the United States* (Boston, 1898), and John W. Burgess, "Private Corporations from the Point of View of Political Science," *Political Science Quarterly*, 13 (June 1898), 211. The reader should also consult such prominent Supreme Court decisions as *Lochner v. New York*, 198 U.S. 45 (1905), and *Coppage v. Kansas*, 236 U.S. 1 (1915).

3. Progressivism and the Legal Profession

Herbert Croly's discussion of the legal profession in *The Promise of American Life* (New York, 1909) is a good starting point for understanding the Progressives' complaint about legal services. Equally important are speeches Woodrow Wilson made to bar groups before becoming President. Many of these can be found in *The Public Papers of Woodrow Wilson: College and State*, 2 vols., ed. Ray Stannard Baker and William E. Dodd (New York, 1925). Theodore Roosevelt's attitudes toward the law and the legal profession are found in his *The New Nationalism* (New York, 1910).

For information on the profession's reaction to these attacks, consult the writings of such bar leaders as Elihu Root. Richard Leopold has a chapter on Root's efforts to upgrade professional ethics, in *Elihu Root and the Conservative Tradition* (Boston, 1953). See also Elihu Root, *Addresses on Government and Citizenship* (Cambridge, Mass., 1916), and Root, "The Layman's Criticism of the Lawyer," *The Green Bag*, 24 (November 1914), 471. See also William H. Taft, *Popular Government: Its Essence, Its Permanence and Its Perils* (New Haven, 1913), and Taft, *Ethics in Service* (New Haven, 1915), for a discussion of the importance of ethics to professional service.

Harlan Fiske Stone's 1915 Hewitt Lectures, published as *Law and Its Administration* (New York, 1924) is an indispensable guide to the profession's efforts to set standards for the administration of justice. Equally important is Julius Henry Cohen, *The Law: Business or Profession?* rev. ed. (New York, 1924). The ABA Canons of Ethics are available in *Reports of the American Bar Association*, 33 (1908), 575.

Other sources on this topic include Everett Abbott, *Justice and the Modern Law* (New York, 1913); Henry Wynans Jessup, *The Professional Ideals of the Lawyer: A Study of Legal Ethics* (New York, 1925), particularly the introduction by Charles Boston; Charles Boston, *Addresses and Writings*, Book II, 1912–1916, New York County Lawyers' Association Collection; Reginald Heber Smith, *Justice for the Poor*, 3rd ed. (New York, 1924); Henry W. Taft, *Occasional Papers and Addresses of an American Lawyer* (New York, 1920); and Taft, *Law Reform: Papers and Addresses by a Practicing Lawyer* (New York, 1926). Finally, "Law and Justice," *Proceedings of the Academy of Political Science*, ed. Herman Oliphant and Parker Thomas Moon (New York, 1923), is a source for information on delays in the law, legal procedure, and the American Law Institute's restatement of the law.

Richard Hofstadter, *Age of Reform* (New York, 1956), pp. 156–164, has a pertinent discussion about the legal profession and the issue of status. Other books dealing generally with the legal profession include J. Willard Hurst, *The Growth of American Law: The Lawmakers* (Boston, 1950); Jerold Auerbach, *Unequal Justice: Lawyers and Social Change in Modern America* (New York, 1976); and Harold J. Laski, *The American Democracy* (New York, 1948), pp. 571–591.

4. Law and Business

The testimony on the formation of the Federal Trade Commission was helpful in understanding the corporate bar's response to government regulation of business. See U.S., Congress, Senate, Committee on Interstate Commerce, *Pursuant to S. Res. 98: A Resolution . . . to Investigate and Report Desirable Changes in the Laws Regulating and Controlling Corporations . . . in Interstate Commerce, Vol. I,* 62nd Congress, 2d sess., 1911–12, page 705. Excerpts from this testimony are available in Samuel Orth (ed.), *Readings on the Relation of Government to Property and Industry* (New York, 1915). This book is also useful because it is a contemporary collection of articles and materials dealing with the relationship between law, business, and the emerging regulatory process. Collections of this kind are generally helpful for understanding the issues of this period. For example, see Walton Hamilton (ed.), *Current Economic Problems: A Series of Readings in the Control of Industrial Development* (Chicago, 1914).

For a discussion of William Jennings Bryan's position on the regulation of trusts, see Paul Glad, "Bryan and the Progressives," in *William Jennings Bryan: A Profile*, ed. Paul Glad (New York, 1968). Other helpful sources on this topic are Victor Morawetz, "The Sherman Antitrust Act," *Proceedings of the American Economic Association*, Third Series, 11 (April 1910), 321; Louis Brandeis, *Business—A Profession* (Boston, 1914), a classic Progressive statement of the lawyer's new social opportunities; and Francis Lynde Stetson, "Government and the Corporations, "*Atlantic Monthly*, July 1912, p. 26; and Stetson, "Lawyer's Livelihood," presidential address before the New York State Bar Association, Buffalo, New York, January 28, 1909.

The program of legal reform urged by Samuel Untermyer, a foe of monopoly, can be gleaned in two speeches, "A Legislative Program to Restore Business Freedom and Confidence," address before the Illinois Manufacturers Association, Chicago, January 4, 1914, and "Some Needed Legislative Reform in Corporate Management," address before the New York County Lawyers Association, New York, January 5, 1911. Also important reading is *Northern Securities Company v. United States*, 193 U.S. 197 (1904), and *Standard Oil Company of New Jersey v. United States*, 221 U.S. 1 (1911).

5. Social Regulation and the Law

There is a wealth of information on the issue of economic regulation and social welfare legislation. The following articles and books proved to be particularly informative: Robert Lee Hale, "Rate Regulation and the Revision of the Property Concept," *Columbia Law Review*, 22 (March 1922), 209; James Bonbright, "Value of the Property as the Basis of Rate Regulation," *Journal of Land and Public Utility Economics*, 2 (July 1926), 276; Leonard Crouch, "Judicial Tendencies of the Court of Appeals During the Encumbency of Chief Judge Hiscock," *Cornell Law Quarterly*, 12 (February 1927), 137; Thomas Reed Powell, "Collective Bargaining Before the Supreme Court," *Political Science Quarterly*, 33 (September 1918), 396; Walton Hamilton, "The Age of Justices," *New Republic*, October 11, 1922, p. 168; Cuthbert Pound, "The Judicial Power," *Harvard Law Review*, 35 (May 1922), 787; Pound, "The Relation of the Practicing Lawyer to the Efficient Administration of Justice," *Cornell Law Quarterly*, 9 (April 1924), 235; Pound, "Constitutional Aspects of Administrative Law," in *Growth of American Administrative Law*, ed. Ernst Freund (St. Louis, 1923), p. 107; Rexford Tugwell, *Economic Basis of Public Interest* (New York, 1968), a reprint of the 1922 edition with a new and pertinent introduction by the author; Felix Frankfurter, "Hours of Labor and Realism in Constitutional Law," *Harvard Law Review*, 29 (February 1916), 351; and "Economics, Philosophy and Morals v. The Court of Appeals," *Survey*, April 8, 1911, p. 77, a symposium of articles and commentary on the issue of legislating social welfare, with emphasis on the famous New York Court of Appeals decision in *Ives v. South Buffalo Railway Company* (1911) declaring unconstitutional a 1910 state compulsory workman's compensation act.

On the subject of the people's attorney, I suggest beginning with Alpheus T. Mason's biography of Louis Brandeis: *Louis Brandeis: A Free Man's Life* (New York, 1946). In addition, I recommend Felix Frankfurter (ed.), *Mr. Justice Brandeis* (New Haven, 1932), an excellent collection of essays on Brandeis. The book has been reprinted. See also *Letters of Louis D. Brandeis, vol. 2: 1907–1912: People's Attorney*, ed. Melvin Urofsky and David Levy (Albany, N.Y., 1972). A. L. Todd, *Justice on Trial: The Case of Louis D. Brandeis* (New York, 1964) is a thorough and fascinating account of the battle waged over Brandeis's nomination to the Supreme Court. Dean Acheson, *Morning and Noon* (Boston, 1965), has a good chapter on Brandeis. Acheson was a clerk to the justice. Paul Freund discusses Brandeis's contribution, in *The Supreme Court of the United States: Its Business, Purposes, and Performance* (Cleveland, 1961). Finally, Alexander Bickel, *The Unpublished Opinions of Mr. Justice Brandeis: The Supreme Court at Work* (Cambridge, Mass., 1957), is valuable for the author's insights into Brandeis's legal ideology. Those interested in the sociological brief should read *Muller v. Oregon*, 208 U.S. 412 (1908).

On the issue of the protocol, and particularly the question of lawyer involvement, see John Dyche, *Bolshevism in American Labor Unions* (New York, 1926); Julius Henry Cohen, *Law and Order in Industry* (New York, 1916); and Cohen, *An American Labor Policy* (New York, 1919). The issue is met head on in Dyche's and Cohen's testimony before the Commission on Industrial Relations. See vol. 19, especially pp. 1039–1045, and vol. 20, especially pp. 577–578 (Sen. Doc. 415, 64th Cong., 1st sess., 1915). On the question of substantive due process, read *German Alliance Company v. Lewis*, 233 U.S. 389 (1914); *Pennsylvania Coal Company v. Mahon*, 260 U.S. 393 (1922); *People ex. rel. Durham Realty Corporation v. La Fetra*, 230 N.Y. 429 (1921); *Marcus Brown Holding Company v. Feldman*, 256 U.S. 170 (1921); *Tyson and Brother v. Banton*, 273 U.S. 418 (1927); and *Nebbia v. New York*, 291 U.S. 502 (1934). Consult *MacPherson v. Buick Motor Company*, 111 N.E. 1050 (1916) for a discussion of product liability.

6. Legal Education, Sociological Jurisprudence, and the Realists

To understand sociological jurisprudence one should start with the following works by Roscoe Pound: *The Spirit of the Common Law* (Francetown, N.H., 1921); *Interpretations of Legal History* (New York, 1923); "The Need of a Sociological Jurisprudence," *Reports of the American Bar Association*, 32 (1907), 911; "Legislation as a Social Function," *Papers and Proceedings American Sociological Society*, 7 (1913), 148; and "The Scope and Purpose of Sociological Jurisprudence, III," *Harvard Law Review*, 35 (April 1912), 489.

The material by and about Oliver Wendell Holmes is indispensable.

Consult Holmes, *Collected Legal Papers* (New York, 1920); Max Lerner, *The Mind and Faith of Justice Holmes* (Boston, 1943); and Felix Frankfurter, *Mr. Justice Holmes and the Supreme Court*, 2d. ed. (Cambridge, Mass., 1961).

On law school education and the emerging administrative state, see Felix Frankfurter, "The Law and the Law Schools," *American Bar Association Journal*, 1 (1915), 537, and Frankfurter, "The Law School and the Public Service," *Harvard Alumni Bulletin*, 17 (November 11, 1914), 115.

For information on legislative drafting and curriculum reform experiments at Columbia Law School, see Julius Goebel, Jr. (ed.), *A History of The School of Law, Columbia University* (New York, 1955). Young B. Smith, "Education and Research," *New York State Bar Association Bulletin*, 2 (April 1930), 189, is a good statement of the relationship between education and research. Herman Oliphant, "On the College Frontier: The New Legal Education," *Nation*, November 5, 1930, p. 493, is also valuable for understanding the curriculum changes proposed by the Columbia Law School realists. See also Gerald Fetner, "The Law Teacher as Legal Reformer: 1900–1945," *Journal of Legal Education*, 28 (1977), 508.

Fred Rodell, *Woe Unto You, Lawyers!* (New York, 1939), is an iconoclastic yet valuable source for understanding this reform attempt. See also Edward Robinson, *Law and the Lawyers* (New York, 1937). A valuable secondary work on this subject is Eugene Rostow, "The Realist Tradition in American Law," in *Paths of American Thought*, ed. Arthur M. Schlesinger, Jr., and Morton White (Boston, 1963).

Several articles by Harlan Fiske Stone provide insight into the conservative nature of legal education and educators. See "The Function of the American University Law School," *Reports of the American Bar Association*, 36 (1911), 768; "Future of Legal Education," *American Bar Association Journal*, 10 (April 1924), 233; "Importance of Actual Experience at the Bar as a Preparation for Law Teaching," *Reports of the American Bar Association*, 37 (1912), 747; "The Lawyer and His Neighbors," *Cornell Law Quarterly*, 4 (June 1919), 175; "The Public Influence of the Bar," *Harvard Law Review*, 48 (November 1934), 1; and, "University Influence," *Columbia Law Quarterly*, 20 (October 1918), 330. Alpheus T. Mason's comprehensive biography, *Harlan Fiske Stone: Pillar of the Law* (New York, 1956), should also be looked at as a basic reference for all legal reform activities during the first half of the century.

Cuthbert Pound, a little-known but nonetheless influential jurist and educator, spoke out on legal education in the following articles: "The Law School Curriculum as Seen by the Bench and Bar," *Cornell Law Quarterly*, 8 (February 1923), 117; "Legal Education and the Education of the Lawyer," *New York State Bar Association Bulletin*, 2 (April 1930), 175; and "A Modern University Law School," *New York State Bar Association Bulletin*, 4 (November 1932), 434.

William Howard Taft, "Legal Education and the University Law School," *Minnesota Law Review*, 10 (May 1926), 554, reveals how this important conservative jurist viewed legal education. Thomas Reed Powell, another neglected but influential legal figure, has two excellent articles, "Law as a Cultural Study," *Reports of the American Bar Association*, 42 (1917), 572, and "Law as a University Study," *Columbia University Quarterly*, 19 (March 1917), 106. Learned Hand, "Have the Bench and Bar Anything to Contribute to the Teaching of Law?" *Michigan Law Review*, 24 (March 1926), 446, examines the growing rapprochement between educators and practitioners in the early twenties.

The Jerome Frank papers at Yale University were helpful in understanding the objective of "legal realists" such as Frank. I found several pieces of correspondence between Frank and Frankfurter relevant to understanding this issue. I also found the relationship between the two men interesting. From their correspondence I sensed that Frank was uncertain about whether legal realism would be accepted. It appeared that he very much wanted Frankfurter's approval, which was not forthcoming. For critiques of legal realism see William O. Douglas, *Democracy and Finance* (New Haven, 1940), and Robert Hutchins, "The Autobiography of an Ex-Law Student," in *No Friendly Voice* (Chicago, 1936), p. 41.

Two books by Benjamin Cardozo, *The Growth of Law* (New Haven, 1924), and *The Paradoxes of Legal Science* (New York, 1928), are gems of legal philosophy. And three works by Samuel Williston, *Life and Law* (Boston, 1941); "The Necessity of Idealism in Teaching Law," *Reports of the American Bar Association*, 33 (1908), 780; and "The Judge and the Professor," *Reports of the American Bar Association*, 58 (1933), 607, are important sources for understanding trends in legal philosophy and education. Morris Cohen, *Law and Social Order* (New York, 1933), is also a valuable book on many contemporary issues of law, philosophy, and education.

7. The Cooperative Movement: In Business, Government, and the Professions

John M. Clark, *Social Control of Business* (Chicago, 1926), should be read for an understanding of the relationship between law and economic development, and the growth of cooperation in business, government, and the professions. Charles E. Clark and William O. Douglas, "Law and Legal Institutions," in *Recent Social Trends in the United States* (New York, 1933), surveys a number of cooperative developments in the twenties. This article is also a valuable reference for understanding many legal developments during the first quarter of the century. I found Joseph Dorfman, *The Economic Mind in American Civilization, 1918–1933*, 2 vols. (New York, 1959), and Louis Hacker, *American Problems of Today: A History of the United States Since the World War* (New York, 1938), important general sources of information on law and social developments. Another helpful survey of developments in this area is Myron Watkins, *Public Regulation of Competitive Practices in Business Enterprise*, 3rd ed. (New York, 1940).

Those interested in pursuing the relationship between trade associations and the law may wish to begin with Benjamin Kirsh, *Trade Associations in Law and Business* (New York, 1938); Benjamin A. Javits, *Business and Public Interest: Trade Associations, The Anti-Trust Law and Industrial Planning* (New York, 1932); and Javits, *The Commonwealth of Industry: The Separation of Industry and the State* (New York, 1936). Julius Henry Cohen, "Ice," *Boston University Law Review*, 13 (January 1933), 1, is a passionate statement calling for revision of the antitrust laws. For cases, see *United States v. United States Steel Corporation*, 251 U.S. 417 (1920); *American Column and Lumber Company v. United States*, 257 U.S. 377 (1921); and *Maple Flooring Manufacturers Association v. United States*, 268 U.S. 563 (1925).

I would supplement these readings with Donald Richberg, *The Rainbow* (Garden City, N.Y., 1936), a personal account discussing the reasons for the failure of the NIRA and the ways in which industrial cooperation might still work. I thought the book was also valuable for highlighting the distinction between regulation by lawyers versus regulation by businessmen. In addition, see David Podell, "Essential Factors in Determining Constitutionality of Recovery Act," *American Bar Association Journal*, 20 (March 1934), 281; Homer S. Cummings, "Modern Tendencies and the Law," *Reports of the American Bar Association*, 58 (1933), 283; and "Proceedings," *Reports of the American Bar Association*, 58 (1933), 197.

Gerard Henderson's *Federal Trade Commission* (New Haven, 1924), the first of the Commonwealth Fund's studies in administrative law, reflects the author's hope that the FTC can become the model for a cooperative relationship between business and government. (The history of the Commonwealth Fund Legal Research Committee can be followed in the fund's annual reports.) A very good summary and discussion of the history and purpose of the FTC is contained in Brandeis's dissenting opinion in *Federal Trade Commission v. Gratz*, 253 U.S. 421 (1920).

A good introduction to the subject of "labor and the law" is a chapter (of the same name) in Irving Bernstein, *The Lean Years: A History of the American Worker, 1920–1933* (Boston, 1960). Felix Frankfurter and Nathan Greene, *The Labor Injunction* (New York, 1930), is important. I also found David Brody, *Labor in Crisis: The Steel Strike of 1919* (Philadelphia, 1965), a good source of information on the position of labor during and after World War I. Relevant cases are *Duplex Printing Press Company v. Deering*, 254 U.S. 443 (1921); *American Steel Foundries v. Tri-City Central Trades Council*, 257 U.S. 184 (1921); *Truax v. Corrigan*, 257 U.S. 312 (1921) and *Coronado Coal Company v. United Mine Workers of America*, 268 U.S. 295 (1925).

The emergence of government as a source of social engineering is portrayed elegantly in Felix Frankfurter, *The Public and Its Government* (New Haven, 1931). Frankfurter's discussion provides a glimpse of government administrative and cooperative trends during the twenties. Also valuable in this respect is Felix Frankfurter and James Landis, "The Compact Clause of the Constitution—A Study in Interstate Adjustments," *Yale Law Journal*, 34 (May 1925), 685. I also recommend Alfred Smith, *The Citizen and His Government* (New York, 1936).

For detailed information on the authority, one should consult the following articles by its legal architect, Julius Henry Cohen: "What Authority Has an Authority," address before the American Association of Port Authorities, Toronto, Canada, September 5, 1933; "The Port of New York Authority— The Evolution of the Authority Plan in Administrative Law," address before the New York University School of Law, March 13, 1940; and "New York Harbor Problem and Its Legal Aspects," *Cornell Law Quarterly*, 5 (May 1920), 373. Gerald Fetner, "Public Power and Professional Responsibility: Julius Henry Cohen and the Origins of the Public Authority," 21 *American Journal of Legal History* (January 1977), 15, examines the use of the authority concept in housing, port development, and hydroelectric power. A celebratory, but nevertheless valuable, statement about the Port of New York Authority is Archibald MacLeish, "Port of New York Authority," *Fortune*, September 1933, pp. 22–31, 118–119. Read *Green v. Frazier*, 253 U.S. 233 (1920), to glimpse the Court's attitude toward public ventures in private enterprise. My discussion of Robert Moses is based on Robert Caro, *The Power Broker: Robert Moses and the Fall of New York* (New York, 1974); on reviews of the book, particularly by William Greider in the *Washington Post*; and on Paul Goldberger's obituaries in the *New York Times*, July 30, 1981, p. 1, and August 2, 1981, p. 21.

Those interested in following the debate over bar integration should consult the issues of *Journal of the American Judicature Society*, 1–10 (1916–1926). The society was a leading proponent of bar incorporation. See also Julius Henry Cohen, "The National Call for the Organization of an All Inclusive Bar," *New York Law Review*, 4 (March 1926), 93, and Robert Jackson, "Compulsory Incorporation of the Bar from the Country Lawyer's Viewpoint," *New York Law Review*, 4 (August 1926), 316. Julius Henry Cohen, "Watchman, What of the Night?," address before the Cincinnati Bar Association, Cincinnati, January 17, 1928, is a strong statement in support of a more socially conscious bar. Another viewpoint on bar incorporation is expressed in William Guthrie, "The Proposed Compulsory Incorporation of the Bar, Part II," *New York Law Review*, 4 (June 1926), 233. A useful secondary account is G. W. Adams, "The Self-Governing Bar," *American Political Science Review*, June 1, 1932, 470. Louis Marshall's views against incorporation were gleaned from his correspondence with Samuel Seabury, president of the New York County Lawyers Association, October 21, 1926, in the Louis Marshall Papers, American Jewish Archives, Cincinnati, Ohio.

8. The Administrative Regulatory Process

For an understanding of the concept of commission regulation in its twentieth-century context, a starting point is A. A. Berle, Jr., "The Expansion of American Administrative Law," *Harvard Law Review*, 30 (March 1917), 430. I found William O. Douglas, *Democracy and Finance* (New Haven, 1940) an important source of information on the relationship between the administrative process and legal education. James Landis, *The Administrative Process* (New Haven, 1938), is also an important statement reflective of the broad, and sometimes euphoric, expectations of 1930s legal reformers. Charles Horsky, *Washington Lawyer*, (Boston, 1952), draws an illuminating portrait of changes taking place in the "Washington" legal community as a result of the creation of New Deal administrative power. Also of value in this connection are two articles by Felix Frankfurter, "The Young Men Go to Washington," *Fortune*, January 1936, p. 87; and "The Task of Administrative Law," *University of Pennsylvania Law Review*, 75 (1927) 614.

Some important New Deal cases include *Schechter Poultry Corp. v. United States*, 295 U.S. 495 (1935); *National Labor Relations Board v. Jones & Laughlin Steel Corporation*, 301 U.S. 1 (1937); *West Coast Hotel Company v. Parrish*, 300 U.S. 379 (1937); *United States v. Carolene Products Company*, 304 U.S. 144 (1938); *United States v. Darby*, 312 U.S. 100 (1941); *Wickard v. Filburn*, 317 U.S. 111 (1942); *Milk Wagon Drivers' Union v. Lake Valley Farm Products*, 311 U.S. 91 (1940), and *Milk Wagon Drivers Union of Chicago v. Meadowmoor Dairies*, 312 U.S. 287 (1941).

Walton Hamilton, "Antitrust in Action," in *Investigation of Concentration of Economic Power*, a study made for the Temporary National Economic Committee, 76th Cong., 3d Sess., Senate Committee Print, Monograph No. 16 (Washington, D.C., 1940), is an excellent portrait of the antitrust process, particularly the distinction between regulation by lawyers versus regulation by businessmen. Hamilton ultimately comes out in favor of commissions rather than courts. In *Politics of Industry* (New York, 1956) he pursues this theme further. Seymour Harris (ed.), *Saving American Capitalism* (New York, 1948), contains a lively series of articles on the subject of government, law, and the economy in the post–World War II era. John Morton Blum has a very good chapter on antitrust during World War II in *V Was For Victory: Politics and American Culture During World War II* (New York, 1976). Finally, read Joseph McGoldrick, *Building Regulation in New York City: A Study in Administrative Law and Procedure* (New York 1944), for an examination of the effect of administration on the average person.

The *Report of the Committee on Administrative Procedure*, Senate

Document No. 8, 77th Congress, 1st Session, 1941, is a sober discussion of weaknesses in the administrative process, with proposed modifications. This report has been reprinted in *Administrative Procedure in Government Agencies* (Charlottesville, Va., 1968). Portions of this book provide a very good explanation of the development and character of commission regulation. Consult Justice Jackson's opinion in *Wong Yang Sung v. McGrath*, 339 U.S. 33 (1949), for a discussion of events leading up to passage of the Administrative Procedures Act. Felix Frankfurter's opinion in *Radio Corporation of America v. United States*, 341 U.S. 412 (1951), is also a sensitive appreciation of the dilemma of regulation and the public interest.

Two articles are essential for those who wish to survey critical attitudes toward the administrative process: Louis Jaffe, "The Effective Limits of the Administrative Process: A Re-evaluation," *Harvard Law Review*, 67 (1954), 1123; and Louis B. Schwartz, "Legal Restriction of Competition in the Regulated Industries: An Abdication of Judicial Responsibility," *Harvard Law Review*, 67 (1954), 474.

Thurman Arnold's works are particularly rich in ideas about law and the economy, and the controversy over regulation of business by courts or commissions. See in particular *The Symbols of Government* (New Haven, 1935); *The Folklore of Capitalism* (New Haven, 1937); *The Bottlenecks of Business* (New York, 1940); *Democracy and Free Enterprise* (Norman, Okla., 1942); and *Fair Fights and Foul* (New York, 1965). *Symbols* and *Folklore* are also important statements of legal realism. In *Fair Fights*, Arnold also addresses the issue of the lawyer in government.

Wendell Berge, *Cartels: Challenge to a Free World* (Washington, D.C., 1944), discusses efforts to prosecute domestic and foreign cartels; Ernst Putthammer (ed.), *War and the Law* (Chicago, 1944), has several good articles on the effect of war on the economy and society; and Richard Hofstadter has a wonderful essay on the transition of antitrust from moral precept to faded passion in *The Paranoid Style in American Politics and Other Essays* (New York, 1965).

9. Individual Rights

While few books discuss the shift from breadbasket issues to individual freedoms during and after World War II, the following materials touch on this development: Walter Schaefer, *The Suspect and Society: Criminal Procedure and Converging Constitutional Doctrines* (Evanston, Ill., 1967); Walter Gellhorn, *Individual Freedom and Governmental Restraint* (Baton Rouge, La., 1956); Nathan Glazer, "A New Look in Social Welfare," *New Society*, No. 58, November 7, 1963, p. 6; Ernst Putthammer (ed.), *War and the Law* (Chicago, 1944); William O. Douglas, *Being an American* (New York, 1948); Max Lerner, *Public Journal: Marginal Notes on Wartime America* (New York, 1945); and James Reston, *Prelude to Victory* (New York, 1942).

A good collection examining changes in the law during this period is Monrad Paulson (ed.), *Legal Institutions Today and Tomorrow* (New York, 1959). Also consult *Conference on Freedom and the Law,* University of Chicago Law School, Conference Series No. 13 (May 7, 1953). The report contains articles by such prominent legal and economic architects as Thurman Arnold, John M. Clark, Benjamin Cardozo, Kenneth Davis, Aaron Director, Paul Freund, John Galbraith, and Arthur Vanderbilt, and deals with the question of freedom in the economic marketplace and in the marketplace of ideas.

For probing examinations of the judicial attitudes of Robert Jackson and postwar legal issues, see Louis Jaffe, "Mr. Justice Jackson," *Harvard Law Review,* 68 (April 1955), 965; and Paul Freund, "Individual and Commonwealth in the Thought of Mr. Justice Jackson," *Stanford Law Review,* 8 (December 1955), 9. Jackson's own writings are important resources on the nature of the Court. In this respect, one should read *The Struggle for Judicial Supremacy: A Study of a Crisis in American Power Politics* (New York: 1941); Jackson, *The Supreme Court in the American System of Government* (Cambridge, Mass., 1962); and "The Task of Maintaining Our Liberties: The Role of the Judiciary," *American Bar Association Journal,* 39 (November 1953), 963. Intra-Court conflict is discussed in Alan Westin, "Liberals and the Supreme Court," *Commentary,* July 1956, p. 23, and in Arthur Schlesinger, Jr., "The Supreme Court: 1947," *Fortune,* January 1947, p. 73.

Some pertinent cases are *Pierce v. Society of Sisters,* 268 U.S. 510 (1925); *Meyer v. Nebraska,* 262 U.S. 390 (1923); *Bartels v. State of Iowa,* 262 U.S. 404 (1923); *Gitlow v. New York,* 268 U.S. 652 (1925); *Palko v. Connecticut,* 302 U.S. 319 (1937); *Minersville School District v. Gobitis,* 310 U.S. 586 (1940); *West Virginia State Board of Education v. Barnette,* 319 U.S. 624 (1943); *Adamson v. California,* 332 U.S. 46 (1947); and *Kunz v. New York,* 340 U.S. 290 (1951).

Gerald Dunne, *Hugo Black and the Judicial Revolution* (New York, 1977), contains some good factual material and judgments but is difficult to read because of the author's unusual writing style. It has a discussion of public opinion following Black's *Griswold* dissent. See Hugo Black, *A Constitutional Faith* (New York, 1969), and also, for a contrasting viewpoint Arthur Goldberg, *Equal Justice: The Warren Era of the Supreme Court* (Evanston, Ill., 1971).

10. The Warren Court and the "New" Legal Activism

Secondary sources of particular value are Alexander Bickel, *The Supreme Court and the Idea of Progress* (New York, 1970), and Bickel, *Politics and the Warren Court* (New York, 1965). *Progress* is a brilliant analysis of why the Warren Court decisions were misguided and represented the wrong concept about progress. Archibald Cox, *The Role of the Supreme Court in American Government* (New York, 1976), is an excellent source. See also J.

Skelly Wright, "Professor Bickel, The Scholarly Tradition, and the Supreme Court," Harvard Law Review, 84 (February 1971), 793.

Particularly valuable are two articles by Anthony Lewis in *The New York Times Magazine*: "A Man Born to Act, Not to Muse," June 30, 1968, p. 9; and "A Talk with Warren On Crime, The Court, The Country," October 19, 1969, p. 34. Lewis's book on the Court, *Gideon's Trumpet*, is wonderful reading. Further conservative criticism can be found in Philip Kurland, "The Court Should Decide Less and Explain More," *New York Times Magazine*, June 9, 1968, p. 34. For an examination of Fortas's role on the Court, one should refer to the testimony before the Senate Judiciary Committee on his nomination to be chief justice. Also helpful is Fred Rodell, "The Complexities of Mr. Justice Fortas," *New York Times Magazine*, July 28, 1968, p. 12.

Other valuable insights into judicial activity during this period are contained in Carl McGowan, *The Organization of Judicial Power in the United States* (Evanston, Ill., 1969); Victor J. Stone (ed.), *Civil Liberties and Civil Rights* (Urbana, Ill., 1977); and Glenn Winters and Edward Schoenbaum (eds.), *American Courts and Justice* (Chicago, 1976). Frank M. Johnson, Jr., "Judicial Activism Is a Duty—Not an Intrusion," *Judges Journal*, 16 (Fall 1977), 5, examines the wisdom of judicial activism.

Some important cases to read are *Brown v. Board of Education of Topeka*, 347 U.S. 483 (1954) and the second *Brown* case, 349 U.S. 294 (1955); *Baker v. Carr*, 369 U.S. 186 (1962); *Gideon v. Wainwright*, 372 U.S. 335 (1963); *National Association for the Advancement of Colored People v. Button*, 371 U.S. 415 (1963); *Reynolds v. Sims*, 377 U.S. 533 (1964); and *Escobedo v. Illinois*, 378 U.S. 478 (1964). *Heart of Atlanta Motel, Inc. v. United States*, 379 U.S. 241 (1964), should be read for the insight it provides about the Civil Rights Act of 1964.

Norman Dorsen (ed.), *The Rights of Americans: What They Are—What They Should Be* (New York, 1970), is a good collection of articles on the "rights" revolution. Dorsen, *The Frontiers of Civil Liberties* (New York, 1968), is an important study of legal activism. Alan Westin's review of the book places in context the work of these new legal reformers. See *New York Times Book Review*, November 24, 1968.

National Conference on Law and Poverty: Conference Proceedings (Washington, D.C., 1965) examines the effort to link civil rights with economic opportunity. Another important source is *Prospect for America: The Rockefeller Panel Reports* (Garden City, N.Y., 1961). Charles Reich, *The Greening of America* (New York, 1970), is an angry statement about the failure of the legal system to create an equitable society. See also Reich, "Individual Rights and Social Welfare: The Emerging Legal Issues," *Yale Law Journal*, 74 (1965), 1245, where Reich argues that lawyers need to take a greater interest in social welfare, particularly with a view to examining critically the substantive and procedural rights of individual beneficiaries. Abigail Thernstrom, "The Odd Evolution of the Voting Rights Act," *Public*

Interest, No. 55, Spring 1979, 49, discusses the controversy over establishing rights in theory and in fact.

11. The Democratization of Legal Services

Elliott Evans Cheatham, *A Lawyer When Needed* (New York, 1963), is a frank call for reform in the provision of legal services. Archibald Cox, "The Lawyer's Public Responsibilites," address before the American Bar Association Section of Individual Rights and Responsibilites, Honolulu, Hawaii, August 14, 1974, is a probing examination of the need for lawyers to alter their traditional approach to the provision of legal services.

For a thoughtful discussion about the need for the bar to retain its self-regulatory prerogatives in the face of growing consumer regulation, see David R. Brink, "Who Will Regulate the Bar?" *American Bar Association Journal*, 61 (August 1975), 936. In contrast, see James R. Silkenat, "Lawyers' *Pro Bono* Duty," *New York Times*, February 6, 1979, p. A12. A good history of the legal services movement is Earl Johnson, Jr., *Justice and Reform: The Formative Years of the OEO Legal Services Program* (New York, 1974). (There is a vast amount of literature on this subject. The national office of the Legal Services Corporation was helpful in sharing library information with me.) Another important article is Edgar Cahn and Jean Cahn, "The War on Poverty: A Civilian Perspective," *Yale Law Journal*, 73 (1964), 1317. Two articles that discuss some of the financial problems of the legal services movement are Thurgood Marshall, "Financing Public Interest Law Practice: The Role of the Organized Bar," *American Bar Association Journal*, 61 (December 1975), 1487, and Sanford Jaffe, "Public Interest Practice—Five Years Later," *American Bar Association Journal*, 62 (1974), 982.

For a discussion about trends toward shutting down access to the federal courts for lawyers pressing civil liberties claims, see Nathan Lewin, "Avoiding the Supreme Court," *New York Times Magazine*, October 17, 1976, p. 3; Louise Weinberg, "A New Judicial Federalism?," *Daedalus*, 107 (Winter 1978), 129; and Tom Wicker, "Closing the Courts," *New York Times*, December 3, 1976, p. A27.

For a discussion of alternate forms of dispute resolution, see *American Bar Association Report on the National Conference on Minor Disputes Resolution*, May 1977, ed. Frank E. A. Sander (Chicago, 1978). Robert B. McKay has a very good article on the problem of providing legal services: "The Self-Regulated Professional and the Public Interest," in *The William O. Douglas Inquiry into the State of Individual Freedom*, ed. Harry Ashmore (Boulder, Colo., 1979).

For a probing discussion of the changing character of professionalism, see Adam Yarmolinsky, "What Future for the Professional in American Society," *Daedalus*, 107 (Winter 1978), 59. The author discusses how consumer demands are putting professionals on the defensive; he also suggests that consumers are demanding a greater voice in professional policy formation (e.g., lay representation on lawyer grievance committees).

Goldfarb v. Virginia State Bar, 421 U.S. 773 (1975); *Virginia State Board of Pharmacy v. Virginia Citizens Consumer Council*, 425 U.S. 748 (1976); and *Bates v. State Bar of Arizona*, 433 U.S. 350 (1977) are essential cases for understanding the assault on the professions.

On developments in legal training, see Charles Reich, "Toward the Humanistic Study of Law," *Yale Law Journal*, 74 (1965), 1402, an eloquent plea for strengthening the law student's perception of the humanistic issues permeating legal conflicts. Reich belongs to a group of legal educators who believe that legal education should adhere more closely to graduate than to professional training. Another good article advocating closer identity between the social sciences and humanities and the law is Robert B. McKay, "Legal Education," in *Annual Survey of American Law, 1977* (New York, 1978), 567. Finally, Learned Hand, "Freedom and the Humanities," *Bulletin of the American Association of University Professors* (Winter 1952–1953), 524, is a sensitive statement of the relationship between law and the humanities.

Bernard Schwartz, "The End of Law in a Changing World," *American Bar Association Journal*, 61 (October 1975), 1240, discusses the emergence of the concept of entitlement. Daniel Boorstin, *The Decline of Radicalism* (New York, 1969), takes a conservative view of professional developments in the area of legal services.

Current changes in antitrust enforcement and the prosecuting role of the Federal Trade Commission are best followed in the daily press, particularly the *New York Times*. I found Samuel Florman, "Standards of Value," *Harper's*, February 1980, p. 62, a very good article on the difficulties the FTC has had in developing standards for industry practices. The author raises the issue of the tendency of agency staff to "legalize" issues. Two other articles to consult: "Is John Sherman's Antitrust Obsolete?" *Business Week*, March 23, 1974, p. 47; and "The Assault on the FTC," *Consumer Reports*, March 1980, p. 149. See *Reiter v. Sonotone Corp.*, 442 U.S. 330 (1979), for a discussion of the expansion of consumer power under the antitrust laws.

Those interested in the issue of privacy should begin with Louis Brandeis and Charles Warren, "The Right of Privacy," *Harvard Law Review*, 4 (December 15, 1890), 215. For a probing discussion of more recent trends, see Richard Sennet, *The Uses of Disorder* (New York, 1970). See also *Personal Privacy in an Information Society: The Report of the Privacy Protection Study Commission* (Washington, D.C., 1977). Cases of importance are *Griswold v. Connecticut*, 381 U.S. 479 (1965), and *Roe v. Wade*, 410 U.S. 113 (1973). Finally, a good collection of articles on the future of the law is Bernard Schwartz (ed.), *American Law: The Third Century* (South Hackensack, N.J., 1976).

Index

215

About the Author

GERALD L. FETNER was born in New York City in 1945. He received his B.A. and M.A. from Queens College of the City University of New York, and his Ph.D. from Brown University. He has served as program officer for the National Endowment for the Humanities, assistant director of The Fund for Public Education of the American Bar Association, director of the ABA Commission on Undergraduate Education in Law and the Humanities, and currently is director of Foundation Relations at the University of Chicago. He has contributed to the *American Journal of Legal History*, *Journal of Legal Education*, and *ABA Journal*. Mr. Fetner lives in Evanston, Illinois, with his wife and two children.

A Note on the Type

The text of this book was set in a computer version of Times Roman, designed by Stanley Morison for *The Times* (London) and first introduced by that newspaper in 1932.

Among typographers and designers of the twentieth century, Stanley Morison has been a strong forming influence as typographical adviser to the English Monotype Corporation, as a director of two distinguished English publishing houses, and as a writer of sensibility, erudition, and keen practical sense.

Typography by Barbara Sturman. Cover design by Maria Epes. Composition by The Saybrook Press, Inc., Old Saybrook, Connecticut. Printed and bound by Banta Company, Menasha, Wisconsin.

BORZOI BOOKS
IN LAW AND AMERICAN SOCIETY

Law and American History

EARLY AMERICAN LAW AND SOCIETY
Stephen Botein, *Michigan State University*

This volume consists of an essay dealing with the nature of law and early American socioeconomic development from the first settlements to 1776. The author shows how many legal traditions sprang both from English experience and from the influence of the New World. He explores the development of transatlantic legal structures in order to show how they helped rationalize intercolonial affairs. Mr. Botein also emphasizes the relationship between law and religion. The volume includes a pertinent group of documents for classroom discussion, and a bibliographic essay.

LAW IN THE NEW REPUBLIC: *Private Law and the Public Estate*
George Dargo, *Brookline, Massachusetts*

Though the American Revolution had an immediate and abiding impact on American public law (e.g., the formation of the federal and state constitutions), its effect on private law (e.g., the law of contracts, tort law) was less direct but of equal importance. Through essay and documents, Mr. Dargo examines post-Revolutionary public and private reform impulses and finds a shifting emphasis from public to private law which he terms "privatization." To further illustrate the tension between public and private law, the author develops a case study (the Batture land controversy in New Orleans) in early nineteenth century legal, economic, and political history. The volume includes a wide selection of documents and a bibliographic essay.

LAW IN ANTEBELLUM SOCIETY: *Legal Change and Economic Expansion*
Jamil Zainaldin, *Washington, D.C.*

This book examines legal change and economic expansion in the first half of the nineteenth century, integrating major themes in the development of law with key historical themes. Through a series of topical essays and the use of primary source materials, it describes how political, social, and economic interests and values influence law making. The book's focus is on legislation and the common law.

LAW AND THE NATION, 1865–1912
Jonathan Lurie, *Rutgers University*

Using the Fourteenth Amendment as the starting point for his essay, Mr. Lurie examines the ramifications of this landmark constitutional provision on the economic and social development of America in the years following the Civil War. He also explores important late nineteenth-century developments in legal education, and concludes his narrative with some insights on law and social change in the first decade of the twentieth century. The volume is highlighted by a documents section containing statutes, judicial opinions, and legal briefs, with appropriate questions for classroom discussion. Mr. Lurie's bibliographic essay provides information to stimulate further investigation of this period.

ORDERED LIBERTY: *Legal Reform in the Twentieth Century*
Gerald L. Fetner, *University of Chicago*

In an interpretive essay, the author examines the relationship between several major twentieth-century reform movements (e.g., Progressivism, New Deal, and the Great Society) and the law. He shows how policy makers turned increasingly to the legal community for assistance in accommodating economic and social conflict, and how the legal profession responded by formulating statutes, administrative agencies, and private arrangements. Mr. Fetner also discusses how the organization and character of the legal profession were affected by these social changes. Excerpts from relevant documents illustrate issues discussed in the essay. A bibliographic essay is included.

Law and Philosophy

DISCRIMINATION AND REVERSE DISCRIMINATION
R. Kent Greenawalt, *Columbia Law School*

Using discrimination and reverse discrimination as a model, Mr. Greenawalt examines the relationship between law and ethics. He finds that the proper role of law cannot be limited to grand theory concerning individual liberty and social restraint, but must address what law can effectively discover and accomplish. Such concepts as distributive and compensatory justice and utility are examined in the context of preferential treatment for blacks and other minorities. The analysis draws heavily on the Supreme Court's Bakke decision. The essay is followed by related documents, primarily judicial opinions, with notes and questions, and a bibliography.

THE LEGAL ENFORCEMENT OF MORALITY
Thomas Grey, *Stanford Law School*

This book deals with the traditional issue of whether morality can be legislated and enforced. It consists of an introductory essay and legal texts on three issues: the enforcement of sexual morality, the treatment of human remains, and the duties of potential rescuers. The author shows how philosophical problems differ from classroom hypotheticals when they are confronted in a legal setting. He illustrates this point using material from statutes, regulations, judicial opinions, and law review commentaries. Mr. Grey reviews the celebrated Hart-Devlin debate over the legitimacy of prohibiting homosexual acts. He places the challenging problem of how to treat dead bodies, arising out of developments in the technology of organ transplantation, in the context of the debate over morals enforcement, and discusses the Good Samaritan as an issue concerning the propriety of the legal enforcement of moral duties.

LEGAL REASONING
Martin Golding, *Duke University*

This volume is a blend of text and readings. The author explores the many sides to legal reasoning—as a study in judicial psychology and, in a more narrow sense, as an inquiry into the "logic" of judicial decision making. He shows how judges justify their rulings, and gives examples of the kinds of arguments they use. He challenges the notion that judicial reasoning is rationalization; instead, he argues that judges are guided by a deep concern for consistency and by a strong need to have their decisions stand as a measure for the future conduct of individuals. *(Forthcoming in 1984)*

Law and American Literature

LAW AND AMERICAN LITERATURE
A one-volume collection of the following three essays:

Law as Form and Theme in American Letters
Carl S. Smith, *Northwestern University*

The author explores the interrelationships between law aned literature generally and between American law and American literature in particular. He explores first the literary qualities of legal writing and then the attitudes of major American writers toward the law. Throughout, he studies the links between the legal and literary imaginations. He finds that legal writing has many literary qualities that are essential to its function, and he points out that American writers have long been wary of the power of the law and its special language, speaking out as a compensating voice for the ideal of justice.

Innocent Criminal or Criminal Innocence: The Trial in American Fiction
John McWilliams, *Middlebury College*

Mr. McWilliams explores how law functions as a standard for conduct in a number of major works of American literature, including Cooper's *The Pioneers,* Melville's *Billy Budd,* Dreiser's *An American Tragedy,* and Wright's *Native Son.* Each of these books ends in a criminal trial, in which the reader is asked to choose between his emotional sympathy for the victim and his rational understanding of society's need for criminal sanctions. The author compares these books with James Gould Cozzens' *The Just and the Unjust,* a study of a small town legal system, in which the people's sense of justice contravenes traditional authority.

Law and Lawyers in American Popular Culture
Maxwell Bloomfield, *Catholic University of America*

Melding law, literature, and the American historical experience into a single essay, Mr. Bloomfield discusses popular images of the lawyer. The author shows how contemporary values and attitudes toward the law are reflected in fiction. He concentrates on two historical periods: antebellum America and the Progressive era. He examines fictional works which were not always literary classics, but which exposed particular legal mores. An example of such a book is Winston Churchill's *A Far Country* (1915), a story of a successful corporation lawyer who abandons his practice to dedicate his life to what he believes are more socially desirable objectives.